Stardust on the Spiritual Path

Trilogy on:

Karma and Vedic Astrology

Relationships and Family Constellations.

Returning to Love

Yildiz Sethi

Copyright ©Yildiz Sethi

All rights reserved. No part of this publication may be reproduced, stored in a retrieval system, or transmitted in any form or by any means electronic, mechanical, photocopy, recording or otherwise, without prior written permission of the copyright owner, except in the case of brief quotations embodied in critical articles or reviews.

Fourth edition

The sketches in this book are by Kylee Dempsey www.heavenlyearthart.com

First edition, Stardust: The Travellers Way, March 2013,

Revised 2019. This book is available in eBook format,

Ingramspark Australia

ISBN: 978-0-6484791-0-9

Dedication

With gratitude to my husband and life partner, Satish, for his love and support, and to my family, children, grandchildren and everyone who has touched my life with their stardust.

Just this morning

Song awakening the heart

Echoing throughout the inner and outer worlds.

The great reminder of what is vital.

There's stardust dancing in these cells.

Yes, the very same as the night jewels.

That heart song takes me up-

Sings me.

Spontaneously arising

One of many voices

All singing that song.

Aladdin Jones

Special Offers

10% off Yildiz's certified online training

If you love the book then consider taking your practice further.

Simply scan the codes below to receive 10% off Yildiz's:

- Certified Family Constellations online training
- Vedic astrology online

Or go to: https://familyconstellations.com.au/buy-fc-training/

Family Constellations Online training with experiential learning- 12 weeks

10% discount coupon **BRFC10**

Or go to: https://vedicastrology.net.au/buy-your-va-course-now

Vedic astrology online 12 week training

10% discount coupon **BRVA10**

Family Constellations training is certified in Australia and allows the student to obtain insurance and immediately start earning income and helping others.

Please read on to learn more about Yildiz's online training courses.

Family Constellations Online training

Family Constellations is a modality that shows the underlying dynamics, entanglements and generational trauma of individuals in their family systems. Also how these manifest in the present in relationships, parenting, patterns, wellbeing and mental health and their ability to fulfil potential.

This may take place in groups and private sessions, in person or online. The process is brief, experiential, psychodynamic, solution-focused, phenomenological and client-centred. A powerful way to re-order our inner perception of who we are into healthier places. The Constellation process works at the core of who we are as human beings, in a way that is limited or inaccessible with other approaches: Particularly in such a brief intervention.

The process works at several levels of awareness and experience simultaneously. Intellectual, visual, somatic, emotional, energetically and generationally. For Relationships, family, parenting, relational bonding, generational patterns, generational (systemic) trauma and incest. This results in several levels of change taking place simultaneously, as multiple levels of neural pathways realign. Suitable for existing and new practitioners.

The training is fully online with experiential learning component.

Learn Vedic Astrology Online

Learn how to read the magic and mystery of Vedic astrology.

How Yildiz developed the course

After Yildiz was introduced to Vedic astrology she spent years in study, research and practice. She went to courses in India, USA and in Australia and took part in lots of personal study and hundreds of Vedic astrology books. She found some information really useful and applicable and lots of information, confused confusing and not helpful or accurate. She has put in hundreds of hours of study and practice to find out what works accurately.

This is what she offers you this this course.

An honest open and practical approach to Vedic astrology in looking at the soul's journey.

Learning Vedic Astrology

You will learn by listening. There is an audio for each lesson.

You will learn by reading. There are course notes and charts for each lesson.

You will learn by doing. There are exercises at the back of 11 lessons for you to test yourself.

You may check your answers with the answers section included.

You may repeat each lesson several times.

You will listen and work through the course notes at your own pace.

Do it as fast or as slow as you want – It's up to you.

The course is designed to build your knowledge as you go through it.

You will be shown how to develop your skills in practical applications as you are shown how to navigate through chart information and build up an analysis.

All that's left after this is, Practice, Practice, Practice and ENJOY

REVIEW

Yildiz Sethi is an Australian woman, who carries the blood of her Turkish and British roots. She is married to a man who carries the history of India in his family. Yildiz is a former teacher of physics and chemistry, a therapist, Vedic astrologer, facilitator of family constellations and a generous spirit. In this book, Stardust on the Spiritual Path, Yildiz shares with us the experience of 'Surya', which is the journey of our soul towards reincarnation. Having a heart that beats with the rhythm of multiculturalism, Yildiz shares with us the cultures and history of those who have long held beliefs and traditions that have been woven with the fibres of past-life influence, and she acknowledges the beliefs of the spiritual traditions that do not include reincarnation as their tenet. To experience her generosity of spirit, one only has to read what she says: "Perhaps there is truth in both beliefs; that this life is unique, a one-off experience that may not be repeated in exactly the same way for everyone. This is the only time that we will have this experience in this body, time, culture and circumstance".

It is a meeting with grace to read this book. We are invited to consider consumerism, global warming and our search for love, as a part of our soul remembering its wisdom. As one familiar with constellations, I relished her descriptions of the work and its application: "From my experience, family constellations take place in a sacred space where many realms can come together for confluence, sharing, connecting and healing. These are realms within realms, like waves rippling out from a central point in a pond, all connected with the vibrations of the splash rippling out seamlessly through one realm into the next, until it is absorbed or neutralised and comes to rest in the greater body of the pond".

Certainly, Sethi provides interesting detail and perspective, but whatever one's belief, vocation, education, or practice, this text provides a gentle and exquisite invitation to evaluate, or at the least, more fully experience the richness of one's own life, right here, right now. This book holds our interest, but perhaps the most beautiful thing is the strength of peace that is left with us once our eyes have left the page.

Francesca Mason Boring, Systems constellation facilitator, author of Connecting to Our Ancestral Past: Healing Through Family Constellation, Ceremony & Ritual.

Table of Contents

Introduction 1
About The Author 3

Chapter 1: A New Dawn 5
Chapter 2: The Soul's Journey On Earth: The Reincarnation Cycle 8

The Wheel Of Karma

Chapter 3: Entering The Wheel Of Destiny And Creation 24
Chapter 4: Karma 34
Chapter 5: Surya As Vidur, The Priest 48
Chapter 6: Free Will And Destiny 53
Chapter 7: Karma And Cosmic Time 62
Chapter 8: Karma And Choice 70
Chapter 9: Mother Earth's Pain 76
Chapter 10: Spirituality And Money 89
Chapter 11: Knowledge 103
Chapter 12: Shedding Your Skin 120

Relationships And Family Constellations

Chapter 13: Karma And The Search For Love 121
Chapter 14: Karma And Family 133
Chapter 15: Merging Fields 145
Chapter 16: The Zen Approach: Family Constellations 153
Chapter 17: Constellations On The Move 160
Chapter 18: Clear Your Heart And Mind For Your Spiritual Path 179
Chapter 18: The How Of Moksha 185

Returning To Love

Chapter 19: Finding Freedom 186

Chapter 20: Essential Ego 205

Chapter 21: Perfection 214

Chapter 22: Becoming One 219

Chapter 23: Surya As Bandhu, The Beggar 229

Chapter 24: Fuel For Growth 233

Chapter 25: The Evolution Of Spiritual Practice 238

Chapter 26: Meditation And Spiritual Practice 243

Chapter 27: Happiness: Coming Home 250

Endnotes 258

Appendix A 262

References 264

INTRODUCTION

This Soul book is a trilogy that covers wide areas of knowledge that can be of assistance as you come to understand yourself and your place in the world and beyond. While you read this book, you can choose to go to an area of particular interest to you, or take it in as a whole.

The first part of the trilogy sets the scene for the spiritual journey, as it presents knowledge and the myths that surround karma through the art and practice of Vedic astrology that are of interest to astrologers and non-astrologers alike.

The second part looks at the spiritual journey through relationships and their pivotal importance along the way, and through a psychotherapeutic process called 'family constellations'.

The third part explores the ways in which we can be fully involved in the transformation process through the act of living.

This is a book that offers the idea that we are made from the stardust that comes from and returns to the universe through the cycle of reincarnation on the spiritual path. My offering is to those of you who are ready to explore and broaden your perspectives to discover new meaning. I have drawn from my knowledge and experiences working with people in my roles as a Vedic astrologer, counsellor, hypnotherapist, family constellations facilitator, family constellations trainer, founder of new modalities (EMI and RCH) and ex-science teacher and from my life as a human being, much like you.

Information and methodologies are included that can be helpful to enable you to become more conscious on your path. There are several true stories throughout this book that serve to show a journey of individual lives through their desire for experiences of all kinds. The importance of emotions and beliefs are explored by looking at how they can become murky and convoluted and how they can be restored and purified to flow freely again, to allow a reconnection to love.

I believe that we are now at a point in our consciousness where many of us are able to bring various fields of knowledge together to help us to see a bigger

INTRODUCTION

picture of who we are and our place in the universe. For this reason, I have brought together certain aspects of Western and Eastern philosophies, science, psychology and personal development. I believe that such knowledge has, for too long, been segregated by traditional ideologies of separatism and that it is now time to integrate them into a philosophy of 'oneness'.

Perhaps, at this time in history, as we have moved into a new millennia, there are enough of us ready to discover what is truly meaningful from a range of knowledge ranging from East to West, ancient to modern, and the mystical areas of life.

Elements of the personal and the relational human journey are explored and, in particular, the value of relationships, to assist us in harmonising and defining ourselves as we grow into our highest potential.

I also include the philosophy of karma in an attempt to dispel common myths about its meaning and function and to provide a fuller explanation of how it is a crucial part of the human experience, in unveiling and utilising our ability to create our reality. I explain the different levels of karma, free will and destiny, as well as their consequences. As an astrologer, my knowledge of karma is largely informed by my experience and practice with clients that involves years of examining astrology charts.

Of course, when I put this book together, I chose from the kaleidoscope of available knowledge that I had acquired in my own limited experience as one human being. I have included an introduction to Vedic astrology ideas and principles because this spiritual science has been a pivotal influence in my approach to the practical areas of daily life. In such areas as relationships, career and finance. I have also included my understanding of science and the human psyche and, in particular, my experience and practice of family constellations, as a way of looking at individual and collective situations that play out in our lives. I believe that these methodologies can be helpful to enable us to become more conscious, as we create, live and follow our paths.

I follow the soul through many experiences, from its point of entry onto the wheel of rebirth and on its long journey towards liberation. By sharing what has assisted me on my own soul journey, it is my wish to offer my perspectives and insights to others through 'Stardust on the Spiritual Path'.

ABOUT THE AUTHOR

Yildiz is a Vedic astrologer, psychotherapist, hypnotherapist and family constellations' practitioner, trainer and educator of counsellors. She has created two new psychotherapies (EMI and RCH). Yildiz holds workshops and training of family constellations and personal development in Australia, teaches Vedic astrology and runs a private practice in Queensland.

She was given the name of Yildiz by her father, which literally translates from Turkish to mean 'star' in English, and Lynne, her middle name, came from her mother. Her father is a Turkish Cypriot and her mother was English. She was born in England, where she married an Indian with whom she has two daughters. The small family moved to Australia in 1986.

Born between cultures and religions and marrying into yet another has provided Yildiz with a broad understanding of different cultures and spiritualities. She trained as a science and multicultural religious teacher and enjoyed her role as a physics and chemistry high school teacher for many years, until a pivotal point in her life when she discovered Vedic astrology.

She became so fascinated with karmic cycles and reincarnation that she began a search for the most effective ways to facilitate deep change. Her exploration of a wide range of methodologies has culminated in specialising in the art and practice of family constellations and the creation of two new psychotherapies (EMI and RCH).

Qualifications

Master of Social Science (counselling), Graduate Diploma in Counselling, Bachelor of Education, Diploma in Clinical Hypnotherapy, Neuro-Linguistic Practitioner, Certificate in Ego State Therapy, extensive training in family constellations.

For more information, see:

www.vedicastrology.net.au
www.familyconstellations.com.au
https://yildizsethi.com
www.rapidcorehealing.com
https://emotionalmindintegration.com

Chapter 1

A New Dawn

Imagine this.

You are in a wondrous place, full of wellbeing and brimming with love and vibrant energy. Your emotions are flowing easily and swiftly. Interestingly, you have no attachment to any feeling, but are able to witness them easily, both as first-hand experiences and, simultaneously, as a bystander. There is a full awareness of colour, sound and many other senses within and around you, and you are at peace, nurtured in the cradle of the universe as you rest between lives. In this state, you can easily view the kaleidoscope of the many lives you've experienced. These lives are scanned so that you can see them in-depth, including the lives containing those significant highs and also the more challenging points of your journey. In this place, you can acknowledge those moments of peace, clarity or joy that made your heart sing. You can recognise those times of song, dance, harmony and love, and also the stench of bloodshed, war and conflict. You can sense your soul developing and deepening through its journey.

You may notice some aspects of your experiences that your human spirit is not assimilating so easily, or still hasn't yet fully understood, while other experiences are deeply etched inside your inner 'knowing' and growing wisdom.

In this seemingly timeless place, you ponder what it is you desire to experience on your next incarnation into the earthly realm. Interestingly, in this state, you have no concern about discomfort or pain of any kind; physical, emotional or mental. Therefore, pain or comfort is not a consideration in what you choose to experience in the next life. Your soul knows that each life is like a drop in the ocean of universal creation and that it lives on regardless, in one form or another. There is no fear, only love, joy and a creative playfulness, with anticipation of the adventure to come.

Now you are ready to join the land of the physical on planet Earth. You already know to whom and where you are to be born - your parents, family and culture.

You already have a sense of how your essence will radiate through your physical form, what you will look like and how you will perceive the world.

You wait until the planets are in exactly the correct position in the solar system to give you the physical body, mental outlook, emotional framework and the physical events that will unfold at particular moments of solar and planetary combinations and cycles. These events are necessary prerequisites for further opportunities to experience and grow in ways that manifest in your growing wisdom.

Lying in the womb, you are aware of the rhythmic booming of your mother's heart. There is an enveloping warmth, darkness and comfort in this place, as you float between worlds, becoming more aware of the physicality of your presence as you grow and develop between realms. Eventually, this state of relative silence and embodied fluidity is sharply jolted, as the gentle nurturing womb becomes an urgently pulsating, squeezing force that thrusts and pushes you out into life, into the light, leaving you gasping in gulps of cold air and screaming into the arms of strangers. There are cries of joy and delight as they look at you and see to your needs. Soon you are clasped in the arms of someone whose heartbeat and smell are familiar and you find yourself sucking with gusto to receive the nectar that will give you the essential nutrients for your first few moments of this new life on Earth.

Knowledge of your spiritual existence has already started to dissipate behind a veil of forgetfulness, called Maya, as you start your new adventure. Your life is already set out before you and, although you may not find out for a while, you also have free will. You have choice in what you create and how you respond to each event or person that you encounter.

You have arrived again and your soul name is Surya. Surya is you and me.

Surya is stardust. Surya means 'sun' in Sanskrit. It is composed of the basic units of the universal matter of hydrogen, the smallest, complete atom. This element is the fundamental building block of matter. It makes up the stars and planets of the universe from seemingly non-living and living matter alike. It is physically embodied into the human form of Surya. Surya is the spiritual name of stardust that now manifests as you, me and humanity.

A human being is an embodied soul that is on a journey through many incarnations that has also experienced eons of time residing in rocks or stones, trees, animals or plants and is now involved in the human cycle of reincarnation. Sometimes Surya is born as a woman and, at other times, a man. Surya always has an insatiable hunger to experience life in all its colours and shades, and its fullness.

You are on a journey, a traveller on your way, following a path, often blindly, not knowing where it leads. You are a creator, part of the creative energy of the planet, the solar system and the universe, even though you might not be aware of it at the beginning of this part of your soul journey.

In this new experience, you bring with you a new innocence and a strong curiosity and desires that are guided by your inner essence; an incessant inner drive called life force. The main point of this life is that it is to be an experience for which you yearn. You have materialised into a physical form in the physical world of planet Earth. Of course, you are also part of a larger picture, as you take your place in a family, race, culture and humanity, and interact with a vast array of living and supposedly 'non-living' forms in your environment. You are, ultimately, a creator who can manifest your thoughts, both pleasurable and painful, into reality. On another level, you are aware of your physical and emotional body and intellectual framework as well.

What an experience! What an adventure! This is the next life of many, perhaps hundreds or thousands of previous lives and probably many more to come.

CHAPTER 2

THE SOUL'S JOURNEY ON EARTH: THE REINCARNATION CYCLE

Surya has been here since the beginning of time as an inseparable part of 'all that is'.

The mystery of the how, when and why of the universe and 'all that is,' may remain a mystery to us on planet Earth. Too vast for us to understand or verify.

How it was formed and when and why it exists, are existential questions that are likely to remain unfathomable for us in our present form. While scientific research takes place and is given some priority the more spiritual aspects of our existence remain elusive. Why we are here and for what purpose is left for each of us to fathom. I offer a perspective for your consideration here.

Perhaps Surya is the end product of a wild outburst of creative energy that we may call 'universal energy.' A force of creation that expresses itself through play and outpourings into manifestations of all kinds. Imagine that universal energy is totally involved with creative outbursts of impulses and experimentation. In the beginning, perhaps creation imagined what it might be like to produce an outpouring of pure energy into empty space; and it was done. The nature of energy is that it is transferrable to many forms and cycles, continually reforming matter into infinite states of being. Hence, a constantly evolving universe is a reality.

Pure energy that is transformed into physical matter and, over aeons of time, morphed into myriads of life forms, with humanity perhaps one of its later creations on planet Earth. Humankind is made up of stardust from the 'Big Bang' that formed a physical creature that encapsulates the energetic essence of 'all that is'. This essence seemingly loses its conscious connection to 'oneness,' as it descends into human form into the physical world.

Our entry into physicality from another state leaves us with a feeling of loss and emptiness. Leaving us with a hint of remembrance of the pure love and bliss that we once knew, that sets us as Surya, on an everlasting search for what 'he' has lost. The loss of oneness created by the fall into amnesia as the connection to 'all that is' is seemingly blocked out. creates a deep emptiness. An emptiness that we all have that drives us in the wild spiritual journey we call life. Human stardust, or Surya, becomes aware of the inner void and seeks distraction from the pain of it through experiences. that distract and invoke creativity through the act of living. Human stardust has infinite opportunities, through the cycle of life, to gradually remember its inner essence. Rediscover who he really is and eventually find its way back to the love. Stardust on the Spiritual Path is a soul journey that becomes an obsession to make meaning of one's existence. This leads to filling one's time with an unlimited range of experiences of all kinds.

This is a long journey on the reincarnation cycle that is driven by the desire for completion, in returning us to 'all that is' that we experience as pure love. Love that is unconditional and ever present, if only we can sense it.

The idea is that we descend into physicality and mortality into a body and mind, as creature beings. We experience a series of lives in an infinite amount of ways. Full of experiences. and when our time is up, we return to our source and again for a new life. This forms the cycle of life that is shaped by destiny and free will to give us the experiences we need to discover who we are. Our experiences enrich us and become part of us on our soul journey as wisdom, until we reach a state of nirvana. This is a state of awakening. Where the need to reincarnate stops as we merge into the embrace of 'all that is.'

Surya, as humankind, entered the cycle of rebirth with the seeds of desire and free will intact, having no knowledge of his spiritual existence once he dropped into the density of this physical realm. He is free to play with fellow beings and the elements of the environment. Initially unaware of his spiritual connection, as he experiences each life as one solitary life until, at death, he dissolves into seeming oblivion and his soul returns to unite with 'all that is' and to a well-deserved rest between lives in the womb of creation.

The soul rests in death and digests and evaluates its experiences until an innate curiosity and desire builds and eventually pulls it back into physicality. This desire grows to a point that can no longer be resisted and the soul is drawn back into the cycle of life once again.

Through the experience of consciousness and physicality and the cycle of rebirth, following the thread of experience through many lives and deaths and resting between lives in the womb of 'all that is', the soul begins to grow in wisdom. Each time, at some stage, Surya contracted with creation to drop into life and forget his spiritual nature to embark on his mysterious quest to find his way back to his source. This journey enables the soul to gradually begin to understand the power of its mind and its ability to create, as a projection of creation, into physical reality.

The cultures of the East have long accepted the idea of reincarnation as it is deeply woven into the fabric of their society. From most Western and many Middle Eastern perspectives, there has traditionally been an acceptance of one finite life, followed by a transition into heaven or hell, depending on the quality, actions or character of individuals.

By considering the validity of the theory of reincarnation, even though I believe that there is compelling evidence supporting its possibility, absolute proof is not available. Just as there is also no proof of one finite life. Perhaps there is truth in both beliefs; that this life is unique, a one-off experience that may not be repeated in exactly the same way for everyone.

This is the only time that we will have this experience in this body, time, culture and circumstance. However, outside this notion of one life, there is that of the cycle of rebirth.

Like the natural cycles within our planet and the universe, the soul revisits life many times through a series of bodies and circumstances, to have more experiences. Perhaps the purpose of such a cycle is for the soul to grow in wisdom through many lives, until it transcends its mortal coil and enter a state of liberation with 'all that is'.

There are many creation stories or metaphors in all cultures and religions that attempt to help our human mind come to some understanding of our connection to our world and beyond. The cycle of rebirth is a fundamental belief that has its foundations in Hinduism, Buddhism and many other Eastern religions, including those of ancient China and Japan. In these cultures, an acceptance of reincarnation is an integral part of the psyche of the people because it is intricately woven into their history, mythology, daily lives and spirituality.

The idea that we are locked in a cycle of reincarnation can be traced back through the mists of time, prior to the formation of many of the main present-day world religions.

As a Vedic astrologer, I look at the ideas of reincarnation through the lens of traditional Indian philosophy. This knowledge comes from an ancient spirituality that is woven into a rich mythology that has been passed down through the generations by word of mouth, since the Vedic era. This dates back from approximately 5,000 years BC in the Indus Valley of India.

The Vedic information was delivered in vast volumes, called the 'Four Vedas'. This knowledge covered many aspects of human life and experience, which is far too vast to explore here. Vedic astrology, known as Jyotish, was revealed in the third arm of the Vedas.

The Vedas contained a wide range of knowledge that was both practical and spiritual and involved many spheres of life, from the sciences through to the arts and spirituality. The mythology and ancient manuscripts of India have records of this knowledge that was channelled by Sri Krishna to the Rishis and Seers of the Vedic era. Sri Krishna is an incarnation of the god lord, Vishnu, while the Rishis were the wise people of the period. It was their task to bring human beings into contact with higher planes of existence, in order to give them the knowledge and tools to harmonise their minds, bodies and souls.

Although this knowledge was primarily passed down by word-of-mouth, some of it was recorded in Sanskrit and can be located in what is left of the remnants of the precious ancient manuscripts in India, as seen in Ved and Techs (2012 online and Appendix A).

Vedic astrology is considered to be the 'eye of the Vedas' because it is able to shine a light on the lives of individuals, in order to guide them on their life journey. The light shows each soul to have an innate life purpose with a range of possibilities. It reveals the desires and passions that the personal soul has chosen to pursue through their purpose.

This is something that the soul wants to experience or a goal that it wishes to achieve. Vedic astrology (Jyotisha) is the science of astronomy and astrology that is considered to be a gift to humanity by providing a way to look through the lens of opaque time at each person's soul path.

The strength and position of each planet at the moment of birth indicates different aspects of the soul's karma, as well as those aspects of the character that are gifts or require further development.

The purpose of introducing Vedic astrology in this book is to highlight this ancient, spiritual science and philosophy and its potential for us in the present. Vedic astrology is part of a holistic system that was woven into the ancient life and culture of the people of the Indus Valley, along with Ayurveda and Yoga.

This trio provides a way to live well by providing effective methodologies and knowledge to assist human beings to look after themselves. It guides them to find balance, in terms of mental, physical and spiritual wellbeing, with astrology providing both practical and spiritual guidance. This was relevant to the people of that time and I believe it is also applicable to us in modern times. Yoga, Ayurveda and Vedic astrology all came from the Vedas.

The healing system of Ayurveda is the ancient, traditional medicine of India that is aimed at helping people balance and harmonise their mind and bodies through food, herbs and body treatments (such as massage), while Yoga is a system of stretching and exercise designed to maximise health and balance. Yoga includes the practice of meditation to help slow and harmonise the mind.

With a quiet mind, it is possible to notice thoughts arising into awareness, so that we can begin the task of understanding ourselves, and start the process of refining or altering our thoughts and freeing our feelings as our consciousness grows.

This trio, Ayurveda, Yoga and Vedic astrology, form a powerful body of knowledge and practice that can be used to enhance the life of humanity by enabling spiritual growth, while maintaining physical and mental health, mobility and strength. A belief in reincarnation is deeply embedded in this culture. This is a theory that believes that we are plunged into physicality, into a state of Maya (illusion). Initially, we are unaware of our spiritual centre as we pass through many lives in order to unveil our true nature in coming back to 'all that is'.

Only when we have the experience of searching for the way back to our spiritual centre do we recognise the deep satisfaction and unconditional love of our source and realise the illusion and the impermanence of our physicality and our deep connection to 'all that is'. The journey itself is full of ups, downs and crises that eventually lead to frustration and a level of suffering of epic proportions, until a point is reached where it is possible to come out of our illusion and truly live in the 'now'.

Only at that point, if we choose to let go, do we experience ourselves to be integral with 'oneness'. At this stage, we understand that we know that we don't need to strive anymore, because we have everything that we need deep inside. In truth, we are already connected and part of 'all that is' but, for some reason, we did't really believe it. Hence, the journey through many lives to rediscover or confirm it.

Recently, there has been a new wave of interest in the idea of reincarnation infiltrating Western culture, spirituality and philosophy. Due to the rising interest in Buddhism in modern Western culture, there is now a growing body of research and documentation in the areas of reincarnation that is contributing to a growing acceptance of this as a possibility. Zammit (2012, online) gives examples of children with such vivid memories of past lives that they have been able to convince their parents to locate and approach former family members from that past life.

In such meetings, they have been able to share unique details of their former life, in a way that only the actual elderly people who they were involved with could, providing proof of their connection. They have demonstrated that they have specific knowledge of their former life and the people who were important to them, that has been verified by historic artefacts or records.

Of course, such vivid memories of past lives is relatively unusual, because most of us experience a form of amnesia at birth, cutting off possible links to the past.

The hypnotherapist, Webster (2001), has also recorded instances of people providing information about former lives through hypnotic regression.

Interestingly, Webster succeeded in having many of the cases he reported validated by having names, places and other relevant evidence verified through historic records. The information was recorded during regressive hypnosis sessions. Many of the people involved in the study appeared to have past lives in other cultures, with some actually speaking in another language while in hypnotic trance, while having no knowledge of the language or connection with those cultures, in their current daily lives.

The notion of reincarnation may not simply be an Eastern philosophical and spiritual belief that has infiltrated New Age thinking. According to Ward (2012, online) in *The Soul Genome, Reincarnation Experiment,* the idea of reincarnation is an ancient one, predating the onset of Judaism and Christianity. It seems the idea of reincarnation has been deeply embedded in many indigenous, pre-Christian and pre-Islamic cultures. There continues to be a great deal of research to provide persuasive evidence of a cycle of reincarnation in many cultured, rather than one finite life.

The work of psychiatrist, Dr Brian Weiss (1988), adds to the growing body of evidence through his book, *Many Lives, Many Masters,* which was written from his experiences with his patients. He discovered, through his therapeutic alliance with them, that many of their psychological disturbances appeared to have roots in previous lives. Dr Weiss said that he had not believed in reincarnation prior to his experiences in psychiatry and psychotherapy.

Furthermore, the Seth books (1994, p274), written by Jane Robertson in *The Eternal Validity of the Soul,* propose another view of reincarnation; that lives are lived in multiple dimensions simultaneously, rather than the limited human perception of linear time. Through this perspective, many lives take place simultaneously through many windows of reality, rather than in a linear, sequential, supposedly human, time-based manner.

From the ancient Indian perspective, we separate from universal energy to assume an individual form and are left in a body to experience physicality, locked in a cycle of rebirth. Thus, we embody an inner essence for which there may be many names and, for the purpose of this book, I have called the personal soul, Surya. At other times, Surya may be such things as humanity, the environment or universal energy. Surya is stardust and can manifest itself in many ways. The personal soul falls into the physical realm for an infinite series of lives, in order to experience itself in a kaleidoscope of experiences.

Once here, the knowledge of former existences and our spiritual nature fades behind a veil, which we can think of as a symbolic door of illusion, which the yogis of India call Maya (illusion). Maya is referred to by many ancient Vedic texts, such as the classical Bhagavad Gita, which was translated and published into English by Bhaktivedanta Swami Prabhupanda in 1978. Of course, just because this belief can be traced back through the mists of time, does not necessarily make it true. It remains the case that, regardless of evidence, a belief in reincarnation ultimately comes down to faith.

A belief in reincarnation or not is an individual choice made by listening to our inner voice about what feels right for us in the face of the available evidence concerning the validity of a range of theories.

Following this belief, you were seemingly separated from your source and dropped into a purely physical plane where you quickly became emerged in physical experiences.

As a child, your body was alive with sensations, such as hunger, thirst, sights and sounds, with emotions sweeping through your mind filled with the anticipation of so many adventures to come. You arrived into the sensations and desires of your human form which initially, were the urgent needs of your body to fill your stomach and quench your thirst. In addition, you have an innate and insatiable curiosity. These qualities spurred you on as you explored, played and experimented with everything around you. At this point in your soul journey, you might not have been aware of anything other than your physicality and the driving need to satisfy your hungers. As a child, you might have been aware of other paradigms that were mysterious and unfathomable, that mostly began to fade as you matured. Gradually, in each new life, your physical presence extended to an awareness of those around you, firstly, to those who looked after your every need.

From this point onwards, you became increasingly aware of your extreme vulnerability and dependence on family, as you were socialised into kinship, culture and community.

As the cycle of life proceeds and you become an older soul, if you are taking note of your experiences, the illusion of Maya starts to dissolve, it seems that the magical aspects of living, begin to re-emerge into your awareness. As you progress on your spiritual journey towards an awakening, you rediscover the mysteriousness and wondrousness of life that extend beyond the physical.

From a Vedic astrology perspective, you separate from your spiritual connection into a state of illusion as you descend into the earthly realm. In this state of disconnection, you attempt to make meaning of it by plunging yourself into experiences in the world. You experience your world through four main areas of life that cover all human experiences in one form or another.

These are Dharma (right action), Kama (desires), Artha (wealth and status) and Moksha (liberation). Kama is desire and is not the same as karma, which will be discussed later.

We miss that feeling of connection, love and bliss that is somewhere in our awareness, if only we could find it. We are repeatedly drawn to an inner feeling of loss or sadness that calls to be filled, that may be likened to a feeling of emptiness. One of our first tasks in mastering life is to master the art of survival, which can preoccupy us for many lives. A search to find what is lost is pursued through an exploration of our senses involving our physicality, including foods, pleasures, relationships and adventures of all kinds

Of course, our first task is that of survival in our physical world, as we begin to create our identity. There is a need to acquire knowledge and skills to secure our survival, which results in a constant search for the next meal, in a desperate bid to relieve our hunger. At this stage of our soul's journey, we might see the world as a great adventure or a scary and hostile place, that is something to be fought and conquered. Who knows how many lives we may spend in this state. A state involved in acquiring the skills and knowledge for survival?

If in previous lives, we've conquered the basic art of survival, While enjoying a level of stability and comfort, its likely that the nagging feeling of emptiness returns to haunt us. We may have enough to eat now, but still have an emptiness that calls for our attention. This can result in attempting to satisfy ourselves with a myriad of desires, goals and achievements, such as acquiring a bigger house, better vehicle, a beautiful partner or a better job.

It is true that we can fill our emptiness, at least for a while, through the pursuit of enjoyment and the achievement of desires or goals through achieving goals or a wide range of experiences, such as knowledge, language, literature, science or mathematics, etc.

Alternatively, we may pursue power through business, politics or military force. Each of our desires is driven by a strong motivation to satisfy our emptiness. It is true that each time we achieve a goal, we do reach a certain state of euphoria and satisfaction for a while, but again, that familiar nagging emptiness eventually returns, sending us, as Surya, onto our next quest, resulting in a seemingly everlasting search for what is missing. At a deep level, we yearn for happiness and love. It seems that there is a figment of remembrance lingering at a cellular or soul level, of something that has more permanent satisfaction than what can be found in the purely physical, material and sensual world.

We may be aware of the drive to rediscover and reconnect with that sense of peace. We, as Surya, are on a quest to satisfy our inner drive and, perhaps, we have not yet recognised that what we are really looking for is love... self-love... universal love and... 'oneness'.

Hence, we continue in a perpetual search in each life, where our soul continues its search and so it continues. On one level, we are searching for a missing part of ourselves and, on another level, we are totally transfixed, consumed and absorbed by the search itself. We distract ourselves with physical, emotional and intellectual challenges. However, our physical experiences are vital to our spiritual journey and growing wisdom. We are all in this process together. We all have beliefs or dreams we are in the process of pursuing. Some of us are still trying to survive, provide the next meal, or find a safe place to sleep. While others are pursuing other goals, having their basic survival needs met, and are seeking tasks to occupy their minds and successfully distracting them from feeling empty.

In other lives, we may have been looking for satisfaction through fulfilling our sensual desires (Kama), in a bid to find comfort and satisfaction with such things as food, sounds, smell, sex, intoxicants, excitement or the acquisition of beauty or knowledge. Each one of these will indeed provide satisfaction or happiness until each experience inevitably wanes and the feeling of emptiness returns.

In each life, we, as Surya, are looking for happiness and love. We often believe that what we are doing will lead us to those ends. Even when we live the life of a murderer, rapist or burglar, we are probably looking for gratification through our feelings of desperation, as we succumb to such qualities as greed and violence in our impatience to achieve gratification. However, even through such destructive behaviours, we are still looking for what is missing, even though we may be going about it in a destructive way.

Of course, in the earlier stages of our soul development, we may not have had a conscience, as feelings of guilt might not yet be aware of right or wrong. We may not yet have realised the consequences of our actions, the deep pain that such actions have on others and ultimately on ourselves. We often don't know that what we do to others is what we do to ourselves. This realisation is an important part of our soul development and experience. How else can we develop a conscience?

In fact, it is likely that being able to draw on past-life experiences is essential for us to be able to feel compassion for those who are choosing difficult paths, while we can also appreciate the necessity for them to live the consequences of their actions. However, even when feeling compassion for those making painful choices, it is wise to realise that what they are drawn to might be a necessary part of their soul journey.

How else are they going to be able to receive the jewel of growth that is available somewhere in each experience? Some people may have to pay for the consequences of their actions through the justice system. Painful though they are, these experiences are all precious for the learning they provide.

It is a worthwhile exercise for all of us to reflect on whether or not we are looking down on, or judging the actions of others, particularly if we consider such behaviour or situations beneath us. If so, we may have forgotten about our own innate, human fallibility. We may have forgotten that any feelings we have of conscience, guilt or innocence, have probably been earned through our own hard-lived experiences, if not in this life, then from the deep soul experiences of past lives. Such deep experiences result in our present 'knowing' and wisdom, so that we can learn to trust our own guidance.

If we believe that we are better than others and above making poor choices, it is likely that our soul has not yet had the experiences or earned the jewel of wisdom required for true humility and compassion. This can show as areas where further growth can take place. Furthermore, by feeling genuine compassion for those who are making destructive choices, we, as Surya, have an understanding that each individual soul needs to experience and learn to take full responsibility for the consequences of their actions.

We are all required to experience the fullness of our actions in all dimensions. At some level, this is a necessary part of our journey and only the experience itself will help us gain the wisdom to mature further.

At a more mature stage of the reincarnation journey, we begin to understand that our experiences, in all their shades, have been instrumental in allowing us to develop the compassion to be less judgmental of ourselves and others. Eventually, as our soul matures, we come to a place of awareness and belief that, in universal law, there is no ultimate good or bad, better or worse, right or wrong. This will be discussed further in the chapters on Karma.

By doing your duty (Dharma), you might find that this only fulfils or satisfies you for a time. The returning feeling of dissatisfaction has the effect of setting you up for the next challenge and motivating your continuing search. If you have made Dharma your main focus in this life, you will be aware of a strong sense of duty and responsibility. There may be an expectation that 'right action' will be rewarded by a sense of peace or good conscience. If this is the case, you might spend your life providing for others and trying to live up to your own, parental or societal expectations as you attempt to live in tune with universal law. You might even go on a crusade and try to 'save the world' in some way.

This is likely to provide you with some satisfaction, but may not deliver you the praise, appreciation or love that you might have hoped for. The deeper inner satisfaction that you desire. A Dharmic life can also involve seeking higher knowledge or aspiring to be involved with justice, or the search for or wish to be a guru or teacher. This is also a search and an experience, like all others.

According to the ancient Vedic and generally Eastern beliefs of rebirth, you are but one soul in a cycle of reincarnation within the soul of humanity and universal energy. According to this philosophy, your soul is with all others, on the same journey. The only difference between one individual soul and another is that some souls are further ahead in their development, through lived experience, than others. We each had to start this journey as stardust as a new soul at some point.

From the Vedic perspective, it is believed that at the end of each life, you return to universal energy in order to review your life and ponder what you've learned.

Therefore, it is you who decides, not an external judging God, what is valuable or necessary for you to experience the next time you are ready to be drawn into physical existence for the next stage of growth on the wheel of life. Ultimately, your soul drops into the reincarnation cycle in the physical world, in order to start a spiritual journey.

You are challenged to gradually find your way back to your spiritual source through experiences that become the main source of your growth and awakening out of illusion (Maya). You are able to dissolve each of the veils of Maya through your pursuit of desires and experiences of life in all its colours and hues, as you push out the boundaries of your reality.

Here is an ancient story that is told in several parts of the East.

> Walking home one evening, a young boy noticed an old man on his hands and knees under a lamp on the street, looking for something on the floor.
>
> The boy noticed the old man's distress and stopped to see if he could help.
>
> He asked, "Sir, can I help you find what it is you are looking for?"
>
> The old man said, "Yes, I have lost something very precious".
>
> The boy asked, "What is it?"

The old man said, "I can't find a name for it or give you a description, but you will know it when you find it. It is very precious. Please help me look".

The boy joined the old man in the search on the floor under the lamp. They continued their search for a long time. Eventually, as the boy began to tire, he said to the old man,

"It is not here, we have searched everywhere. Where did you lose it?"

The old man said,

"I lost it in my house, but it is too dark in there to look, so I decided to look out here, where I could see under the lamp.

The moral of this story is that, once you have begun to exhaust your search and experiences in your outer world, you will have nowhere else to look but within. Once you come to this point, you will have started your journey home to your source.

Your consciousness can now start to expand and you can be more fully present in your physical, emotional, intellectual and spiritual elements. You are now on your way to 'waking up,' although you might still have many lives to complete the process of purifying your thoughts and emotions. This can seem like an endless, timeless task, as you learn to trust each step into unknown territory but, what a journey and what an experience!

From a Vedic perspective, the human soul journey is about coming to know our true nature and potential, our 'satiate', which is a Sanskrit word for grace or energy. Satiate means 'bestowing the energy or lighting the lamp'. In reality, this requires so many experiences of all kinds and is, therefore, far too wide and deep to be covered in one lifetime. The human soul needs to experience itself in myriads of ways in order to obtain the knowledge that it needs for growth and maturation. Once the soul has reached this point of grace, it can let go of its mortal coil and enter into a state of liberation.

Interestingly, the great present-day master, Eckhart Tolle's (2009) message to us, is that each person has the capacity to let go of suffering and move into a higher state of consciousness at any moment.

There is no need to wait or to do anything but make a choice. He explains that, even though the human soul always has the potential to return to its source, most of us are so entangled and identified in the 'stories' we have of ourselves and the limiting constructs of our minds, that often only extreme suffering is enough to push us to the point of transcending and letting it go. However, we must be sufficiently mature and have suffered enough to be able to transcend to a higher state of consciousness. From the Vedic perspective again, the experiences are themselves an essential part of the journey that is potent with possibilities for transformation at every level and at any time. There is hope for us all in this.

The Wheel of Karma

The cycle of life and death, where we live what we create.

CHAPTER 3:

ENTERING THE WHEEL OF DESTINY AND CREATION

Imagine that in a former life, around 5,000 years BC, Surya was born as an Indian in the Indus Valley in India. There, where the people of that time were very much in awe of their world and aspired to bring their bodies, minds and spiritual natures into balance with the wheels of nature and the solar system. They were adept astronomers and great observers of the cycles of nature, who had an awareness of their connection with the cosmos and its effects on their minds and lives. They followed the movements of the stars in the sky with great precision. The astronomers developed the complex and sophisticated spiritual science of Vedic astrology (Jyotish). This astrology grew out of a study of astronomy and became combined with the mythology and folklore of the times, by people who were very much in tune with the rhythm and pulses of the Earth, the cosmos and their own body rhythms. In the study and observation of Jyotish, learned men and women noticed that the patterns and combinations of the planets somehow correlated and reflected the lives of the people below. A common saying of that time was, "as above, so below".

This chapter will be of interest to those of you who appreciate the philosophical, practical and technical aspects of astrology, and those who are sceptical. I introduce the main differences between the Western and the Indian systems. If this topic is not of interest to you, you might want to skip to the next chapter on karma. However, much of my understanding of karma has come through my study and practise of Indian astrology and philosophy, and my experiences observing karmic cycles that play out in my own and other people's lives through reading charts. It is impossible for me to separate karma from astrology because Vedic astrology is a karmic map of the soul's progression.

My fascination with astrology started at an early time in my life when, as a girl, I was drawn to its mystery. Somehow, I couldn't connect with the Western version of astrology, because it didn't speak to me at a soul level.

Perhaps it wasn't the right time, or I needed to connect with an astrology that was familiar to my particular soul journey. As a young woman, I became engaged with the events in my life as it progressed in another direction. Although I had always maintained a desire to become an astrologer, I knew that the time had to be right. I believe that there is a time for everything.

The time for me to be introduced to this spiritual science came when I was at the end of one astrological cycle and was just about to enter another that involved a life- changing situation, with a strong focus on higher learning, and involving the academic, the mystical and the psychological. In my studies of astrology, I became aware that the soul enters into physical life at a point in cosmic time that is marked by the arrangements of planets around the geographic place of birth.

The arrangement of planets that form a cosmic map (astrological chart) show the progress of the soul journey from its inception through to the progression of various stages towards liberation.

The people of the Indus Valley discovered that, if they knew the pattern of the planets or stars at the time and over the place of their birth, they could understand a lot about individuals, in terms of personality, psychology, physique, health, success, relationships and much more. The formation of the stars became the blueprint of their inner and outer lives and the motivations of individuals were an essential tool for the people of this civilisation to understand themselves, their purposes and their choices.

Vedic astrology is a science that is deeply spiritual because it reveals the progress of the soul's journey through many lives. It provides a way to view the wheel of life through which the soul enters and leaves repeatedly, and maintains a cosmic record of the collective karma (action) for each person. The combinations of the planets in the cosmos form the psychological and energetic codes by which the soul enters, through the fusion of the feminine and the masculine, in the consummation of desire and love (our parents) in the service of creation.

The soul enters into a family and culture at a particular time and moment in history, in order to give it all of the experiences it requires in this life. The spiritual science of astrology maintains the connection of the golden thread between 'all that is' and the journey towards liberation.

The astrology of ancient India is part of ancient Hindu religious and spiritual teachings that come from the Vedas. The Hindu religion, according to Flaherty (2001, online) in a transcript from an interview with him, makes the point that Vedic astrology "is ultimately concerned with Moksha (enlightenment), which means the process of reaching the point of leaving the wheel of birth, death and rebirth".

Astrology is only one area of knowledge coming from the Vedas.

There are other ancient spiritual teachings that have been passed down orally through the generations prior to 3,000 years BC. There are many Vedic texts, the most known of which is probably the Bhagavad Gita, which was translated and published in English by Swami Prabhupada Bhaktivendanta in 1978. This is a text that recorded oral teachings that were passed down from the Rishis of the Indus Valley from a golden period of humanity prior to 3,000 BC.

During this period, Rishis (advanced human beings), channelled teachings from higher realms for the guidance and benefit of humanity to form what is known as Vedic knowledge. A Rishi is a seer who is a highly developed human being, to whom the Vedas were revealed through states of higher consciousness. Interestingly, Chandler (2012) reported Deepak Chopra, stating that between 20 and 37 of these seers were women or Rishikas. The most widely used Indian astrology system, Parashara, was delivered by the great seer, Parashara, probably between 5,000-3,000 BC. It is clear from the history and knowledge of that period that these ancient Indians were highly advanced astronomers and astrologers. The knowledge of Vedic astrology itself continues to be delivered to the Indians, largely from ancient times through the classical Vedic book, Brihat Para Sara Hora Shastra. It is a compendium of Vedic Girish Chand astrology, containing two volumes, translated and published by Sharma (2010). In modern times, this information has been made more readily available to the West by many English-speaking writers and teachers.

Such research and writing has served as a conduit to connect ancient spiritual knowledge to modern Western thinking.

In this book, I explore mainly the esoteric and spiritual aspects of astrology and how these can inform us about our soul journey. The position of the planets over the place and time of birth becomes an astrology chart when using the Vedic sidereal system (fixed-star system). This shows the exact position of planets in the sky with the same accuracy that a present-day astronomer might look out at the stars using a modern telescope. It is an accurate form of astrology that holds deep wisdom from which we can gain a great deal of guidance in a climate where, particularly in the West, metaphysics and astrology are often viewed with suspicion, at best, or the people who believe in it are described as being 'off with the fairies', at worst. There are many well-educated, modern and technical people for whom metaphysics and astrology are either taboo or of insignificant value. For this reason, I draw attention to the difference between Western and Vedic astrology, showing why many scientists might have a tainted view of astrology in general, from a technical standpoint.

This might be due to the anomaly between the astronomic accuracy of the location of planets at given points in time, compared to tropical Western calculations, thereby discounting the credibility of all astrology. It does not consider that there are some systems that are astronomically accurate, such as Vedic astrology. One of the differences between the two systems is that one is based on the tropical moving-star system and the other is based on the sidereal fixed-star system. Generally, Vedic astrology and a small percentage of Western astrologers use the sidereal fixed-system, while the majority of Western astrologers use the tropical moving system. The tropical system is governed by the precession of the equinoxes, while the sidereal system is governed by the position of a fixed star beyond the solar system and is unrelated to the equinoxes. The sidereal system remains fixed and does not move in relation to Earth. The Western tropical system is located within the movement of the precession of the equinoxes, which move in a large arc over a 25,000-year period. This is why it is called the moving-star system.

The tropical Western moving-star system has moved away from the sidereal Vedic fixed-star system by a difference of nearly 24 degrees and is continuing to move away. I acknowledge that there are some Western astrologers who choose to use the sidereal system for accuracy. There is no discrepancy between sidereal Western and sidereal Vedic astrology on this point. There is only a discrepancy between sidereal and tropical astrology because the charts produced by the two systems are significantly different.

Dr. David Frawley, the well-known and reputable scholar of Vedic Sciences, explains some of the fundamental differences between sidereal (Vedic) astrology and tropical (Western) astrology:

"This is because the signs of the Tropical zodiac are based upon the equinoxes, not the fixed stars. The beginning of the Tropical zodiac, its first degree of Aries, is always identical with the point of the vernal equinox, the place of the Sun at the first day of spring, and not with any specific group of stars. The orientation of the equinoxes to the fixed stars changes over time according to the precession of the Earth on its axis. This phenomenon, a changing of the tilt of the Earth, causes the point of the Earth, relative to the fixed stars, to move backwards in the zodiac. Over a period of around 5,000 years, the point of the Earth, relative to the fixed stars, makes a full circuit of the zodiac. The zodiac that corresponds to the actual constellations, or the fixed stars, is called "the Sidereal zodiac".

Vedic astrology uses this, as does Western Sidereal astrology, which derives its orientation from the Indian mode.

Around 2,000 years ago, when Western astrology was in its formative stage, the two zodiacs coincided. Since then, with the precession, the two zodiacs have been slowly moving apart, around 50 arc seconds per year. Hence, the tropical zodiac shows the actual astronomical positions of some 2,000 years ago."

Frawley (1990, p44)

So, the sidereal system has remained accurate because it does not depend on the precession of the equinoxes, while the tropical system has moved significantly from its real location and continues to do so.

Both systems use the twelve-sign zodiac, which is a series of constellations that are located in a band around the Earth. The constellations appear to move as a result of the rotation of the Earth each day and the path of the Earth in orbit around the sun. The constellations are always in view from Earth. This means that, over any point on Earth, there is a constellation sign over the horizon. This changes approximately every two hours, due to the rotation of the Earth. In this way, the 12 signs of the zodiac (constellations) will pass over a point on Earth over a 24-hour period. This means that babies born at the same geographic point may be born with a possibility of any of the 12 zodiac signs on the horizon, at their birth time.

The constellation on the horizon at the time of birth becomes the rising sign and is significant in the personality of each person.

For example, a child that is born in Sydney at 6 am, when the Aries constellation is on the horizon, has a rising sign personality of Aries, whereas another child born two hours later at the same spot, when the Taurus constellation is on the horizon, has a rising sign personality of Taurus. The two children born on the same day and in the same place have different rising signs and therefore different personalities and life paths.

The constellation that happened to be on the horizon at the moment of your birth becomes your rising sign. This could be any one of the following:

Aries, Taurus, Gemini, Cancer, Leo, Virgo, Libra, Scorpio, Sagittarius, Capricorn, Aquarius, Pisces.

There are many books that provide information on the qualities of zodiac signs, so I won't go into that here. The pattern or combinations of planets over the birthplace becomes a symbolic map on the astrology chart of an individual, with the rising sign becoming the first house of the chart, with the next zodiac sign forming the next house and so on until the twelfth and final house.

The zodiac signs are considered to be the backdrop on which the planets are positioned.

The planets used in the Vedic system are:

Sun, Moon, Mars, Rahu (North node of the Moon), Jupiter, Saturn, Mercury, Ketu (South Node of the Moon) and Venus
(Pluto, Uranus and Neptune are not used in this system).

In Vedic astrology, the rising sign represents the personality of the individual that is shown to the world. This means that if a person has a rising sign at 10 degrees Leo in the Vedic sidereal fixed-star system, it will be shown as 4 degrees Virgo in the Western tropical moving-star system (due to the tropical system being nearly 24 degrees ahead of the Vedic sidereal system, as explained earlier).

This difference means that all of the planets in the chart will have a difference of nearly 24 degrees and can be placed in different zodiac signs between the two systems. This means that there will be two very different charts for the same birth details between the two systems.

Both systems were in unison around 2,000 years ago due to the return of the precession of the equinoxes at that time. Since then, the cycle of the precession of the equinoxes that takes approximately 25,000 years to complete, has continued to move the tropical system further away from the actual position of planets (sidereal). This movement away will continue for many thousands of years before it starts to move closer again.

I believe that this discrepancy between the two systems has enabled many Western scientists to discount astrology as a legitimate area of knowledge. Whereas, Vedic astrology in India has largely remained accepted by the community, among many of the well-educated and scientifically minded, as well as the poorer masses, continuing to use it to guide them in such things as relationships, marriage, fertility, health and the more esoteric or spiritual aspects of their lives.

The main difference between the sidereal Vedic and the tropical Western systems is the 23-24 degree difference between them. Other differences are that Indian astrology is a moon-based system, whereas Western astrology is sun-based.

The Western system primarily refers to the sun sign of an individual and may also consider the rising sign as well, whereas the Vedic system refers to the moon and rising sign. Both systems use transits (rotation) of planets around the Earth. In addition, Vedic astrology contains many other systems, tools and techniques to fine-tune the quality, accuracy, prediction and analysis of a chart. One of the main systems used is the moon-based Nakshatra system. The Nakshatra system is a 27-house system based on the cycle of the moon that preceded the sun-based zodiac system. Vedic astrology uses both systems. The Nakshatra system forms the basis of the planetary period (Vimshottari Dasha) that indicates the planetary periods' influence on each part of life. In addition, there are also up to 60 divisional (harmonic) charts used for looking at the many different aspects of life. For example, within these divisional charts, there are specific charts for marriage, children and so forth.

In India, if someone asks for your astrology sign, they will most often be referring to your moon zodiac sign (the zodiac sign where your moon is placed in the sidereal system), or alternatively, the Nakshatra sign of your moon (the Nakshatra where your moon was placed at birth). Whereas, in the West, most people primarily refer to the sun sign. Of course, by now, it is obvious that I prefer Vedic astrology because of its accuracy and perhaps because it appeals to my scientific background and my need to use a system that I find reliable and predictable on both practical and spiritual levels.

Using Vedic astrology, I have been able to put my present life into the perspective of my greater soul journey and come to understand my karmic cycles. However, I do also respect the validity of Western astrology, Chinese astrology and many other systems that are being practised around the world, because I believe that they all have a place in serving their people.

The combination of planets at a point in time is a perfect vehicle or map for a soul to utilise as it comes into life on planet Earth. Finding exactly the right moment to come into each life to provide exactly the experiences required, while the combinations of planets continue to orbit around the Earth, creating constantly changing conditions for new souls to enter life, is quite incredible. Each soul enters a specific set of life experiences.

This is an accurate way of looking at your current soul development and it can give you a glimpse of your collective karma and what is set to come into fruition in this life. It is a highly sophisticated, accurate and comprehensive astrology system that has many tools at its disposal.

It is spiritual because it reflects the soul's journey and challenges for this life.

It is scientific because the planets and combinations of planets form predictable patterns and combinations according to their constant motion, creating symbols, revealing your character, life purpose and the events to be poured out as time passes.

In short, as a Vedic astrologer, I have found over many years that all I need is the date, time and place of birth of someone prior to meeting with them, in order to see their psychology, personality, emotional resilience, capacity for common sense or logical thinking, intelligence and specific areas of interest and capabilities, such as family, relationships, career, finance, higher learning etc. When I see a chart that shows a strong interest in healing, this person is a doctor, nurse or alternative healer, and when I see a chart that has a primary interest in higher learning, this person is pursuing a career that supports this interest. When I see a chart of a real estate agent or entrepreneur, this is shown clearly in their chart. I can also see where a person is finding it hard to find their life purpose or commit to a path. This analysis takes place prior to meeting the person with no other information than their birth details. As an ex-science-based person, this continues to amaze me.

I have been drawn to Vedic astrology because it is accurate and practical. In the Western tropical system, my sun is in Leo and my Jupiter (in conjunction with the moon) is in Taurus in the tenth house of career, which indicates a very easy career of high status.

Whereas, in the Vedic sidereal system, my moon with Jupiter is in the ninth house of higher learning and my sun is in Cancer, the twelfth house of spirituality, unconscious matters, grief and loss. The Western chart shows much more success than my Vedic chart and does not reflect my life. My interests, passions and career are clearly more accurately shown in the Vedic chart, as I have been very involved with learning, teaching and helping others. At the time of writing, I am not famous, although I am known in my field and locality as a competent practitioner and teacher. Success in the Vedic chart is indicated much later in life. This anomaly continues for each planet between the two systems, with the Vedic system clearly reflecting my life, actions and psychology accurately.

In addition, the Vedic system uses another tool, the Vimshottari Dasha planetary-period system, which reflects the influences and focus of my life perfectly at each stage.

For those who would like to know more about Vedic astrology theory and practice, or where to find a suitable astrologer, I have provided links in the endnotes.

CHAPTER 4:

KARMA

As Surya, you are a co-creator with 'all that is' and are constantly throwing your spear of intent, thought, word or action into your world. These always have effects and consequences. Nothing is lost in the universe. Energy is constantly being transformed from one kind to another; there is nothing lost. Karmic law is much like Newton's law of thermodynamics, which states that for any action, there is an equal and opposite reaction. As Surya, on your soul journey, you are here to create and experience karma on the cycle of life.

The word, 'karma', was first seen around 3,000 BC in the Bhagavad Gita (in Sanskrit, which translates to 'the song of god') that, according to Indian mythology, was delivered by Lord Krishna. Karma means action. Simply, this can be considered to be 'what goes around comes around'. The theory of karma is relatively simple, but the range of its consequences can be intricate and mysterious. As you are reading this book, it is likely that you already have some awareness of karma and have a sense of yourself as stardust on your spiritual journey. You will be creating and living the fruits of your karma at all times. Put another way, what you create is what you experience. This relates to your intentions, actions, thoughts, beliefs and emotions. You are constantly projecting these into your environment, consciously and also unconsciously. Your projections flow from you and eventually come back to you, either immediately, or later in your current or a future life. Therefore, it is helpful for you to become aware of your projections of thought, word and action, and even aware of your most involuntary private thoughts as well. It will take many souls a very long time to be able to believe this, because they cannot see the link between their thoughts, desires and actions and their physical reality. They might not realise that much of what comes their way is coming, not only from this life, but from previous lives too; a mixture of past and present creations. It might take many people a long time to realise that they are creators. In addition, they might eventually realise that it is not an external god or creator that judges their karma, but their personal soul, particularly between lives.

You may, of course, look at your karma at a conscious level at any stage of life, if you have the courage to do so. There is no right or wrong or black or white in karma. It just IS; it is action. Karma is not punishment.

It is impossible for me to separate karma from Vedic astrology because the position of the planets over the place of birth (forming a birth chart) determines each personality and also the events that are due to unfold at particular points in life. People will come into our life that we are due to meet at particular periods in time, according to karmic and astrological lore. Our karma will unfold in perfect time. Some people will be new to us in our soul's journey, while others will be those with whom we have 'unfinished business' from previous lives that seek completion. These can be a love affair that ended badly or was not consummated due to choices, social restrictions or any other limitation, or possibly a business partner, parent or child with whom something is not yet resolved satisfactorily. Each of these experiences provide us with the ability to make choices and to experiment with different outcomes. From the beginning, events and situations will seemingly happen to us as Surya. We might or might not have an attentive and loving mother or not, be born into a war or famine or into an abundant and soft environment. At a soul level, these events will be pre-ordained. Our gender is chosen to provide the necessary, specific experiences we require, even though gender, as we know it, is not a part of the spirit-world experience. Gender is an important part of our physical earthly experience. These are the situations that will help to shape us through the events of our life and create more karma.

There are many kinds of karma. You have personal karma, but you are also involved in much collective karma, such as your family karma and also the other collective karma involving race, culture, religion and generations. There are experiences to learn from on many levels simultaneously. You are seemingly thrown into your life and have chosen to experience it for many reasons. It is possible that you may find your family loving and harmonious or so challenging or distasteful that you would like to cut them off. However, being born into this family is no accident. It is very much part of your spiritual journey, regardless of its ease, dysfunction or pain. Simply disowning family or relationships will not be enough to release you from the karmic connection. There is a need to experience it for what it is and realise what does not belong with you and the value of coming to the best place you can with it. This means acknowledging the shortfalls in others as well as yourself. Perhaps then you may be able to understand it, integrate and let it go.

By letting go of the negative pattern you are changing your destiny (karma). Go into a different way of being, by becoming truer to who you are and emerging richer from the experience.

With collective karma, you may need to acknowledge your collective destiny with others to accept them and yourself as part of the group. You are experiencing the consequences of what has gone before for some reason, in a personal way, and also from what was set in motion from previous generations in your genetic line. Such karmas are played out in the rise and fall of nations or the spread or demise of religions and the waging of wars.

Through being part of so many different karmic experiences, you are involved in karma in many spheres of life including family, society and politics which is part of your karmic map. We are locked in a cycle of cause and effect. 'What goes around comes around'. This means, at best, you have the opportunity to face your karma and attempt to resolve it, which can only provide valuable growth.

Particularly through the spiritual teachings of Vedic Astrology, I have learned that there is a mixture of karma to unfold in life that comes in three basic strengths. These are fixed, mixed or light karmas. Fixed karma cannot be changed, will not move and is strongly destined to take place.

There is no getting away from it, because it has been set up over many lives. It is a pattern or action that has been set up repeatedly, is deeply ingrained, can't be avoided in this life and must come back to be experienced. It can be anything ranging from pain to joy. Such karma is meant to take place.

Perhaps, no matter what, you are destined to be famous or rich with seemingly little effort, or to find key people who can smooth your path to a particular goal, so you enter at the right time and place. A chance meeting may result in doors of opportunity that open easily for you.

Alternatively, it may be that you can't rise above or divert poverty, tragedy or difficult circumstances, no matter how hard you try. You may find that, even with the greatest effort, you are never at the right place and time to meet the people who can help you. Even when you plan everything meticulously, something happens to block your path.

Or, alternatively, you may have a mediocre kind of life where there are no huge rises or falls for you. No matter what you do, you remain unnoticed and not particularly successful or tragic. This is fixed karma, but it is not necessarily uncomfortable.

Fixed karma can't be changed, whether it is pleasant or painful. However, even in fixed-karma situations, even though you can't change the karma heading your way, you still have a choice. You get to choose how you respond, converting the experience into a valuable lesson that provides the opportunity for personal and spiritual growth.

You might have been born handicapped or into a particularly abusive of deprived family, or experience other difficult situations that your powerless to change. At some level, your soul has decided that this experience is essential for you. It's coming from previous actions or beliefs and has already been set in motion, so it must be experienced. What is sent out must return. This is universal karmic law.

Fixed karma can show itself in a childless couple, who would otherwise have made wonderful parents on the strength of their character and integrity, while others have children easily, with some being violent or negligent with them. Other examples of fixed karma can be extreme poverty or wealth, chronic illness or disability, or alternatively, really good health. We've all heard of people who are healthy into old age, even though they drink and smoke. The length of life is often fixed karma and cannot be avoided, such as the early death of children or young adults. Many highly gifted and accomplished artists, musicians and singers are inspirational and creative but, for some reason, do not get appropriate recognition, while less talented people are elevated to fame easily. It's hard to fathom with our earthly mind what the reasons could be for such outcomes. It might not be easy to understand and often it can feel unjust. That's because we can't see the details of the karmic trail that has been formed over many lives and the underlying need that our soul has for going through these experiences, unless we look at it with a competent and compassionate Vedic astrologer.

This is a true story of a dear friend of mine. I have changed some details to preserve his privacy.

> *There was a man called Geoff, from Sydney, who was a successful builder and also a very good Vedic astrologer. He noticed a tragedy coming up in his chart that would change his fortune and destroy his business. As the period approached, he did everything he could to make sure that he was on good terms with everyone around him and was mindful to treat each customer as well as he could. Immediately prior to the time when this catastrophic event was due to take place astrologically, Geoff was feeling confident that he could avoid the predicted disaster. He couldn't imagine what could go wrong.*
>
> *Then, one Monday during the predicted period, he received a deluge of cancellations by customers, while at the same time, tradesmen and suppliers withdrew their services to him. After some research, he found that another company in the same area with a similar name had gone bankrupt. Even though he did let everyone know that this was not his business, the tradesmen, suppliers and customers stayed away and he went bankrupt anyway. He couldn't avert his fixed karma and had to experience it fully, even though he did his best to stop it.*

The second kind of karma is mixed, (medium-strength) karma, which is also relatively strong, but not as strong as fixed. With mixed, medium-strength karma, it is likely that actions or events will play out in life unless huge efforts are made to make the changes required to avert them. If the mixed, medium-strength karma indicates eventual success, then with some effort, success may be achieved. You may have many obstacles in your path and rejections along the way and might need to make many internal changes, but eventually you may break through and fulfil your goal. If the mixed, medium-strength karma indicates eventual failure, then you might create that too with chaotic, mixed messages. Mixed, medium-strength karma requires great effort to change. However, change is possible with a good attitude and perseverance.

In mixed, medium-strength karmic situations, you will be challenged to stay with it or, in order to change it, you might need to change beliefs that no longer serve you. You might need to re-evaluate your values or change your behaviour and intentions. None of these are easy tasks. They involve looking at yourself honestly and deeply to notice your thoughts, beliefs and intentions, evaluating your behaviour and coming to see your blind spots. This process can take a lifetime to make significant change and relies very much on your ability to honestly self-evaluate, let go and move on.

At times, you might have to consider only yourself while, at other times, you will need to consider the consequences of your actions on others.

It is possible that change can take place relatively quickly once all of the required elements are brought into alignment through your efforts. You can make the changes if you are prepared to search your heart and soul for the best possible responses, which will result in growth. It can be that difficult love relationships are resolved with genuine soul searching if you are prepared for the reflection and change that this requires.

From this point on, you are likely to make different choices in how you respond to the situations that come your way, even if you can't avert the actual karmic situation.

The third type of karma is light karma, which can easily be changed by altering your thoughts, intentions, beliefs or actions. Light karma can be changed quickly and is more directly under your conscious control.

This can be wonderful, tragic or chaotic karma and everything in between, in any area of life, because everything is karma and it is your response that is most important. By the way you react, you are likely to gain a relatively quick response, either positive or negative. With light karma, you have the power to change situations quickly and you can become much more aware of the law of 'cause and effect' as it plays out in your life in a visible way. You may, if you take time to reflect, begin to realise that your intentions are a key component of your Karma and what you create. Your intentions are coming from your desire and are executed through your values, beliefs, thoughts, words and actions. This may be considered free will.

You always have a choice.

In truth, you always have a mixture of these three karmas (fixed, mixed and light) entwined through every aspect of your life experience, with some in greater measure than others, in particular areas of your life. One person might find their relationships have some particularly heavy, fixed and difficult karma, while their career flows really well after some hard work and perseverance, showing mixed-strength karma; for others health is good, even though they eat junk food for most of their life. For some people, a knowledge of karma has led them to live in fear and lose trust in themselves. These people may be so terrified of creating difficult karma that they put off making decisions and give their power to others. At the end of such a life, they might realise that their decision to not make decisions is still a decision in itself that may have more to do with fear and lack of courage. A decision to avoid life's challenges and, hence, its potential for experience and growth, in attempting to remain safe, can result in feelings of regret, resentment or anger over lost opportunities at the end of life. Alternatively, there may be a misplaced reliance on others to somehow make decisions. In other words, not making decisions and leaving them to others, is not helpful for us or others, in terms of karma.

Such a situation has the effect of putting impossible expectations on others that often result in disappointment, anger and resentment on both sides, when expectations are not fulfilled. One party feels powerless with unmet expectations, while the other feels frustrated by the unrealistic responsibility of being expected to make someone else happy. This is, of course, a valuable life experience, although frustrating and painful for both parties.

At some level, you have elected to live now in this moment in time and to be part of this family, culture, race and the consciousness of humanity at this period of evolution, and to be a part of this mass consciousness. You are multi-dimensional, existing in many spheres and all of these elements are part of your spiritual path, without exception; a separate entity and also part of the world and the 'oneness' of the universe. We are all connected and our souls are connected through time and space, through many realms. This means that by being kind to others, you are being kind to yourself and by hurting others, you are hurting yourself. You end up hurting yourself because 'others' maybe you in another place and time. Similarly, by being genuinely compassionate, you are being compassionate to yourself. Your karma is personal, relational, family, ancestral, cultural, national and religious, and is also involved with the planet Earth and the universe.

The human psyche is very complex because much knowledge is stored subliminally. The main theme in Peter Novak's book (1997, p207), *The Division of Consciousness,* is that karma that is too painful for conscious awareness is repressed and stored in the unconscious mind, where it is exposed for investigation by the soul after death, unless the person has been ready to connect with it, or process it, in life. Novak examines many near-death experiences and discusses the afterlife of the human psyche, while exploring his ideas of how the mind judges itself after death. He suggests that painful, repressed experiences become our idea of hell, while joyful experiences become our idea of heaven, which creates a division of consciousness at death. Novak proposes the idea that consciousness divides in death to experience these polarities in full, before making a final analysis about what is to be experienced in the next cycle of life.

Painful karma is often a result of actions taken due to unhealthy belief systems, unresolved and stuck emotions, or poor choices. These will often form blockages or restrictions to making more healthy or comfortable choices, leaving you stuck in an entangled and complex cycle. It takes courage, determination and often guidance to disentangle your soul from such encumbrances.

However, having reached this point, it may be possible to return towards finding your true nature and potential by being able to make better choices. These can be less troubling decisions that lead to more comfortable karmic consequences. This is the ultimate purpose of your physical life, to become immersed in your material world and to discover how you create your reality and find your spiritual centre. To this end, it is necessary for you to experiment with your physicality and your power to create in this reality.

You may create chaotically for a long period of time on your spiritual journey as Stardust and then, eventually, refine your thoughts and actions to create more consciously, until you find your way home to your spiritual self and your ability to co-create with 'all that is'.

In some lives, we are meant to experience quiet, while in others, we will have specific goals that we would like to achieve or challenges to face. Some souls are here to experience poverty and pain, which is unfathomable to our earthly minds. Through these experiences, we have the opportunity to develop the courage or confidence to face our karmic patterns and to look at ourselves and choose how to respond.

You might not be aware that you have the opportunity to change much of your karma at every point of your life, by just choosing to do so. In particular, by your response. You have the power to make much of your karma easier or more challenging, softer or harder, pleasant or more painful, knowing it will complete its cycle and come back to meet you. As your understanding of karma grows, you will become increasingly aware of the effects of your actions on those around you and, ultimately, on yourself.

We all need to be mindful of what we are creating for ourselves by the way we live and interact with others. During a tour in India with an astrology group, I was given time with an astrologer who ran a notable Vedic astrology institution in India for Indian middle and upper-caste boys. We met in his office in Delhi in the year 2000 and after a brief chat he offered to look at the charts of the people in the group. I was surprised to find his overall performance to be quite rudimentary and unreliable, as he made some reasonably accurate analyses and predictions mixed with several grossly inaccurate ones. I took off my wedding ring and asked three questions:

Will I be married?

Will I have children?

Will I become an astrologer?

Many traditional, Indian Vedic astrologers prefer to be asked questions in this manner. His answer to each question was a resounding "No".

He said that he couldn't see much of merit in my chart in any of those areas. He said that because the chart had several planets in the twelfth house, many of my choices would be poor, sinful, destructive and wasteful. Therefore, I would not be able to do astrology successfully. Upon looking at marriage and children, he also said that I would be in my second, if not third marriage by now, and that I would have no children, but possibly some abortions or miscarriages. I informed him that I was indeed married to my first husband, had two children and had been an astrologer for several years, to which he responded that my husband's good karma must have saved me from a poor fate.

This was a valuable learning experience for me to observe how he had allowed his personal and cultural conditioning, and also his prejudices, to filter through into his astrology readings. Regardless of his position at the school, he was not such an accomplished astrologer. He said that many Western women did not stay committed to marriage and, therefore, he had assumed that, with Saturn being the ruler of the Seventh house of husband in the second house of family, there would be tough times in marriage that would result in me having three divorces and no children. He found it hard to imagine that some Western women might have the motivation to try to sort things out, rather than moving on. In my chart, Jupiter and Venus are very strong planets, aspecting and occupying respectively, the first (ascendant) house and also the seventh house of marriage, which both indicate the strong possibility of longevity in marriage. In addition, the other possible astrological interpretation for many planets in the twelfth house is a strong focus on Moksha, spiritual liberation and subconscious matters. The combination of planets in my chart was a fairly typical indication of an interest and ability in astrology. His obviously deep, cultural conditioning had coloured his view of the merit of women, and Western women in particular, in regards to what they may aspire to do or be. In his school, only boys were admitted to learn the Vedic sciences.

He had a conservative, patriarchal and cultural view of relationships, astrology, career and children. This meant that he didn't consider the more positive possibilities as a credible outcome. Perhaps a spiritual ego was also operating that involved some arrogance about being part of a culture that had a long historical tradition of spiritual practice.

This story serves to show that it is imperative for an astrologer to be both personally and spiritually developed and open minded in any branch of astrology. In my opinion, it is not very important to be schooled in a particular knowledge or technique, or to come from a particular family, caste or race, in order to be competent or capable in this area.

In fact, from my point of view, not coming from within the tradition of an astrology system but having an innate passion or natural ability for it, may be more important and more authentic, at a soul level. In the same way that an astrologer forecasting death at a particular time that turns out to be false, can cause great stress to the person concerned, so too can the declaration of a lack of capability or success for someone in a particular area of life for which they feel a calling, be extremely damaging. This can sow seeds of impending doom, thereby undermining life purpose and be extremely damaging for the person concerned.

The mind is very powerful. So powerful that statements or expectations can plant seeds that can easily manifest into reality through fear. Whatever you focus on has the power to change your reality and your destiny, especially with light or mixed-strength karma. Someone with perceived power or knowledge, who makes a prediction about you, may have a huge influence on your reality. This was a great lesson to me and a reminder that if I use such powers thoughtlessly, or with an inflated ego, or poor judgement, it will surely create negative karma for myself as well as cause damage to others.

Denis Flaherty (2001) talks about the problem of astrologers feeling the need to make accurate predictions being related to their inflated egos and the need to impress when, in reality, much of the karma in a chart is not fixed and is open to choice. In such cases, it is the astrologer who is working in his or her own interest of needing to impress, rather than that of helping or guiding others in their life path and possible choices.

This was a great example of 'what not to do'. From this experience, I have learned to be conscious of attempting not to make pre-judgements as much as possible when reading a chart. Rather, it is best to consider all of its possible interpretations, as well as the range of choices available to the person concerned. Each chart is full of challenges and gifts and under the influence of the cycles of karma that are destined to unfold. My intention is to help those people who come to me for readings and to understand the cycles that they are involved in, while pointing out their various options and how they might make the most of each particular period, particularly the more challenging ones.

As an astrologer, I know that there is no reason to reveal a difficult period of life to a person without also giving guidance as to how they can best cope with it. I feel that it is the astrologer's duty to leave each person with the potential to take responsibility for themselves and to help them with their challenges so that they can be empowered by their ability to make choices to navigate their life.

I believe that a good Vedic astrologer will be intuitive and knowledgeable by being able to look at the psychology, emotional state, relationships, career, health, karmic cycles and many other matters to help people to deal with them without an agenda or prejudgement.

When I see a chart unfolding in the life of a person, with its accuracy, idiosyncrasies and poignancy, I am constantly reminded of my 'smallness' in the scheme of things. This reminds me that there are realms operating outside of my awareness that are impossible for me to comprehend from this human form, consisting of cycles within cycles and possibly other realms of existence. I am a grain of stardust in the universe and a part of 'all that is'.

We are all creating karma through our actions, regardless of our role in this life, so it is important to remain mindful of our intentions and actions and their impact on others.

You are an individual and also 'at one with all that is', so whatever you do has an effect on you and, as you go through the long process of rebirth, your soul will begin to realise your true power as a creator. Eventually, through karmic law, you will begin to understand that, at some level, you are responsible for creating your own experiences. You reap what you sew. As your consciousness expands, so does your wisdom and mastery, until you begin to refine your intentions, which leads to more conscious actions. In this way, you may be drawn back on your journey, consciously towards 'all that is', once you've had many earthly experiences and refined and clarified your thoughts and emotions.

Look at your life. What are the themes?

Which areas of your life appear to involve:

- Fixed Karma
- Mixed Karma
- Light karma

In terms of relationships, consider the quality of each type of connection in your life. Look at your relationships in each of the following areas and consider if you have positive (pleasurable) or negative (painful) karma in each kind relationship.

Relationship Karma:

- Family
- Friends
- Lovers or partners
- Colleagues

Consider if the karma feels like it is fixed, mixed-strength or light karma.

Can you see any patterns in these relationships?

If so, notice the patterns:

List them

Consider how you are contributing to them and what you can change

Make changes in the next week and extend it to a month or beyond

If it's not possible to change - consider how you can change your perception of it.

Career and Finance Karma:

Consider if the karma feels like fixed, mixed-strength or light karma.

1. How is your financial position?
2. Are you happy in your work?

3. Do you have a career?

4. Did you receive an adequate education?

5. Do you have good employment opportunities?

6. Do you have the good fortune to be in the right place and time?

7. Do you receive recognition for your work? Or

8. Do you find that there are few opportunities, even with substantial efforts, resulting in no recognition and a chequered resume?

Write down your answers.

Consider how you are contributing to the situation.

Consider what you can change.

Make the change or changes in the next week and extend it to a month or beyond.

If you can't change the situation, then you can work at changing your perception and reaction to it.

1. Are there some areas of life that you don't have to concern yourself with because they run smoothly, for the most part?

2. Are there some patterns that, regardless of how much you try, continue to be troublesome?

Write down those areas of life that appear to be outside your control.

Continue picking new areas to focus on in the forthcoming year. In this way, you can become more aware of your patterns and your karma and consciously set up new patterns or karma, even in those areas that are fixed. Remember that changing perception is a positive change.

The list of opportunities is endless once you start to consider it.

If you tabulate your results you will find an indication of areas of life that may be classified as Light Mixed or Fixed karma.

CHAPTER 5:

SURYA AS VIDUR, THE PRIEST

Surya is the soul of man on its cycle through many lives. On the banks of the Ganges River, in a place called Haridwar in north India, is a place where many religious ceremonies and rituals take place. The Ganges River (also known as Ganga) is considered to be the lifeblood of India and is worshipped for its bountifulness. It is said that the deceased will reside in heaven as long as a portion of that person's remains are sanctified by the Ganga waters.

Here I am giving an account of a real situation that I witnessed, in order to show karma playing out and being set up in a real-life situation, that is just a glimpse of the actions of one priest. This is an example of someone who is blessed with very comfortable karma by their birth and their resultant position in life, who allows greed or deeper unconscious motives to over-ride genuine Dharma or right action. Be aware that I am not suggesting that this is an example of all or many priests.

> *On any day along the banks of the Ganges there are throngs of people. Many are there to receive its vibrant energy and to meditate, put a candle out onto the river or to cleanse their sins by bathing in the holy water. This is one of the places along the Ganges where family members go to help their deceased loved ones return to their source, by pouring their ashes into the river to release them to join the spirit world. An Indian performing at least some of the sraddha (funeral rites) rituals in India receives the satisfaction of having done the best they can do to bring peace for the soul of their deceased family member. It is a journey home, both for the deceased and the living; a spiritual as well as an emotional pilgrimage. It is the desire of most Hindus to have their ashes scattered in the sacred Ganges. Following this, there has often been a tradition for grieving members to visit their family pundit (scholar) after the funeral ritual in order to update the record of family names. These are written in a scroll that goes back hundreds of years.*

In this particular case, the man involved had taken his father's ashes from England to India.

The ritual symbolically connects the dead and the living family members with their ancestral, religious and cultural roots. Haridwar is an ancient spiritual centre where tourists, grieving relatives and local people go on pilgrimage. In this place, there are also many poor people who come to receive from the generosity of the grieving visitors that are advised to donate food and small amounts of money to them, as part of the funeral rites. The donation is part of the funeral ritual and is seen as a way of paving a good spiritual path for the grieving family and the loved ones in the afterlife.

On this particular cold morning, there was a commotion. There was an Indian-looking, well-built man in his late 50s called Shukthi. He had grey hair, thinning on top, was stripped to the waste and wearing swimming shorts. He was kneeling on a stool, looking at the man sitting in front of him and shouting, "No! That's not what we agreed. No more! I am here to send my father off and I don't want to be pestered for more money. I am here for my father. This is my last gift to him".

The man facing him was of a medium build and around 30 years old. He was sitting cross-legged on a cloth, wearing a cream-coloured turban and a large loose collarless shirt with dark trousers. This is Surya and his name in this life is Vidur. He was a Brahmin priest that had been hired, only a short time before, by the grieving Shukthi to perform the last rites for his father. A hefty price had been agreed and paid and, since then, three different men had interrupted the ceremony to add 'vital' ingredients or artefacts, with Vidur's approval, at different stages of the ceremony. Each time disturbing the ritual for further payments from the grieving Shukthi.

Shukthi angrily said again, "No more. That's what we agreed. I don't want anyone else interrupting the ceremony for money".

Vidur replied, "That is a necessary part of the ceremony".

Shukthi replied, "I have paid you. I am not paying any more and I don't want any more interruptions asking for money".

"Ok, ok...", said Vidu reluctantly, and continued with his mantras and rituals for a few more minutes in front of Shukthi, who slowly closed his eyes again and began to relax.

Vidur got Shukthi to repeat a chant several times and then said, "Put that gold chain you are wearing into the water".

Shukthi opened his eyes, looked confused and, when Vidur repeated his request, he grew angry again.

Vidur was saying, "It is a small sacrifice to ensure the safe passing of your father and a good rebirth. Don't you want that for him?"

Shukthi said firmly, "Gold will make no difference to my father's passing".

He knew that wealth, in that way, is a human earthly perception and would not help his father in the spirit world. After more demands and rejections, Vidur said,

"Alright, it's your choice, but your sacrifice would have made a great offering to Krishna for your father".

Shukthi said, "No more".

"Ok, ok", the priest replied.

Shukthi settled on his stool again, looking ruffled and uncomfortable, but accepting of what was left of the service, while Vidur continued speaking in Sanskrit, pouring water from a bowl at different points and splashing it in the air, onto Shukthi's hands, temples, third eye and crown.

After a few minutes, Vidur told Shukthi to tip the ashes into the river from his urn. At that moment, Vidur's mobile phone rang. He answered it, giving curt instructions about arrangements for an evening meeting. Shukthi looked at Vidur on the phone and his anger returned. This was a special moment for him, and his priest was talking on the phone about his social arrangements.

Vidur was a Brahmin priest. Brahmins are the highest of four classes (varnas) of Indian culture. Brahmin is the priest class, although not all Brahmins are priests. However, to become a priest, an individual must be a Brahmin in this culture. Being born a Brahmin is considered to be of great fortune and virtue. It is common knowledge in India that being born into this lineage demonstrates good karma and a close relationship to the state of enlightenment, as well as a special relationship with the gods. Such a person is most likely to have received a privileged education, where he would have learned Sanskrit, mantras, rituals and the spiritual teachings from the ancient, sacred, spiritual texts.

The priest, noticing Shukthi's irritation, put away his phone and said, "OK, go on, tip all the ashes into the water".

As he did so, another flurry of activity involving shouts and laughter from another group pierced the air. Shukthi decided to focus on the task at hand in spite of the noise and interruptions, and gently tapped his father's ashes into the flowing water. This was a special moment for him. His relationship with his father had been difficult and estranged for most of his life, but had become reconciled, more respectful and loving in recent years. He and his brother had travelled a long way for this moment. He felt the privilege (with his brother) of being the one of six siblings to bring their father's ashes from London to the Ganges, where his family's ashes had been placed for many generations. Vidur looked around him impatiently, wishing Shukthi would hurry up, as his next customer was waiting in the background.

As he looked down the river, he caught the eye of a boy of around 12 or 13, standing in the cold, running water of the river. The boy looked up at him, winked, smiled and pointed to his full pockets. The boy held a piece of glass about 15 cm square, resting on the river bed, where the water flowed over it. This provided a strong magnification where he was able to see the glint of jewellery as it flowed down the floor of the river towards him, where he scooped it up with lightning speed and put it in his pocket. A team of boys just like him were waiting downstream and were able to pick up gold bangles, chains, rings and other valuables that had been surrendered into the water by grieving families.

This boy looked very poor and was probably providing for his family in the best way he could.

Vidur looked back at Shukthi, who had tears on his face, after emptying his father's ashes into the river. Vidur told Shukthi to go into the water and immerse himself three times in order to complete the ceremony and be cleansed of his sins, and he then moved on to his next customer without any further communication.

Vidur had an air of arrogance and entitlement that assumed the right to treat people the way he did. I had a vision of him going to his meeting later, feeling quite content with his day, and then drifting off peacefully to sleep that night. Here is a true example of someone who is born into a high station in life, who is revealing his true character through his intentions, beliefs and actions. He is experiencing good karma while he creates some very difficult karma through his conduct.

Perhaps the more comfortable and powerful circumstances we find ourselves in are a very good place from which to allow the real quality of our personality to arise for all to see. No one escapes having to live the consequence of their karma.

CHAPTER 6:

FREE WILL AND DESTINY

Here is an old tale.

> There was a beautiful bird trapped in a cage. He was well looked after and comfortable. One day, his owner put the cage outside and inadvertently left the door open. The bird didn't notice that he was free to go and carried on as he always did in his small enclosure, until another bird swooped down and invited him to come out and join him soaring in the wind. The other bird tried to let him know what he was missing. The caged bird thought about it for a while and looked out onto the vegetation and the expansive sky and decided to stay, as that amount of freedom was too much for him to comprehend.

How many of us do this? How many of us limit ourselves?

We always have free will. Free will and karma go hand-in-hand. We might often feel that we are at the mercy of life, buffeted by situations or the will of others, sometimes violently and, at other times, more gently. We don't always realise that there are many times when we can change our destiny by using our free will to refocus our intentions and make changes. Perhaps we don't know, while we are still a new or younger soul, that we have more power than we could imagine. Our journey is partially about discovering our true nature and our ability to be a co-creator. To move in synchronicity in a dynamic unfolding universe and interact with the elements of our experiences using our free will.

We are all connected to each other and the cycles of nature and each new day, as stardust. Surya, as stardust, is pure energy that is part of 'all that is', dancing in the shimmering light of the early morning, basking in the freshness and potency of each day. Surya observes the wonder of life through the sparkling dewdrops on a leaf and the dancing light on water. Surya is present in the shafts of gold light hitting the forest floor from the thick canopy above. Marvelling at the stillness and mystery of the velvety darkness of the night and its hypnotic power that draws us evocatively into slumber, so that our body can renew itself while our consciousness escapes into the realm of dreams.

From the beginning of human existence, your soul, as Surya, has manifested into the physical bodies of men and women and stared through many different eyes at the sky. Looking at the sun, the moon and the stars, in search of meaning or connection with the world and its cycles, and the vastness of what lies beyond. In female form, we may have been aware of how closely our body is entwined with the lunar cycles, the Earth's fertility and the richness of the harvests and the flow of the seasons. As men, we may have been aware of our masculinity and our connection with the power of cosmic forces and the majesty of the sun.

Your soul has long been aware of the gift of warmth and light that the sun bestows on you and the mystery and beauty of the elusive moon, as it waxes and wanes in its lunar cycle. You become aware early in each life, of the early morning light bathing your eyes and touching your skin as it brings you back into consciousness each day. A day where each moment can create a new possibility.

As Surya, the woman, we have been aware of the heat of the midday sun on our backs as we tend our vegetable gardens and observe it setting into the horizon each evening. We have felt the coolness and comfort of the light from the milky moon and enjoyed observing its daily movement, as it flows through its lunar orbit in the night sky, waxing and waning. We have followed our curiosity by looking for its location and noticing its fullness or slimness each night. In those lives as women or men, we have felt our 'smallness' in connection to our environment and the mystery of the rhythms of the universe in our blood and bone marrow, knowing at an intuitive level that our meridians are inseparably entwined with those of the Earth and the universe.

In modern times, scientists have discovered that the element, hydrogen, is the basic building block of matter that congeals or coalesces to form larger atoms of supposedly non-living gas, liquids or solids, and also living cells. Furthermore, by trying to understand the science behind the 'big bang' theory, scientists have and are attempting to understand and even replicate the conditions necessary for such an event by looking at matter subjected to such factors as lightning, pressure and other replicable forces. However, the mystery of what and where the magical spark of life comes from to enable life to form, is still beyond scientific comprehension. What it is that transforms a clump of atoms into a living cell is still unknown. The magic of the origin of the creative driving force that enables matter to morph into life is still a mystery, so too is its ability to evolve into an abundant range of species, is still hard to fully comprehend in a post-Darwinian era.

A creativity that has produced such a vast array of plant and animal species that populate the oceans and landmasses of planet Earth may be too vast for the human mind to fully grasp.

From the beginning, our choices were entwined with our natural biorhythms and those of our environment. Since that time, modern trends have had the effect of distancing us from our earthly roots through industrialisation and the rise of formal world religions. Religions have evolved that often place clergy between ourselves and 'all that is', with an unspoken suggestion that ordinary people cannot be trusted to have a direct relationship with God or universal energy. It is assumed that ordinary people need a hierarchy to interpret the often-simple messages of love and peace that are at the basis of most religions.

X In the present, science and technology has become the primary reliable set of knowledge that has almost a religion in itself for many people, by being the only way to answer the big questions of life. This has had the effect of reducing many of the big questions of life to intellectual technological reasoning, that further separates us from the natural, prolific, fertile and creative chaos of the universe. This body of knowledge rely on rational thinking that is devoid of any creative or mystical elements, is having the effect of distancing us even further from our place on our planet and the ecosystem, and even has the effect of denying our spiritual nature. Surya, as much of humanity, has lost contact with the knowledge and roots that have been central to sustaining and nurturing a vital part of us as human beings, in a way that purely factual, logical and linear knowledge cannot. Much of current humankind has such an inflated egocentric view of itself, that it often forgets that the wheels of creation were established long before its entry into this world as a species. We are a product of myriads of forces, many too complex and convoluted, or even possibly, too simple, for our human brain to comprehend. Surya is only one speck of stardust in the universe.

During our more recent incarnations into more rational and scientific thinking, we may have largely forgotten that imagination and creativity are an innate and essential part of our being, even though this is still touchingly evident when we observe the wonder of new life in a new-born baby, children lost in play, an artist deep in a frenzy of creative energy, or a musician lost in a melody. Many of us have disregarded the natural capacity of our minds for intuition, inner knowing, the mysterious language of dreaming in symbols, the power and validity of emotions and the impact of colour and smell. As a result of our need to be logical above everything else, many of us have disowned, relegated or suppressed these parts of our psyche.

This includes emotional or intuitive factors that have the capacity to see the symbolic 'white elephant' in the room, but chooses to rely on pure rational and intellectual logic above matters of the heart and intuition.

Matters of the heart and intuition continue to be relegated to the background in favour of the ability to utilise linear thinking because we have forgotten or not realised that both rational and intuitive knowledge have the capacity to provide a fuller picture. We have largely been seduced into the convenience, comfort, gadgetry and 'progress' of modern times and have forgotten that we are also creative, symbolic, emotional beings and a product of the Earth and the cosmos. In fact, we are much more than a logical, intellectual entity if we connect with all parts of our being and potential.

As Surya, you are a co-creator and involved in the wheel of reincarnation and karma (action), with free will in what you choose in your responses. You have the power to choose even when you are part of mass consciousness. When you align yourself with the masses of people who have thoughts or beliefs based on fear, greed or victimisation, these experiences can be materialised into reality relatively easily, which demonstrates how beliefs have the power to create reality and sway movements. Mass consciousness can be formed and constantly reformed by groups of people with similar ideas or feelings, whether they are uplifting or depressing in quality. If these values or beliefs are clouded by misconceptions, social conditioning or religious doctrine, then this becomes a powerful force that can be manipulated for the benefit of those in power. However, the force of mas consciousness influences us more than we can know. We are involved in collective and also personal choices and, therefore, all have some responsibility for creating our own reality through our choices. Even when we choose not to acknowledge responsibility for ourselves through laziness, apathy, lack of education or the conditioning of a society that strongly denies freethinking, we are still making a choice. Even not making a choice is a choice and has its consequences. We sometimes forget that we have free will.

At times, we may be unwittingly involved in a mass consciousness that supports a reality that does not promote justice, human dignity or freedom. In these situations, we have to share some responsibility for co-creating the chaos and inequality that permeates the 21st Century. Alternatively, we might, at times, have been part of a fair and equitable system that, over time, has become corrupt while we were to comfortable or complacent to notice the gradual shifts in attitude that resulted in civil rights being taken away in the name of national security, or some other fear-raising moral panic.

As more people become sufficiently aware, they are choosing to take back the power of their minds and free will and come out of their conditioning as much as possible in changing their lives. This results in gaining more clarity in choices, so that a new reality can emerge.

For this reason, I have chosen to help individuals on the path to knowing themselves through therapy, personal development and Vedic astrology. The aim of these methodologies is to help myself and others make use of our potential to live fuller, freer lives; hence, to help create a new wave of higher consciousness from which a new reality can emerge.

What follows is a narrative of two people that shows how small choices can result in large changes. Just as a ship on the ocean can make a change of a few degrees and set a direction that results in reaching a totally different location. Any choices we make can change our path. There is a symbiosis of free will and destiny in each of our lives. This is an account of Surya in the form of two men showing how their free will and ability for imagination shaped their lives.

> *Andrew was born to a hardworking family in London in the 1950s. He was the middle child of three siblings, his father was a boilermaker and his mother mostly kept house. He lived at a time when life was improving in England after the hardship of the war years that his parents had lived through. He was grateful to have an education,*

although he didn't feel particularly bright or clever, but went through school in a mediocre way, making a few friends and playing football on the weekends. He got his first job as an apprentice toolmaker with his old school friend and neighbour, John, and dutifully worked hard, not asking too many questions, making many demands or having any expectations beyond his day-to-day existence. His wages were so small that he had no choice but to remain living at home and his work hours were long. He and John continued their friendship. Eventually, as the apprenticeship came to an end, he was promoted to the role of toolmaker and his wages significantly increased. He found that he suddenly had more money and freedom to make choices. To his surprise and dismay, his old friend, John, left to become an accountant. John had been doing a course at a local technical college part-time to gain qualifications to further his career. He had mentioned this to Andrew, but Andrew had not taken it seriously. Andrew hated the idea of study. By then, Andrew had been seeing a local girl for a while who had a pleasant enough appearance and was homely and kind. They married, had a family and moved into their own home nearby. Meanwhile, John had moved out of the neighbourhood for work and they lost contact with each other.

A few years went by and Andrew gradually worked his way up to the position of top toolmaker in the firm, and was often called into the office to consult with them about the jobs to be completed in the factory.

Eventually, Andrew was offered a job in the office as an assistant, responsible for organising the work for the day for the workforce. During this period, he learned some office skills.

Then a period of unrest swept through England. Strikes and power cuts became the norm as the government of the day was intent on changing the face of England, with the hard face of capitalism and economics becoming prominent in all decisions in the reshaping of the nation. This led to shutting down significant areas of industry in the country, such as mining, smelting and the production of nuts and bolts, resulting in the rise of manual-labour redundancies. Many jobs related to the industrial heartland of the country became obsolete.

When his firm folded, Andrew was one of the lucky few who was able to get a job as an office worker with the local city council. He took a job manning the phones and dealing with files and queries from the public. By then, he was around 40 or so and very grateful to have landed such a job. Many of his peers and family members, who had been fiercely independent and proud of their working-class heritage, had been reduced to the shame of having to accept social security payments for the rest of their working lives.

Andrew settled into his new role. He took his sandwiches to work each day, sat at the same desk and ate lunch and read the newspaper at the same table for the next 20 years. Much changed in that time. People came and went and systems changed and were eventually computerised and Andrew frequently had to adapt, although often reluctantly, because he didn't like change.

Andrew remained dutiful, reliable and compliant. However, there were many times when he found himself becoming bored by the monotony and the predictability of his days and he began to dream of driving past the council building as he approached in the morning. He had visions of spending the day walking on a beach, sitting in a forest, going fishing or being on a barge on the canal. He thought of his mortgage, his wife and her reliance on him to provide for the family, as well as the comfort of their home, and a feeling of resignation came over him. He pushed aside these dreams of wanting to escape and felt the numbness in his head and a familiar dull ache in his belly return.

He often found himself feeling angry over simple things, such as the tone or attitude of a customer, or the lack of efficiency of his workmates in not following procedure. Again, he pushed his irritations aside, put on a smile while clenching his teeth and reading his newspaper over his lunch and then he went home at the same time each day.

Then, one day, while shopping on the weekend, Andrew bumped into his old friend, John. They were both now in their early 60s, but somehow there was still something about each of them that made them recognise each other.

There was a familiar glint in the eye, a way of moving, a facial expression that was too subtle to analyse, but undeniably present. Over a cup of coffee, they spent time talking, renewing their friendship and sharing some of the events of their lives.

John was now a managing director of a printing firm. He had changed careers several times during that period. He had become an accountant and that had served him well for a while, until monotony had set in for him and he realised that he didn't want to do that for the rest of his life, even though it paid well. He began to look around at his options and realised that he had really enjoyed his TAFE studies, so he had decided to look around for further educational opportunities. He came upon Open University correspondence courses, embarked on a course part-time and completed a degree in business studies. He then moved out into a management role in a different industry and, feeling satisfied with this way of advancing himself, he was drawn towards more study.

He had discovered that he enjoyed stretching his mind and learning, even though he had not excelled at school. He had found that once he was learning about areas that interested him, he enjoyed study and so he had completed a Master's degree. This led to greater opportunities opening up for him and he was presently in a management role that he found challenging and enjoyable. He was on a good salary, took regular holidays overseas and looked happy and content. Andrew noticed the twinkle in John's eyes that contained a zest for life that included humour and satisfaction.

When John looked at Andrew, he noticed a flatness and sense of sadness in his friend, mixed with the genuine pleasure at this chance meeting. Andrew was genuinely happy to meet his friend, but found it hard to fully comprehend how he had managed to create so much for *himself. He wondered how it was that he had had the imagination, courage and commitment to select and achieve his goals in the way he had and to have taken so many risks along the way. John shared that his life had not been without challenges and disappointments. John's first marriage had broken up in his 20s because a rift had developed between him and his wife, probably due to his studies and his growing knowledge and aspirations that she didn't share.*

He had also been made redundant at one stage, which had led to another period of study before finding his next position. In another job, he had been sacked because he had been too outspoken with his boss. He laughed as he spoke of the ups and downs of his life and said he was fine now. He had remarried and had a family and lived a comfortable middle-class life, owning a house in a good part of town. The friends separated, wishing each other well, knowing that they probably wouldn't meet again, as things were so different between them now as a result of the different paths and choices they had made.

Here we have two men who started life in a very similar way, but through their choices, became separated and had very different outcomes, in terms of life path and satisfaction. There is poignancy in the tale over their lost connection and how their choices had separated them to such a point that they realised that they no longer had enough commonality to maintain their friendship.

It is true that many of us don't know that we have choice. At earlier stages of our spiritual journey, and even now, we may feel that we are totally at the mercy of the elements, the gods and the forces of good and evil.

Gradually, as our wisdom grows, we begin to realise that although we may not always be able to change strong karmic situations, we do have choices in how we deal with them.

We also have lots of choice in choosing our path at the many crossroads of our thoughts, especially as we regain our ability to think freely and come out of our conditioning. If we can begin this process, we can gain more clarity and begin to understand ourselves more fully and become clearer about our intentions, so that we can more clearly manifest our reality. From this point onwards, we have much more free will to create our lives.

CHAPTER 7:

KARMA AND COSMIC TIME

This is a chapter that delves into the more technical, practical and spiritual aspects of Vedic astrology tools and application. If you find this of interest, please read on. If this is not of interest to you, just move onto the next chapter.

The karmic imprint of a chart is a perfect vehicle or map for a soul to utilise in coming into physical life by finding exactly the right moment to enter, so as to provide exactly the experiences required for this stage of the spiritual journey. The combination of planets orbiting the Earth continues to create constantly changing planetary combinations that trigger life events in the present, while continuing to provide a conduit through which other souls may enter through birth. Each person comes in at a slightly different combination of planets for their own specific life requirements. In this chapter, Surya is male. He arrives at a particular combination of planets around the Earth. This is a pattern that symbolises all areas of his being.

(I am using English names for the planets and they also have Vedic names.)

In his chart, the position of Surya's:

Sun shows his soul and potential for majesty and ability to shine and be seen. It also shows the level of his pride and healthy ego.
Moon demonstrates his emotional resilience and ability to give and receive love, and shows his the balance and capacity of his mind.
Mars shows his courage, motivation, life force, determination and zest for life.
Jupiter shows his capacity for wisdom, generosity, knowledge, luck and good karma.
Saturn shows his restrictions or challenges in life and ability for patience, structure, discipline and humility.
Mercury shows his intelligence, attitude and abilities with finance, communication, versatility and humour.
Venus demonstrates his appreciation for love and romance, beauty and the arts, and sensual enjoyment.

As an astrologer, I am always interested to see how the planets are dancing in relation to each other in each chart. How they relate to form a unique psychic imprint displaying the gifts and strengths, challenges and limitations of each individual. Connecting a body, mind and soul. This is a map of a soul's collective karma and how it is set to unfold over time, with the strength, weakness or position of each planet providing crucial information to guide each individual to their areas and events in life.

The chart is simply a symbolic map of your psyche, body, mind and soul.

You are the living chart.

Vedic Astrology is sometimes criticised for being overly predictive and deterministic. It does show both the positive and also the challenging aspects that I have mentioned before. It is important to find an astrologer who can show you those areas in your life where you have choice, so that you can be empowered by the reading in looking at your choices, rather than feeling like a victim of destiny.

The purpose of the karmic cycle, from this perspective, is to experience and grow until we transcend the limitations of the chart we come in on. A life well-lived will see you leaving with a different set of karma to that which you came in with. You always have a choice to look for the jewel of growth, at each point. Remember, only fixed karma can't be avoided. You have the power to change mixed and light karma at any time. You also have the choice to change your perspective on fixed karma too, so that you may experience it differently and, therefore, change it for the future.

Each life is mapped out from the beginning to the end, with the main themes and desires interwoven in the planetary-period system of your chart. This is initiated by the position of the moon at your time of birth. This provides a way of looking at the timing of your karma as it unfolds. The planetary periods are triggered into action by the energy of the planets (in their orbits as transits) as they pass over particular points of sensitivity over the position of planets in the chart. In reality, your chart is encompassed in your being. Hence, the combination of transiting planets and unfolding karmic periods provide constantly changing experiences throughout your life. The Vedic chart consists of 12 signs (zodiac) and also 27 sub-signs called Nakshatras or moon signs, each governed by one of the planets. To see how karma unfolds, the chart must be examined with the planetary periods that are integral to the system, to get more detail about the energies of the period. The planet ruling the moon Nakshatra sign becomes the first planetary period that the person enters into, with the other periods following in sequence, according to the following table on Planetary periods.

Planet	Years
Sun	6 Years
Moon	10 years
Mars	7 years
Rahu (north node of the Moon)	19 years
Jupiter	16 years
Saturn	19 years
Mercury	17 years
Ketu (south node of the moon)	7 years
Venus	20 years

Each planetary period has the seeds of events or people that are due to come into your life at particular points, so that experiences may come to fruition. The nine planetary periods cover a life-span of up to 121 years, which is thought, from the Vedic perspective, to be the life span of human beings. Imagine the planetary periods joining at each end to make a circle, with a soul entering at one point and leaving at another point at death, according to their designated life span.

This is the wheel of time for each life. Each period has a flavour and energy, according to the planetary strength and position in the chart and the houses it rules. The planetary periods have varying lengths. We each enter a planetary period at a specific point for our soul journey, rising sign and, in particular, our moon. The position of the moon and its placement in Nakshatra provides the starting planetary period for each soul. Of course, these will all be unique.

Some people may start life in a Mars period, others in a Jupiter period and so on.

Further, in looking at the energetic qualities of each planetary period, it is possible to gain insight as to the primary areas of focus for each period of life.

For the planetary periods, the energy of:

Sun represents the experience of prestige, power, ego and success.
Moon represents the experience of emotion, nurturing and the mind
Mars represents the experience of will, determination and action.
Rahu (north node of the moon) represents the experience of ambition and illusion.
Jupiter represents the experience of expansion, knowledge and luck.
Saturn represents the experience of obstacles, tough lessons and wisdom.
Mercury represents the experience of communication, knowledge and finance.
Ketu (south node of the moon) represents the experience of past-life connections and letting go.
Venus represents the experience of love, romance and enjoyment.
In my case, the Nakshatra of my moon is governed by Venus, so my first planetary period was Venus, followed by the Sun, Moon, Mars, Rahu, Jupiter and so on.

Furthermore, by looking at the energetic qualities of each planetary period, it is possible to gain an insight into the primary areas of focus for each period of life.

The unfolding dasha (planetary) periods provide constantly changing experiences over your lifespan. There is a time for everything; a time for happiness, sadness, loss, gain, adventure, courage, romance, success, failure and learning. There are synchronicities and opportunities that you will either recognise or not and, at times, you will act on it and, at other times, you may doubt yourself.

These are the crossroads in your life; those times when you can make changes in your life direction as your life is fated to be AND you also have choice.

The moon-based (Nakshatra) system consists of 27 sub-signs, called Nakshatras This was the original astronomical or astrological calendar for the ancient people of the Indus Valley in the Vedic era, which was the cosmic clock for rural people. It enabled them to be in tune with the cycles of the planets in the solar system and the flowing seasons on Earth. The position of the moon in the Nakshatras became the means by which people kept lunar time. They used this cosmic lunar calendar to find the best times for planting, marriage, ceremonies and rituals in their daily lives.

The position of the moon's Nakshatra in an astrological chart has a deep significance for each soul. The mythology and knowledge surrounding the Nakshatras are still very much a part of the cultural, spiritual and daily lives of traditional Indians and it is the original rich astrology system of India. It is steeped in mythology and spirituality, providing deep meaning and characteristics within each Nakshatra that are available to guide people in many ways. The position of the moon's Nakshatra in an astrological chart has deep significance for because it shows a deeper view of the soul's progress. It was later that the sun-based, 12-zodiac sign was assimilated into the Indian astrology system, within the sidereal fixed-star system.

The sun represents the soul and the moon represents the mind and emotions. As the soul (sun) is hard to see or grasp in concrete terms, so at some point, decided it was more practical, to observe the sun's energy through the moon. The moon is illuminated by the light of the sun; therefore, by looking at the moon, you are seeing the reflected energy of the sun in the action, mind and motivation of each person. The soul's energy is experienced through the moon (mind) in thoughts, actions and emotions, in a way that can be seen and felt in a physical way.

Generally, it is said that the planet of your planetary period 'grabs' you in moving your focus to the areas of life that are ready to be experienced, in opening the door to karmic connections.

As I observe the way my life has been shaped according to my chart and planetary periods, I can see that I was married in my moon planetary period, which has a connection in my chart to fertility, because it sits with my fifth house planet, Jupiter.

In my chart Jupiter is the ruler of the house of fertility and is the symbol of children. Even though, prior to this period, having a family was the last thing on my mind, once I entered this period, my mindset changed and I intentionally had two children. The following period was ruled by Mars, the ruler of the fourth house of home in my chart, which resulted in me becoming a homemaker for several years. While it was satisfying in many respects, because I love my children, it was also a frustrating period for me because I had to put my desire for further education and career on hold to support my husband and family. Life changed as I entered the next major planetary period of Rahu as it's in the sixth house of work and connected to the house of education. I was able to follow my desire and entered into study and, eventually, taught physics and chemistry. During this period, we migrated to Australia, where I continued teaching until the end of my Rahu period, when I met two Vedic astrologers in one week, signalling a change in life path as I entered my next major planetary period of Jupiter. Jupiter is in the ninth house (higher learning) of my chart, with my moon, indicating higher learning, counselling, teaching, astrology and spirituality, because the moon is the ruler of the mysterious twelfth house.

I don't feel I can go further without mentioning the significance of the karmic axis of Rahu and Ketu. Rahu (north node of the Moon) and Ketu (south node of the Moon) who are always 180 degrees from each other.

They are shadowy energetic points, rather than planets, that rotate in an axis against the regular direction of the orbits of planets around the Earth. Effectively, they stir up the planets as they approach and move through them.

The position of Rahu and Ketu axis in the birth chart is highly significant, as Rahu shows the focus or life purpose and Ketu is the connection with past-life experiences and knowledge. This is the means the path by which past-life situations or knowledge come into life. The Rahu and Ketu axis transiting or orbiting the Earth becomes even more potent when they transit sensitive points of your chart, such as planets and, in particular, your own Rahu Ketu axis. This stirs up the planets and what they represent in your life and providing the perfect conditions of stress and ultimately, possible transformation.

In my case, I entered into a Rahu planetary period and into further education and my teaching career, as the Rahu Ketu axis transited the Rahu Ketu of my chart. This triggered my entry into a career and our migration from England to Australia soon after, This was highly influential as it took place across my houses in chart that represented work and travel in my chart. I have a chart that shows a specific planetary combination that indicates a desire to leave my homeland in moving to a foreign country.

Eighteen years later, the same Rahu Ketu transit took place again as I was at the end of my Rahu period. I was introduced to Vedic astrology as I entered into my next period, the period of Jupiter. I left school teaching to enter the world of astrology and, eventually, psychotherapy.

Ketu, in my chart, is in conjunction (combination in the same house) with Mercury (knowledge) and the sun (ego/soul) in the mysterious psychological and spiritual twelfth house, This indicates a strong connection with which past-life knowledge of such things as astrology and healing to enter this life. I became aware that I had been a Vedic astrologer before.

I believe that in a previous life as a male Vedic astrologer, I hadn't had the understanding or communication to convey the ideas that reflection and inner change was what was mostly required by the simple people I served, in order to help them cope with life challenges. People who were steeped in tradition, culture, mythology and superstition, for the most part, looked outside themselves for their solutions, rather than inside. I was aware that I had not been able to help them at a deeper level to assist them in making changes to their thinking, so they could stop creating chaos and drama in their lives. Indeed, I would have liked to have made changes in myself too, but didn't know how.

As I lay on my deathbed reflecting, I made a vow to myself along the lines of, "Next time, I will do astrology, but I will attempt to help those who genuinely seek change, to make deeper, permanent changes to find more freedom on their spiritual path".

This remembrance came to me in a meditation and I understood it fully. Some of you may wonder if I had dreamed this or if I was making it up? Who knows? I followed what I felt to be my inner voice. Yes, I would do astrology and it would help me on my own spiritual journey, and I would also help others through it, to understand themselves, their psychology and deeper unconscious motivations. It would also help me to understand the cycles of my life path and my unfolding purpose. To understand myself, gifts and challenges and karmic cycles and how to deal with them. I would be happy to share this with others.

Help them make those psychological and emotional changes that would guide them towards their true nature and spiritual centre.

I avidly developed the knowledge and techniques of Vedic astrology and started to put them into practice with astrology clients. However, it wasn't long until I realised my limitations in helping people at a deeper level of consciousness. This led me to studies in counselling, which I found invaluable as a first step into therapy and transformation, because my primary objective was 'to do no harm' and, preferably, to assist those who came to me through counselling or astrology.

CHAPTER 8:

KARMA AND CHOICE

Surya is here to immerse himself with the physical elements of his world, following his purpose and karmic road. A road that ranges from being wide to narrow at places, with many forks and crossroads along the way. He has many opportunities to stay on the main road of familiar territory, or to go into unchartered territory. He may often look up from his path to see visions of himself walking high up in the hills, experiencing the exhilaration of the climb and observing the landscape from different viewpoints.

You are bound to the wheel of life, but you have choices. This means you're not totally bound by pre-ordained destiny. You are making choices at all times, whether you are aware of it or not. Even not making a choice is still a choice and has consequences. Most of you are free in what meaning you make of, or how you respond to each situation. Sometimes your choices require little thought, consideration or effort as they flow easily and fit well with your thinking and values. Familiarity is often attractive as it has an element of comfort about it, which requires less effort. Therefore, it is often easier to continue in the same job, relationship, lifestyle or even destructive addiction or obsession, than make a change.

At other times, we come to points in our life where continuing in the same way is no longer the easy option. It now outweighs any perceived benefits and is limiting or blocking other possibilities. At these times, our inner essence or life force pushes us to move into a new way of being and yearns for new experiences. Perhaps we have experienced enough of our present choices or habits, or simply learnt all we can from the situation. We are ready for change. However, change requires energy, motivation, courage and also persistence. If we feel that we don't have the resources and resilience to make the change or, at another level, don't feel we deserve better, we are likely to sabotage our efforts for change and never make that next step. We may end up looking back on our life in later years and feel trapped, cheated or victimised by circumstances or our decisions, with feelings of apathy, depression, anger or resignation. Surya is still at the stage of his evolution where his greatest need is to be accepted by others, family or community and his greatest fear is isolation or rejection. He needs to experience staying within the group or living up to others' expectations in order to find out if this helps him to find the happiness he is seeking. There are, in fact, no good or bad choices. They are just choices and he has to live with the consequences.

In some lives, Surya may look back with regret, perhaps realising, in retrospect, that he could have made other choices. At other times, his soul may have required a quieter, more restful and predictable life. Perhaps this is what is needed after the drama and turbulence of former lives. Sometimes Surya's soul has chosen to rest.

However, even though the main theme or themes of life may have been set before birth, it's possible at any point to make new choices. It's never too late to change a value, belief, word or action. There are always choices, event for those who are unjustly accused and sent to prison. The choice is to respond with anger, bitterness or revenge. Or accept responsibility for your actions and let go of what is outside your capacity to change. You could view this restriction or downturn in life as an opportunity for study, exercise or contemplation. Or you could view it as an opportunity for transformation on many levels, so that you can resume your life with more potential and a different perspective when the time is right. This is how you can reach the end of your life with some personal satisfaction and dignity. You always have these choices.

The purpose of life, from my perspective, is to realise ourselves in our entirety. We come from love and light and our ultimate purpose is to find our way back, to love and light. Our task is to release ourselves from all the negative intentions, thoughts and feelings that separate us from 'all that is'. Release ourselves from all that holds us back from love and our creative potential, so that we can embrace who we are. Making a choice is always a dichotomy. There are always gains and losses.

Here is the story of Surya coming into contact with his life purpose and desire and daring to aspire through his choices. This is a true story of someone I know, who was able to change his life by choice, determination and effort.

Ben is a man who came from the north England of working-class in the 1970's. His parents were divorced and he'd lived mainly with his mother growing up. He'd had little contact with his father. His father struggled to stay in work and was often unemployed, while his mother worked hard to raise him and his sister and had done her best. Ben had found education at the local comprehensive school tedious and mostly irrelevant to his life and had left as soon as he could. This makes Ben sound a little depressing, though this is far from the truth, as he was a happy go lucky sort of boy. He often noticed something inside him bubbling up saying 'Your life is special; you just have to find the way to shine'.

Ben was a sociable and loyal boy and easily created a strong group of friends around him, who spent a lot of time together listening to music. They liked rhythm and blues, gospel and reggae, mainly.

He and his friends felt a strong allegiance to the beat, lyrics and rhythms of these songs, often holding the singers and songwriters in high esteem and even putting them on a pedestal.

At school, the only areas that had seemed less tedious, and even enjoyable to Ben, had been the music and art classes. He was reasonably smart, but no other subjects had touched him like they did. There was something about music, in particular, that filled him in a way that nothing else did. He knew that his mother couldn't afford a musical instrument or lessons because she was struggling to keep them afloat, so he never mentioned his love of music to her.

On leaving school, he applied for many jobs, but was always passed over. Somehow, he didn't make the right impression. No one would give him a chance to prove himself so, by the age of 20, he was feeling quite depressed and worthless. He remembered standing at a bus stop one afternoon, looking at the cars going by, thinking that he would never be able to afford a car of his own or become a respectable or legitimate part of society. He thought that he would never have a job, family or home. He felt excluded from society and disappointed with himself and the way his life was going.

A couple of weeks later, he was involved in a car accident, as a pedestrian. A car raced through a pedestrian crossing, hit him and drove on, leaving him with a broken leg and shoulder. He had to spend time in hospital to recover. Once he was well enough, he had to go through the court system in the prosecution of the hit-and-run driver. Ben was awarded 3,000 pounds in compensation.

For Ben, this was a pivotal day in his life. He had never had more than a few pounds at a time until that point.

He cashed the cheque, went around to the local music shop and bought several instruments. A couple of guitars, a saxophone, two sets of drums and a microphone with a PA system. He then called his friends for a meeting. His friends were in similar, poor situations, most not working, with lots of time on their hands and no money. They were filled with excitement as they listened to Ben and his vision of creating a band.

Ben painted a picture of them becoming musicians and becoming successful. They happily accepted their place in this newly formed group. With that, Ben and his friends now considered themselves as having a job and spent the next few months learning to play their instruments and beginning to put tunes and lyrics together.

They started early each day and went long into the night, seven days a week. They realised that their efforts were paying off as they developed a distinctive sound and had created a few songs that were quite original. Eventually, after a particularly good practice session, Ben felt confident about approaching the neighbouring pubs to audition for gigs, and they were given an opportunity.

Their first performance went quite well, with a relatively small audience in the pub on a Saturday lunchtime. They soon began to attract bigger audiences as the weeks went by. It wasn't long before they found that they were in demand in their local town and felt ready to audition in larger venues further afield.

It was only one year later that they were just about to cut their first record and were nervously waiting for their agent to play their album, fresh off the press. The record was switched on and the young men sat back to listen to the sound they'd produced. A deep feeling of satisfaction and delight was bubbling up in Ben and his fellow musicians as they listened to what they had created.

They had each achieved so much individually, by mastering their instruments and working together as a team. They had found out where each of them could make a positive contribution to the band and their performance. They had worked out who could play each instrument and who could sing, write lyrics or specialise in sound production, as well as who was best suited for marketing and approaching prospective agents and music promoters. They had all been on a steep learning curve and, as yet, had made very little money, but were very happy to be working together in an area that they loved and where each person could develop their natural abilities.

Ben remained one of the primary drivers in the group, being the lead singer, and was deeply involved in writing lyrics. One of his colleagues turned out to be highly intuitive in knowing who and how to contact the people they needed in order to connect with those 'in the know' in the music world. Very soon their record was being heard on the local radio stations and was picked up by national music stations. They were invited onto the famous Top of the Pops TV program and their record climbed the popular music charts.

Standing in front of the TV cameras and playing their music to their hearts' delight, all members of the group looked at each other as they finished their song, knowing that they had succeeded. They had dared to dream and to put in the effort to make their dreams come true. Later, as they celebrated at the pub, they all turned to Ben and thanked him for having the vision to put his small windfall of money to good use. Ben is now a middle-aged man, still living in the north of England in a similar area to where he was born. He chose to stay. He could have left, as his accountant advised, but for him, his hometown and his close friends and family were too precious to leave behind.

He has a family of his own and a home.

The music band had undergone many changes as the men developed and grew, but they were still popular and still making money. Ben had values that he lived by that had connected him with his community and his roots, while also allowing him to pursue his passion. He was an opportunist who seized the chance to change his life and take destiny into his hands in forging his own path. Many people around him made different choices and looked at his success with envy and disbelief. They said that he had been lucky in life. This is true. Ben had been lucky, but he had also made significant choices and been prepared to stand by them and do what was necessary to make them work.

In this example of karma and choice, we have a person who dared to follow a vision of himself and somehow knew that he was worth more than the life he appeared destined to live. By following his passion, he grabbed a key opportunity fully and, by learning the appropriate skills, he was able to find success and also maintain his sense of belonging and take his friends along with him. Ben had mixed karma that needed him to connect with his vision and passion and look out for any opportunity that could help him take the next step.

He was conscious of maintaining those values he held dear, thereby creating nice karma too. He found a way of maintaining the relationships he considered important and resisted the temptation to move overseas to a tax haven, because of his deep connection to his homeland. Ben had a strong sense of Dharma because he had a sense of duty, Artha, because he wanted to create wealth and Kama, in that he had desires that he wanted to fulfil. Perhaps he had a sense of Moksha (liberation) too, but he didn't discuss that.

This true story shows how a mixture of karma, choice and following your dream in a conscious, determined, and structured way, can shape a life well-lived.

CHAPTER 9:

MOTHER EARTH'S PAIN

At times, as Surya, you have been born into ancient civilisations and a rich mythology that is interwoven with the movements of heavenly bodies, the flow of seasons and the constant cycle of fertility and fruitfulness in the lives of you and your people. These natural elements link your soul with the collective souls of your ancestors and the landscape. In these lives, your people developed ways of looking at the stars and interpreting the messages that were encoded in them. The constellations visible from Earth were perceived to be inextricably woven into your practical and spiritual daily life. At these times, the soul of Surya instinctively knew that he or she was part of the universe, well before the advent of present-day knowledge, science and technology, or organised religions. The people of that time didn't know the science that tells us that the elements making up the universe, are those that form the building blocks of all matter. Living and nonliving. Cells of all living things, plants, animals, human beings and the basic units of matter; air, rock, soil, water, and universal matter, all formed by the same basic chemical units. All matter evolved from universal energy and created from stardust.

I believe that in a book that is about your spiritual journey on Earth, I cannot avoid addressing the crisis that we, as humanity, are facing at this time. I refer to global warming and the over-consumption and excessive use of fossil fuels. Over-population and the growing inequality of wealth and resources, and food security. However, in this chapter, I will be addressing the issue of global warming primarily. This is only one part of the karma that humanity is creating on the planet.

I am addressing this from my perspective, which I appreciate, may not be yours. I know that there are many views on this topic that range from informed, logical and evidence-based, to purely personal opinion and rumour. Often based on vested interest, emotion and fear. I am aware that there is much knowledge about this issue of environmental sustainability already out there, but many people know only some of the facts surrounding this issue and often do not understand the science involved. If you are interested in understanding more about the science of global warming, read on. If not, feel free to move to the next chapter.

I am not a member of any political party, although I have strong green and humanitarian leanings and have knowledge as a former physics and chemistry teacher which informs my own perspective.

From a Vedic perspective, we are in the Kali Yuga, the Iron period of humankind. The lowest and crudest point of humanity. This is a long and challenging period, but perhaps an important one, in which we are challenged to define ourselves and make choices.

Surya is the stardust of the universe and planet Earth. The stardust that makes up all living and non-living matter.

Stardust that is constantly recreating itself into many forms. This same stardust collecting and forming into minerals, gems and compounds over millions of years that lies dormant in seams in the Earth's crust, until Surya, as the pioneer and industrialist, discovers the value of fossil fuels in plentiful supply, just for the taking. There is no cost to be counted or considered, it seems.

Surya became engrossed in the pursuit of fossil fuels with the inevitable scarring of the landscape and pollution of the air and the delicate ecosystem, at a time when it seemed like a great gift and a bountiful supply with few setbacks. It fired the bellows of the industrial revolution towards progress. Surya, the pioneer, didn't know that there were even greater treasures in the elements, such as sunlight, wind and water, available for use. Ways that could provide a way of living sustainably and in harmony with mother Earth. Fossil fuel supplies have been a bounty that has transformed the culture and daily lives of most of us in a very short time. This has resulted in millions of people being conscripted into the promise of a better life, where Surya, the worker, toils his life away often for subsistence only, while the industrialists and financiers become engorged with wealth. Everyone is so seduced by their task that they are oblivious to the plight of fossil fuels being plundered to extinction, as well as the degradation and pollution it causes to the very elements that sustain life: the land, water and air.

Meanwhile, Surya, as other faces of humanity, consisting of philosophers, scientists and observers of this rampant addiction to fossil fuels, call attention to the fragility of the ecosystem.

At the same time, courageous and aware economists draw attention to the world's unsustainable financial structures and our over- reliance on fossil fuel resources, only to be discounted or ridiculed as spoilers, by those who have been seduced by the idea that this bounty will go on forever. Many scientists draw attention to the free energy available in the sun, wind and water, with little or no cost to the environment, and they are often dismissed as idealistic and impractical, even in the face of hard scientific evidence supporting the viability of renewable energies as sustainable and ecologically friendly. Many industrialists and workers alike do not want to believe that the bounty is over, or that they are damaging their havens, the very air they breathe and the balance of the natural cycles that they rely on for life itself.

The planet Earth is a collection of stardust that has matured and mellowed from its fiery formation following the 'big bang' around four and a half billion years ago, when it became one of several planets thrown into orbit around its star, the sun. The planets were initially a collection of gases consisting of mainly hydrogen and helium. This was a bilious and stormy period where lightning frequently charged and discharged through the rich elementary gaseous mixture, causing atomic collisions under high temperatures and pressures, which gradually formed a kaleidoscope of larger, dense atoms and molecules. Molecules that began to settle into more solid matter within the gaseous atmosphere. This was the beginning of the formation of the crust and core of planet Earth.

After the turbulence of the big bang, the Earth was given a smaller twin planet that was locked into its gravitational pull to revolve around it in a monthly cycle. This smaller sister planet that we know as the moon, is in constant motion around the Earth, while the Earth and the other planets of the solar system are similarly locked into the gravitational orbit of the sun. Each planet in the solar system revolves at its own speed and distance from the sun, with the sun itself being similarly pulled by the gravitational pull from its position within the revolving galaxy; cycles within cycles.

By the second stage of its formation, the atmosphere of the Earth had evolved from hydrogen and helium to mainly carbon dioxide (96%) and ammonia (3.5%). For billions of years, this seemingly toxic atmosphere continued to evolve to form the crusts and layers of the planet. This eventually gave rise to a dense atmosphere, where vapour and gases were continuously expelled during the degassing of the Earth's interior through an unstable crust, mainly through volcanic eruptions. During this period, there was no free oxygen present in the atmosphere, because hydrogen would readily combine with any available oxygen to form water vapour.

As the Earth began to cool as the process of water vapour (condensation) began to take place and it began to collect in mass into rivers, seas and oceans.

This evolution continued until around 2.7 billion years ago, when anaerobic microbes (microbes that don't need oxygen), formed the first cells of life. These microbes have the ability to combine water and carbon dioxide with the aid of the sun's energy. This created a chemical reaction using the catalyst, chlorophyll (the green colour in plants), to form glucose and oxygen. This is the process of photosynthesis. This point in evolution was a pivotal stage of development. The miracle of life had jumped from the purely physical to the next-phase, living cells. This was a period that provided the conditions to produce and sustain life, with photosynthesis as its foundation.

The living plant cells were producing oxygen from photosynthetic reactions in cells to form the start of our oxygen-rich atmosphere. From this point, over the next 600 million years, the levels of carbon dioxide reduced, as the levels of oxygen increased to our current levels. Carbon dioxide and water were being converted into glucose and carbohydrates into plant cells and tissues, while, at the same time, releasing free oxygen into the atmosphere.

This process of photosynthesis has resulted in the Earth's current atmosphere of 78% nitrogen, 21% oxygen, 0.03% carbon dioxide and 0.07% of all the other miscellaneous gases. This has been the approximate ratio for many millions of years, until now. Plants producing food and oxygen, in symbiosis with animals feeding off them and being able to utilise oxygen and food in respiration, has been in a delicate balance for a long time. A balance that has supported our very existence on this planet, mother Earth.

It is true that the levels of gases in the atmosphere have fluctuated from time to time, due to specific events, such as volcanic activity and meteoric collisions. Earth has gone in and out of ice ages and periods of warming and cooling. This has supported many different species during its life, many that have become extinct, as newer species have continued to evolve. It supported dinosaurs from 250 million to 65 million years ago through the Cretaceous, Jurassic and Triassic periods. These periods are shown through carbon dating, to have ended after the Earth suffered collisions by meteorites. Collisions that threw up dust that obliterated sunlight from Earth's atmosphere, resulting in a mass extinction of species. No light, no food, no warmth.

Mother Earth has endured many changes, including the wobble and shift of the poles and possibly a complete reversal of the poles, at times.

In addition, the crust has belched out gases through volcanoes and the continental plates have continued to move, crumple and slide against each other to form mountains on one side and new crusts on the other, with fresh lava pouring out to cool and solidify into new land. Planet Earth continues to shift, change and evolve.

Surya was there as stardust, as the Earth formed, heaved and developed its many layers. Surya was present in the elements of wind, water and rock formation, and during the period 350 million to 50 million years ago when the Earth was covered by dense, rich forests enriching the atmosphere with oxygen through photosynthesis that produced carbohydrates to be stored as plant material. This provided a fertile base for life as we know it and for the continued evolution of new species in the oxygen-rich atmosphere. Huge forests captured the sun's energy and transferred the simple elements of carbon dioxide and water, with the aid of chlorophyll, to glucose (carbohydrate plant material) and oxygen over millions of years.

Surya, as stardust, has watched layers of dead trees over many millions of years fall into swampy water and the very slow process of fossilisation, under specific conditions, take place over millennia, to produce preserved, concentrated hydrocarbons of coal and peat. Simultaneously, Surya has witnessed sea animals and plants trapped between layers of rocks, under specifically perfect conditions in the oceans, to form pressurised fossil fuels of gas and petroleum over millions of years. This has occurred over periods of time that are far too long for us to appreciate fully.

From these ancient times, the carbon-rich fossil fuels have laid deep in the crust of the Earth, being used in tiny amounts by tribes and small groups of people at a sustainable, minimal levels until around 2000 years ago.

From the 1800s, at the beginning of the industrial revolution, and up to now, the fossil-rich fuels that have been lying in rich folds in the Earth's crust for millions of years, have been dug up and burnt almost completely, over a relatively short space of time.

Three hundred and fifty million years of fossil fuel reserves of trapped sunlight and carbon-rich fuels, coal, oil and gas have been ripped out of the crust of mother Earth, to be burnt. Providing the energy for electricity, for the production of metals and fuel for cars, trucks, ships and planes, and for the manufacture of many products. Nearly all of the stores of fossil fuels have been mined and combusted (burnt) almost to extinction in the last 200 years. Surya, as mankind, will soon have to find another method of harnessing energy for its energy-hungry lifestyle.

All fossil fuels are primarily composed of carbon and hydrogen through photosynthesis. From a chemical perspective, the only difference between coal, oil and gas is the size of the molecule and the density of the substance. Coal is the largest molecule and the densest, containing up to 120- 130 carbon atoms in one molecule. Oil is less dense, containing an average of 11-20 carbon atoms in one molecule, and methane gas is the least dense, containing one carbon atom in each molecule.

Generally speaking, the higher the number of carbon atoms per molecule, the higher the density of the fossil fuel and the more potential energy or heat is trapped in its collective bonds.

However, the denser the compound, the harder it is to provide enough air (oxygen) to allow full combustion, burning to occur. This means that denser fuels have limitations in their ability to release their full potential of energy and, instead, release lots of unburnt fuel as smoke. The trapped sun energy is released from the fossil fuels through combustion, to produce energy that can turn the turbines of the power stations for electrical power. The chemical reaction of burning, emits carbon dioxide and water, primarily. However, because the molecule of coal, in particular, is so large and cannot come into contact with sufficient oxygen for full combustion of available carbon, most of it is expelled as coal dust or smoke. The energy being released is the trapped sun energy of millions of years of photosynthesis into plant material that became fossilised over millions of years: Now being expelled, primarily, as coal dust or smoke. This is precious energy being wasted.

This means that the combustion of coal is extremely inefficient. The average composition of coal is approximately 90% carbon, 3% oxygen and 1% nitrogen.

Converting the sun's energy trapped in coal is inefficient due to the high density of the carbon molecule. Even when a plentiful supply of air is available, in the combustion of coal, it is only approximately 0.75% efficient in releasing heat energy. Due to the smaller molecule in oil, it is possible to obtain a higher efficiency rate of combustion, with methane gas being the most efficient at being able to convert a lot more of its potential energy to heat. However, regardless of the efficiency of combustion in producing heat energy, all fossil fuels produce carbon dioxide as a result of burning.

The combustion of fossil fuels is a reversal of the photosynthesis process, which involves the sun's energy being naturally trapped by plants, along with atmospheric carbon dioxide in the reaction to make carbohydrate (plant matter) and oxygen. In reversal, fossil fuels (coal, oil and gas), are all hydrocarbon molecules, which, when burnt in oxygen, release carbon dioxide, water and energy.

Photosynthesis in plants

water + carbon dioxide light (sun energy) = carbohydrates (fuel) +oxygen.

Combustion and respiration

carbohydrates (fuel) + oxygen = sun energy (heat) + carbon dioxide and water.

These two processes are no longer in balance, due to the excessive combustion of fossil fuels.

The fossil records show that there was anything up to an average of 270 parts per million of carbon dioxide in the atmosphere, going up and down several times over the last 400,000 years and rising to an average of over 370 parts per million over the last 200 years. This shows that there has been a 27% increase in carbon dioxide levels in our atmosphere in only 200 years. Coincidentally, this is the same 200 years that the Earths' fossil fuel has been mined and burnt.

Carbon dioxide is normally only 0.03% of our atmosphere, which is very finely and delicately balanced with the other elements of the atmosphere, to maintain the temperature of the planet. These statistics are important, because carbon dioxide is very powerful, in small quantities, at absorbing and emitting infrared radiation. Carbon Dioxide has been labelled a major component in greenhouse gases, along with water and methane, by most of the leading, reputable scientists of the world. Therefore, the massive increase in carbon dioxide levels and the rise in global temperature has been forecast to upset the delicate balance of the atmosphere and lead to significant global warming if carbon dioxide emissions remain at their current level or continue to rise. Relatively small changes in temperature can lead to large climatic changes, as can be seen by the 2-3 degree change in temperature that resulted in the ice ages.

Much of modern society is very reliant on fossil fuel energy at national and global levels, and also at personal levels. The global financial structures are based primarily on the fossil fuel industry. We are in crisis. You and I are facing a crisis that involves many different species at the crisis point of extinction in the present century. While extinction is normally a natural process Surya's impact as humanity in pouring too much carbon dioxide into the atmosphere has created conditions for extinction of many species of plants and animals.

At the same time as humankind has been mining and burning most of the Earth's reserves of fossil fuels and pouring millions of years of storage of fossilised carbon out as carbon dioxide, into the atmosphere over a 200-year period, Surya has been cutting down the lungs of the Earth by felling most of its forests. The part of the ecosystem that could be the most useful in helping to absorb excess carbon dioxide in the atmosphere naturally through photosynthesis, has been and is continuing to be cut down.

In addition, carbon, sulphur and nitrogen that is released from burning fossil fuels, are forming acid rain as they come into contact with atmospheric water vapour in becoming acidic. This falls on ecosystems and create acidic soils. Fossil fuels contain mainly carbon, hydrogen and oxygen and also sulphur and nitrogen, in smaller amounts. Species of plants and animals are becoming extinct at alarming rates, as their ecosystems retreat or are fatally damaged and polluted.

The excess quantities of carbon, forming carbon dioxide, sulphur, forming sulphur dioxide and nitrogen-forming nitrous oxide in the atmosphere form carbonic, nitrous and sulphuric acids, respectively, as they become absorbed in atmospheric water vapour and fall as acid rain. This changes the pH (acidity) of soils, rivers and oceans, kills forests and damages the delicate ecosystems of the oceans.

Interestingly, at the same time, the ice caps are melting at alarming rates, probably due to the temperature rise from rising greenhouse gases is resulting in water levels rising and the flooding of low-lying nations.

While it's true that the ice caps have increased and decreased many times in the Earth's history, it's interesting that this is taking place now, after 200 years of excessive greenhouse gas emissions caused by us.

An excessive release of the sun energy store in plants into the ecosystem, is taking place.

In addition, the financial institutions of the world that have embraced neo-capitalist policies built on an unsustainable model of exponential profit growth is based on a level of consumption that has resulted to this point of crisis is close to collapse. At present, there is growing social unrest resulting in, poverty, hunger, instability and corrupt political power. People left helpless and hopeless seeking refuge in mass migration, while the world's population continues to explode at unprecedented rates.

We are informed by most reliable and 'unbiased' scientific predictions that continued global warming is set to change the climate of the world, causing vast changes and devastation over the next few decades. By 'unbiased', I mean, not being paid to do research by or for the coal, gas, or oil producers or by those who profit or have vested interests in those industries, or by those involved in renewable energies.

They are involved in scientific research funded by educational or purely scientific-based bodies, such as The Union of Concerned Scientists (2012, online, Citizens and Scientists for Environmental Solutions). They are simply a group of people concerned about what we are doing to our planet and worried about our survival.

We are being challenged to look at our lifestyle and the choices we make, and often our behaviour of not acknowledging the big issues were facing. Unfortunately, those in positions of power and wealth have vested interests in maintaining the political, technological and financial structures, as they are.

In the meantime, we are at the mercy of escalating prices of energy, according to Strahan (2008, p176) in The Last Oil Shock, as those with the power to guide us towards renewable energy technologies, hold fast to the old, failing fossil fuel industry. Humankind's addiction to its comfortable consumerist lifestyle and its entrapment in the cycle of debt, ensures that those in charge of the present political and financial system maintain their power and wealth. In the meantime, they are also involved in promoting the spread of misinformation and 'spin,' in order to denigrate genuine scientific findings and create fear and confusion in the minds of world populations.

Of course, it will be expensive to make change, but change is vital if we are to survive the mess we've created.

You as Surya are challenged to wake up and to join the groundswell of people in the world who are concerned for themselves, their children, grandchildren, humanity and the ecology of the planet. You are faced with the choice, to carry on just as you are, as many governments and capitalists of the world would prefer, in pursuing personal power and profit, or to concentrate on the best possible future for coming generations. Most governments plan for only a few years ahead, having mandated short terms in office. This creates a short-term, rather than a longer-term vision that could result in more responsible political decisions, that don't just consider finance and power for the immediate future. Longer vision is urgently needed. You have the choice to reconsider the way your living. You might consider making the change towards sustainable energy and lobbying for more sustainable options in that regard, such as solar, wind, wave and geothermal energy. Or you may choose to stay as you are.

Sustainable energy sources involving the Earth's elements of sun, wind and water are freely available and sustainable and need to be creatively and successfully researched and applied by the inventors, scientists and technicians of the world.

Instead, those who are don't accept the science, are often involved in releasing scare campaigns suggesting that the scientific world is not to be trusted in its predictions. In the meantime, many are not sure what or who to believe and so choose to maintain the status quo. Survival is their goal, jobs, paying bills and putting food on their tables for one more day, week or year, rather than facing the long-term consequences looming ahead. I can understand that. However, if you look at the likely impending change that is on its way, the move to new technologies can provide a whole new set of industries and jobs and a new, more sustainable economy, once the transition is made. There is money to be made and a good financial base to be formed in sustainable energy.

You can contribute to the change that is coming, by making small changes in your lifestyle. Perhaps consider using sustainable public transport or electric cars that you can recharge using green sustainable energy, or even walk or use a pushbike. In addition, you can choose to live closer to work or consider creating a sustainable living in your home or land, where you grow your own food, as food prices are destined to rise due to predicted fuel shortages (Strahan 2008 p243).

You can choose to join the new wave of consciousness that is beginning to swell and dare to make your voice heard in forming new movements in local and national governments, until the growth in mass consciousness reaches a critical mass, from which everything can change relatively quickly, towards a new way of living. A way of living on planet Earth that gives humanity and other species a chance of survival. The Earth itself will survive, as it has endured many catastrophes in the past. It is our species, that has polluted the environment, that is in danger of extinction, unless we make radical changes quickly. Cause and effect is a reality. We are creating karma.

We, as humankind, are at a crossroad. We can carry on as we are, pursuing fossil fuels and our existing lifestyle in the hope that all will be fine; that it will work out well, somehow. Some believe the majority of the environmental world scientists are wrong and that everything will continue as it is. However, the scientific prediction the present excess of carbon dioxide will take at least 1,000 years to stabilise, if excess carbon dioxide emissions stop now. Even now, the climate is likely to change significantly, due to what we have do so far, creating more droughts and floods to low-lying lands with more mosquitoes and epidemics forecasted. When the fuels run out or become scarce, the cost of food and transport becomes too expensive, many of us will find it hard to survive.

If you decide to join growing mass consciousness in our world, demanding change and proactive, experimental and imaginative in creating the changes that are required for survival, you stand a chance of having your grandchildren survive.

You as Surya are at a crossroad. If you make the change to sustainable living, you will probably live in a sustainable home and community, where you and others can be actively involved in permaculture in your locality, providing locally grown produce.

Your home will make all of the energy you require through renewable energies that may include two or three different types, at least, in each home, such as, solar, wind, geothermal or wave energy. You can collect rainwater for drinking and recycle grey water for washing and toilets. In addition, you can work from home or travel on sustainable public transport, or in your own electric vehicle, fuelled by renewable energy. The technology for all of these ideas is already available and is operating effectively in some communities.

In this new world, you can be employed by the vast network of jobs created in renewable energy fields, or in the vast array of service industries within your community. It is also likely that your home and community will be surrounded by newly planted forests. The financial markets will operate and the political governments of the world will be elected on the strength of their vision, effectiveness, sustainability, humanitarian and ethical intentions and practices.

While this is a very serious and sobering subject, I believe that there is hope if enough of us wake up and do what we can individually, to reduce our impact on the planet by becoming involved with local and national governments to demand change. It is we who elect the governments of nations and we do have power individually and collectively if we use it.

Surya is creating karma with the environment.

We have a choice. I wonder what we will choose.

CHAPTER 10:

SPIRITUALITY AND MONEY

This is a huge, complex area. We often have an idea of spirituality that is symbolised by a deep imprint on our psyche, of a perfection, simplicity, compassion and an endless capacity for giving, while having low expectations for ourselves. Icons such as Ghandi and Mother Theresa continue to be ideals to aspire to, for many people. Simultaneously, there is a rise in consumerism and a reduction of social services for the poor in many countries, due to an increase in capitalism and the notion of the 'survival of the fittest'. This is driven by the structures of industry, finance and politics, resulting in the growing divisions between rich and poor.

The slogan that became popular in the late 1900s that said 'greed is good', has taken seed in an unrelenting exploitation of the gross profiteering of people, situations and the environment by people in power.

Here are some of the roots of the conflicts that we experience between spirituality and money. It may appear that we are challenged to take sides, to either be spiritual or wealthy. To aspire to spiritual ideals or become ruthless and selfish in our fight for survival. In reality, we are all an integral part of the physical, material, social and financial world, where we have to pay for food, services, goods, social involvement and entertainment in order to live. Our body needs sustenance for survival. We have to pay for it somehow.

Therein lies the deep psychological conflict of many. We are aware of the need for practical, survival involving our personal and social responsibilities and also our spirituality. We influence by our culture and religion, this may be frugal, ranging to grandiose. Religion is also frequently at the centre of society and culture, instilling a deep imprint of fear imparted from an image of a strict or vengeful God. A God who watches our every move and keeps a tally of the positives and negatives of our actions and attitudes, to see if we go to heaven or hell. Such psychological and religious structures maintain the status quo in most societies. Structures that maintain control and stability, with fear. Many people fear exclusion from their group if they stray too far from its accepted norm.

We are often locked in a struggle between a desire for ease and abundance with a fear of poverty and struggle and also a fear of the responsibility required to use our power of creativity well. This can leave many of us 'sitting on the fence' and not daring to move on to abundance, while simultaneously craving it. Perhaps, for some people, it is 'safer' spiritually to stay poor, for fear of unleashing the hidden monster of greed and avarice within.

Also, many of us have a deep unconscious loyalty to the poor, hungry and struggling masses of the world, perhaps due to our cellular memory or the collective consciousness of humanity. An underlying remembrance of times when our ancestors did perish in hunger and poverty. Our hearts are at one with the image of suffering. So, how can we aspire for more, if we are so deeply entangled with such feelings? Such feelings will surely form unconscious limitations or blocks to success.

One way to find some peace with this conflict between those struggling and the desire for more abundance, is to find photos or artefacts of past generations involving poverty where you can look at them from time to time and make peace with them. A good exercise to help you with this is to look at the images and express your deep gratitude for their struggle to make your life possible and easier in the present. Without them, you would not be here as Surya. Perhaps, tell them that when you are successful, you won't forget where you come from and that they all come with you in your joy and prosperity. They are already in your genes. This is an acceptable way of thinking because most ancestors want the best for their offspring. This is largely what their struggle was about.

In addition, you may also find that donating a small percentage of your earnings to charities on a regular basis is beneficial, because the more you earn, the more you can help others. In these ways, you can maintain this loyalty and respect for those in need and also help those in the present, as you become more successful, thereby reducing your sense of guilt.

From a Vedic perspective, some people are here to focus on creating wealth. That is their main purpose for this life. Just realising this is a vital step in personal development because it involves acknowledgement of the need for survival in the physical, material realm. The task of survival requires skills and knowledge and action to be taken and sustained, to set up and attain goals. There is a need for practicality. These factors have to be constantly reviewed and, if necessary, adjusted or changed in order to be sustainable.

Once survival is achieved in a sustainable way, there is often room in life to turn your attention elsewhere, such as further learning, travel or pure enjoyment and adventures.

While it is true that money in itself cannot make us happy, becoming accomplished in wealth creation means that we can be sufficiently free to focus on other aspects of living.

Being able to utilise the elements of the practical, social and financial worlds is a primary first step on our spiritual journey.

There are many people who think that they can skip this first step in their spiritual growth and proceed to what they perceive to be the purely spiritual, without having gone through the process of developing their material (financial) and creative powers. It is true that some of us have already conquered the material world in being able to sustain ourselves in previous lives, so don't feel this as a primary concern in this life. However, such people can easily sustain themselves with what they do, so they can be content and enjoy their lives in whichever way they wish. They are fundamentally in a good place with money.

However, the importance of this first stage in developing the resources we need, is how we grow our wings, to fly. These are the resources we need to create our reality and cannot be under-estimated. Once this is mastered and we no longer have to worry about our bank balance or paying the bills, the skills and structure learned through acquiring wealth mastery will allow us to create in other ways.

Many people believe that they can become wealthy by short-cutting the traditional steps required, such as education, acquisition of skills perseverance or work experience, or gradually rising up the ranks. People progress in any of the above ways.

There are also people working outside the system in an underground or black economy, but such work is blighted, as they can't be open about what they do, because of the need to remain unnoticed by the authorities. Therefore, these people cannot become too successful and unconsciously sabotage their potential, due to fear of exposure and not feeling good enough.

In short, wealth creation is part of our spiritual journey, a basic task to be performed as a precursor to further advancement by providing a minefield of experience from which to grow. It is a challenge.

If you are struggling, it could be that, even though you may be very much aware of your spiritual path (as you are reading this book), you may benefit from focussing on becoming financially stable. This process, in itself, can be vital in developing your ability for co-creation.

Every living thing is challenged with the task of mastering its environment for survival. A lion cub has no choice but to learn how to hunt if it is to survive in its natural habitat. In the same way, we, as social, intellectual and spiritual creatures, are challenged to manage our social, material and financial worlds before we can be free to pursue other realms with ease.

In truth, aspects of your true character can emerge for all to see, by how you earn money and also how you live with your wealth. Those who hoard or are miserly may have learned how to acquire wealth, but are still very much tied to the mentality of 'not enough,' or the mistrust of the natural flow of the give-and-take of abundance. Somehow, they fear that it might be taken away again, or that they didn't deserve it in the first place. Alternatively, those who are overly generous with their wealth may inhibit the growth of the people they seek to help.

Compassion that also includes what's in the best interest of the others, cannot only be about giving money to appease. While this may appease feelings of guilt over inequity, may not be in the long term best interests of who they seek to help. Giving too much is rarely helpful to those in need, or for the relationship between the two parties. Perhaps some funds are required, but so is the structure required for work to build autonomy and self-respect. This is likely to be more complex for the giver, rather than simply donating money. It requires thought and collaboration with those in need, in order to be more sustainably productive for the giver and receiver. On our soul journey, we need to find balance in our ability to create and use our abundance well. This is very much part of our spiritual growth.

If you look at your life from a financial aspect, you may reflect on how well you are able to generate an income.

Rate it between 0-5, with 5 being the highest. If it's high, then you are already mastering this area of development. If it's low, then there is room for growth.

Money is simply a commodity. Karmically, there needs to be a fair karmic exchange between a giver and a receiver. Goods and services do not have equal value. We need to be able to differential the value of goods or services to estimate their worth. This is where we come to self-esteem. We need to consider what we believe we deserve. The biggest factor in wealth creation is self-esteem. Many people do not believe that they are worthy of more. Also, many have limited beliefs about what is possible for them to achieve.

Some of you might be wondering what this has got to do with spirituality. On our physical, material path as stardust, we are forced to engage with and master the elements of our planet and our social and material worlds. We enter the wheel of karma into illusion and every part of it is spiritual. We need to come out of illusion in every area of human experience. It's important to learn how to sustain ourselves first. This includes practicality and being grounded and requires resources, finance.

Relationships are also important here. The relationship with self and others on our spiritual path. Clarity in these fundamentals of what it is to be human on planet earth is required to utilise the skills to create wealth. It is important to experience it all in every hue, to provide us with the opportunity for growth and wisdom. Practical, earthly life is not separate from spirituality; it is at one with it.

Self-worth is pivotal to the ability to acquire wealth. Self-worth or worthiness is pivotal for the ability to grow and aspire to abundance and freedom. Self-worth is about the amount of permission that we give to ourselves to aspire to greatness. On the journey, we need to have the ability to expand our perception of ourselves in many realms. Such a rudimentary commodity as money, and the ability to create and manifest it, is a prerequisite and very much part of our spiritual realisation and growth.

I was born into a poor family in England. My parents worked hard to provide for seven children, of whom I am the eldest. We lived in rented house and went to the local school. I believe that I had good karma by being born in England, where education was freely available, during a time in the 1960s when the social world was opening up and making it possible for people like myself to move to other socio-economic groups, through education.

My first experience of work was at the age of 13 when I took on a Saturday job shampooing hair in a salon. When I left school, I became a medical laboratory technician. I married and we bought a home and, after the birth of our children, I studied and became a teacher. Soon after that, we moved to Australia where I continued to teach.

As a teacher, I worked hard to master the knowledge and skills needed to inspire my students to create their own dreams, until I reached a crossroad in my life. It was a call from my soul for change and it came through an introduction to Vedic astrology. I was being guided to know that it was time to move on from the comfort and security of my role as a teacher, to something else that was not yet clear, but was extremely inviting. Fascination pulled me into the study of Vedic astrology and into developing the skills necessary to help people with their karmic cycles. I let go of a regular income to start again and had to apply imagination, focus, time and effort to build my knowledge, skill and confidence in a new area, so that I could start to earn an income again.

This led to further studies in counselling and psychotherapy to give me the knowledge and skills to help my clients further. Study provided more knowledge and growth as I explored and expanded. On this path, as in my teaching, I've been on a constant path of learning and improving my skills , allowing me to provide the best services I can so I can provide the best service I can.

I had come from a regular salary as a teacher to being self-employed. This was a huge shift in thinking as I had to become a small business woman and while wanted to earn an income from what I offered I most wanted to provide a good service those who came to see me. This involved having to promote, market and organising myself, as well as continually refining my skills and knowledge to be able to provide the highest quality services I could. This was a challenging period for me, that required a lot of personal growth in gaining clarity about who I am, my purpose, intentions and goals and most of all my sense of worth.

In addition to earning money, I am conscious of being mindful of doing so ethically, because I appreciate being able to sleep well at night. Here is one spiritual journey of co-creation. Each of my siblings have followed their own paths and, on looking back, I believe the starting point as a poor family, was perfect to help us define ourselves in preparation for life.

I have made both poor and good choices along the way and will continue to do so, as I grow and refine. However, when I look back and reflect, I find that I have used the ten rules of creation. These can be applied to any aspiration or career, whether you're a banker, business person, nurse, tradesperson or anything else. Your ability to create an income is an important part of your life on Earth and very much part of your spiritual path. These rules may be found in my book Be Rich AND Spiritual.

Here is a story of Surya as Achak, the medicine man.

> *Achak had gained status and respect with his people and naturally grew into his role as a healer as his skills and wisdom became apparent to those around him during his youth. He found it easy to learn about what ails people and the healing qualities of the ecosystem in their ancestral lands and happily and respectfully learned from those wiser and older than himself. He had the power to hear, see and feel energy and merge into other realities of the spirit world in his healing work and personal meditations. His people valued him and happily provided him with a house and paid him in food or goods, because he was considered an asset to the community. He provided guidance, healing, rituals and rites of passage. He helped the community to stay in tune with their lives and their ecosystem, so they could live in sustainable, peace and abundance.*

Interestingly, Achak always requested payment for his services and rarely gave them away freely. He knew that if people were genuine in their need for healing, they would appreciate what he offered and pay him appropriately. He knew that if their souls were ready for healing or growth, they would be able to benefit from his services, knowing he was guided by 'all that is'. Payment of their hard-earned commodities was a fair exchange to invoke the cooperation of the spirit world with the skills and knowledge of the healer. The villagers knew that the tribe was held together by each of them fulfilling their role in the community. Each necessary in their contribution of knowledge and skills.

They also knew that some of them had more skills and knowledge than others and could rightly demand more payment. With the help of the healer, they knew they were engaging the forces of life and death and forging a connection with their ancestors in the spirit realm.

Achak knew that his people could not receive energetically, any healing, in full, unless they made payment. There had to be a karmic exchange of energies, if the person concerned was to be able to take it in, at a soul level. To help them without payment would put them into a karmic debt with him, which he didn't want for himself or them.

Therefore, Achak always asked for payment in food, plants or minerals from the surrounding area, that often required some effort or diligence to attain. They would seek and find the food, plant, rock or other specific artefact as payment and Achak knew that this preparing them for their healing. Through this, they fine-tuned their commitment to their own or loved one's healing process. It was commonly known that if no payment was made, that no effort or commitment was spent, thereby reducing the probability of a good outcome.

By agreeing to the payment, the healing process started and the soul of the person and their ancestors stirred and collected in anticipation of the forthcoming healing ritual. They had agreed to the karmic exchange and were able to receive any appropriate healing, in full, knowing it was a fair exchange for what the medicine man facilitated with the powers that be. Of course, they also knew, as Achak the healer knew, that all healing is self-healing and that nothing is guaranteed, and the healer was in service of the individual and the larger forces at work. Only a mediator of their soul with 'all that is'. Guarantees could not be given. There is a requirement of surrender for both healer and the sick in the process.

For those cases where Achak knew a family's genuine need for help, where they couldn't to pay, he contracted with them or the family to do such jobs as repainting his house, digging his garden, or weaving his next item of clothing over the following months. In this way, his services were available to all and the karmic exchange was complete in ways that allowed everyone to hold their heads up with dignity in the community.

In addition, Achak was careful to find out what level of help each person required and sought in relationship to what their soul was able to receive through his intuition.

When someone was not yet ready to look at the choices, beliefs or emotions that were contributing to their dis-ease, he often offered different levels of help in the form of dietary advice, lotions or potions to assist in relieving symptoms. Knowing that to offer more is inappropriate, because all healing is self-healing and can only take place once readiness, responsibility and awareness are also present. They wanted help without doing the appropriate work. A quick fix.

Whereas, when Achak found someone ready to face the 'dark night of the soul,' in order to let go, resolve, or make any deep, spiritual or psychological or bodily shift, he would commit to deep healing work, knowing they were in the right state of readiness to accept what healing was possible.

In short, Achak the healer compassionately offered what each person was ready and able to receive, knowing that to offer more was inappropriate and pointless, and very much dependent on their soul development. He respected each soul's journey, knowing he too at former points of his own soul development, in former lives. was also not ready and had to be left to the hard task of living and growing. There is no short cut to growing wisdom.

In any work that you perform, you are using your time. Time IS your life, so it's up to you to use it well. The greatest gift we have to offer others is ourselves, our skills and our time. Healers and helpers in today's society often find themselves in a conflicted position of wanting to give, but also needing to sustain themselves.

This can often result in working very long hours or, alternatively, doing more than one job and possibly living under a great deal of stress. Those who are providing services that are of benefit to others need to have sufficient respect for themselves and their work to be able to charge an appropriate fee for their services, rather than being locked in a confused or frozen attitude around spirituality and money. Potential customers and employers pick up on feelings of confusion; lack of confidence or poor self-worth. This is a source of huge potential and essential growth for each of us, regardless of our station in life. Our ability to sustain ourselves is very much in line with our spiritual path and with Maslow's Hierarchy of Needs (1943, online).

Maslow demonstrates, through his pyramid, how human beings on the path to self-actualisation, need to first master physical survival before they can take care of issues of safety and feelings of belonging, and building self-esteem. Having mastered the basic elements to sustain life, it is then possible to use all of that experience, knowledge and growth gained, for the pursuit of inner talents, exploring creativity and fulfilment towards self-actualisation.

In our society, film stars, media personalities, popular singers and sports people are often held in the highest esteem, with trades people often paid more than healers, teachers and philosophers. In a society where money is seen to equate to value or worth, perhaps Surya, as humanity, is challenged to re-evaluate its priorities.

Perhaps it is also a time for such people to claim their rightful place and not be embarrassed by stepping into their own true worth, as medicine men and women who help others and value their worth, much like Achak, in a compassionate and grounded manner.

Having a good relationship with money is important because it shows your sense of presence and self-assuredness by being able to co-create in the physical world, and your sense of worthiness in being able to receive the rewards of your efforts.

Worthiness is a vital component in your relationship with money or wealth. This feeling of or lack of worthiness may often be linked to your family system or may come down to more personal beliefs around:

- Money and wealth
- Spirituality
- Readiness to take responsibility
- Your connection to your life purpose

You might be lucky and know who or what you are and have a clear vision of what you want to achieve. This means that you can start co-creating with universal energy from a very young age to achieve your goals. Alternatively, you might not feel such clarity because you might have a multi-stranded life purpose and have many things to sort out before you can be more focused about what is required for now. This means that you might have several different purposes at different stages of your life.

If you have dreams and goals, but can't or don't make them materialise, this could be due to:

- Not being connected to your life purpose
- Having a poor relationship with money
- Having a lack of clear goals
- Goals that are out of step with your values or beliefs
- Priorities out of order with your goals
- No plan to achieve your goals
- An inner sense of unworthiness
- Conflicts and confusion around spirituality and wealth
- Not ready to take full responsibility for yourself in all aspects of life
- Lack of action

In short, these can be reduced to four main areas.

1. **Connection with your life purpose.** Consider what excites you, what you enjoy. What makes you feel good about yourself? Envision how you start to build your life, perhaps gradually, at first.

2. **Set your priorities.** Write them down. Rank them. Set a general timeline for the most important ones.

3. **Develop a belief system that works for you.** This will open you up to more positive possibilities.

4. **Take action.**

Your ability and willingness to manifest prosperity comes from your self-esteem, values, beliefs and emotional state, as well as your ability to say 'yes' to the world, as it is, and create from there. By saying 'yes', you are able to utilise what your physical world has to offer. This is an essential foundation for your spiritual journey. By listening to the beat of your heart, the flow of your breath and what lights you up and gives you fascination, joy, laughter and fun, you may be able to find a path that provides you with experience, growth, wisdom and prosperity. For much more on this topic, see my book "Be Rich AND Spiritual".

Ten Guidelines to becoming comfortable with spirituality and money

1. Imagination

Imagination involves having a vision. Having an idea or ideas of how you want things to be. This is a vital component of co- creation and manifestation. Unless you can form a vision of how you would like things to be, your creative power will be stuck and unfocussed. Some people prefer to drift through life and wait for an opportunity to come their way. If you have strong positive karma coming your way, this is fine. However, many of us have mixed-strength karma. This requires focus and effort and for us to create the right conditions, because there is no one who can do it for us. Imagination is the first step in creation. Get a clear picture and go back to it often and fine-tune or change it, if your intention shifts. Put an approximate timeline for the vision to be manifested.

Write down your vision

2. Intention

Intention may come before or after imagination and involves the underlying driver for what you are creating. Perhaps you want to be wealthy or self-sufficient or independent, or you want to be the best at what you do, or the best that you can be.

Alternatively, you may want to provide a good service or product. Perhaps you want fame, or something else…

Write down the intention of the vision.

3. Skills

Consider the skills required to create your vision.

Plan how you are going to gain those skills.

Make the plan concrete, step by step.

Outline the skills required.

Consider where and how you can get them.

Consider the cost in time or money, or both in acquiring skills.

4. Knowledge

Consider the knowledge you need in order to realise the vision.

Make a plan of how you are going to gain the knowledge.

5. Courage

Change requires courage.

Are you prepared to face and overcome and challenges that might be between you and your vision?

6. Motivation.

What is your level of motivation for the vision you have on a 0-10 scale?

If it is 8 or above, you are motivated. If it is lower, you may need to go back to the intention or vision and change or adjust it, until you find a vision that has a higher than 8 motivation for you.

Motivation creates excitement and excitement creates motivation.

7. Structure

What are the steps you need to put into place in order to allow your vision to materialise? A vision often requires some structure on which to form.

8. Perseverance

How persistent are you in pursuing your goals and dreams?

Will you continue to re-assess and find other ways of going forward if you don't succeed the first few times, or will you give up?

9. Responsibility

Take full responsibility for yourself and what you have and are creating.

This means taking responsibility for what goes well and also what does not.

10. Action.

Act today. Set this manifestation list into action by DOING.

CHAPTER 11:

KNOWLEDGE

Knowledge is wide and deep with many facets and flavours. As Surya, you have lived in many ancient cultures that appreciate the significance of the sun and moon and their relationship to the annual cycles, tides and fertility. These are lives where the celestial bodies and the changing seasons have been central to your life. As Surya in these cultures, you have folklore, mythology and rituals interwoven in each part of your life through cooking, childrearing, planting, harvesting, singing, dancing and making love, in the vastness of the cycles of mother Earth. In some of your lives, you've been fearful of nature and sought to appease a perception of an all-powerful and fearful, judging creator. At other times in your incarnations as Surya, you have worshipped the sun and moon and the natural elements out of pure gratitude and joy for the abundance you have around you.

You felt awe and gratitude for the primary elements on which your life depends. The cycles of rain and the gush and flow of rivers in wet seasons, that somehow transform into the heat of summer, where the landscape withers into a parched drought. Pushing nature's life force to the brink of existence. Then somehow the cycle 'remembers' to repeat itself and the seasons roll out, one more time. Your soul and mine have seen the flow of wind across fertile meadows and desert dunes, through valleys, over mountains and across vast bodies of water. The wind picking up water and carrying it as mist and clouds over large distances, where it rises to higher ground and drops its load. Large drops splashing onto the parched earth, absorbing to saturation, before draining off into rivers and out into the sea. A perfect forum where nature, choice and destiny flow together.

Surya is always seeking knowledge that she hopes will help her make sense of her world and give her the tools to enter new experiences on her spiritual journey.

This is an ancient story that originates in India.

The Elephant and the Blind Men

KNOWLEDGE

Once an elephant came to a small town. The people of the town had read and heard of elephants, but no one in the town had ever seen one. So, a huge crowd gathered around the elephant and it became an occasion of great fun for everyone. Five blind men lived in the town and were eager to find out more about the elephant. As the blind men stood in front of the elephant, someone suggested if they each feel the elephant with their hands, they would get an idea of what it looks like. The five blind men went to touch the elephant and later sat to discuss their experiences. One blind man, who had touched the trunk, said that the elephant must be like a thick tree branch. Another, who had touched the tail, said it probably looked like a snake or rope. The third man, who touched the leg, said the shape of the elephant must be like a pillar. The fourth man, who touched the ear, said that it must be like a big fan, while the fifth man, who touched the elephant's side, said it must be like a wall. They sat for hours and argued with each other, each sure that he was correct. Obviously, they were all correct, from their own standpoint, but no one was willing to listen to the others. Finally, they decided to go to the wiseman of the town to ask him who was right. The wise man said that each of them was right and each was wrong, because they had each touched only one part of the elephant and, therefore, only had a partial perception of it. If they put all of their perceptions together, they would get a better idea of what the elephant looks like.

The moral of the story is that each one of us sees things exclusive within one stand point. If we try to understand other people's points of view, we might gain a wider perspective of the whole.

As far as I know, there are no boundaries or limitations to knowledge and my main purpose in writing this book is to bring a few areas of knowledge together by looking at the spiritual journey of Surya, as stardust, a traveller on her way. I am bringing together areas of knowledge that are legitimate in their own right. My hope is that by looking at the spiritual journey through the Vedic perspective of ancient India and modern science, psychology and the latest areas of knowledge as energy fields, it might be possible to create a more holistic view of our place in the universe. I am aware that there are many more views I could have included and that I am being selective in my choices.

Since the period of enlightenment (1735-1819), involving the industrial revolution, there was an upsurge in the growth of knowledge. This ranged from the scientific, rational and technological that took precedence over previous forms of knowledge, such as religion, mythology and folklore. In the present, science has become an ultimate source of knowledge in its attempt to explain the big questions of life that we, as Surya, have always asked. These are questions about humanity, the universe and the natural world that science attempts to answer through experimentation in collecting evidence on which to base theories. Theories supported by empirical methodologies in a search for predictable evidence-based patterns and laws.

There is no doubt that this has resulted in a swing in favour of technology and medicine that has revolutionised our lifestyle, with a decline in place for human values and concerns. Values of humanity, emotion, conscience, creativity, faith, religion, mythology, art, wisdom, culture and folklore.

Science has almost become a fundamental religion in its own right, with many people having total faith in its ability to answer all humanity's deepest questions.

Other cultures appear to have maintained more balance in their value of knowledge. The knowledge from ancient India dating from 3,000 BC (over 5,000 years ago), contained a wide variety of artistic, scientific (math, astronomy and medicine) as well as, the arts, music, dance, appreciation of history and story and spiritual knowledge, according to Appendix A at the back of this book. This is true of other ancient culture also.

As has been discussed, astronomy and astrology came from the same root of knowledge in the Vedic era, where many areas of knowledge were able to coexist equitably and respectfully in providing a bigger view of the 'elephant' to its people. However, attempting to assess the validity of Vedic astrology, in particular, in terms of present day quantitative research, has been problematic, due to difficulties in standardising all of the factors and techniques involved. This is because it's not simply a science, like mathematics. It also depends on the astrologer's level of knowledge, analytical ability, as well as personal development, and their ability to tap into a chart with precision and intuition. Finding ways to measure these factors with accuracy and reliability continues to be problematic, because present scientific research doesn't yet have the tools or knowledge to be able to assess both the practical and also the mystical elements involved.

By looking at how astrology works, it has been noted that the cycles of the moon have an observable effect on the tides of large bodies of water on Earth, in a predictable and measurable manner. In addition, there is a great deal of mythology worldwide that relates to the effects of the moon on planting and fertility. In particular, the effect of the full moon on the psyche of individuals, has long been noticed and has been noted as an interesting phenomenon, but not been seriously researched. The cycles of the waxing and waning of the moon have a direct effect on tides in the ocean. Could the effects of the moon on many humans be due to the fact that we are composed of between 70% and 80% water and so we may be affected like the tides?

The mythology around the effects that the moon has on us is so strong that the word 'lunatic' has been adopted in common language to describe those vulnerable to lunar cycles. If this is the case for the effects of the moon, why is it not also logical and highly possible that other transiting planets around earth might also have a direct effect on the minds and bodies of people and events, as we are, it is all stardust? Stardust in the universe is always being affected or having an effect on other masses of stardust, so why wouldn't such movements influence us too?

In terms of scientific research, I would like to draw attention to the fact that there are many fields of knowledge that have not yet been researched. There is an endless amount of knowledge yet to be discovered and, as knowledgeable as we think we are, we know only a small fraction of all there is to know.

So, where there is no scientifically verified evidence to justify and explain a particular phenomenon as yet, it does not necessarily mean that it's invalid or untrue. It simply means that it hasn't been researched and verified, or we don't yet have the tools, knowledge or motivation to research and understand it.

There was a time when the Earth was thought to be flat and to be the centre of the universe, when the concept of gravity had not been realised. The pioneers of the idea that the earth was a sphere rather than flat, were challenged and ridiculed and had to be resilient and courageous in facing attack and vilification for presenting radical truths, that flew in the face of the 'accepted knowledge' of religious and philosophical people of the time. Interestingly, not so long ago, it was inconceivable to think that we would be able to talk to friends around the world through a small hand-held device or to enter cyberspace. The reality of how the laws of science and nature are constantly being reshaped, as new knowledge is discovered and verified, are timely reminders for us to continue to be vigilant and maintain something of a curious attitude towards present scientific knowledge and being mindful of its limitations and the fact that it an ever unfolding entity.

Coming from a scientific background I believe does has some advantages of the appreciation of evidence- based laws and practice, I believe that this helps me in discrimination and the ability to sift through and assimilate claims, facts and figures, and appreciate philosophies, theories and practices that work well in a logical and reliable way.

However, I don't always rely on published scientific or psychological research for approval or verification, before exploring or taking on new ideas and beliefs, if I find them feasible and reliable in my practice.

I come from a mixed cultural background, which gave me a fascination for culture and religion generally, and a natural interest in science, which resulted in my choice to become a physics, chemistry and multicultural, religious teacher. These areas gave me an awareness of a wide range of possibilities including the value of both the right and left brain. The left brain with its logical and scientific elements and the right brain with its creative, artistic, feeling and spiritual qualities.

By wanting a bigger and more expansive view of 'the elephant' I widen my perspective. I don't see why both sides of the brain shouldn't operate together, with left and right brain aspects equally valid in our human experience.

Psychology (the science of the mind) relies very heavily for its validity on so-called evidence-based research to adopt what can be loosely called 'the medical model'. B. Duncan (2012), who is a psychologist, has written a book published by The American Psychological Society that critiques and challenges the language, quality and practice of existing evidence-based psychological research. He draws attention to the fact that many evidence-based approaches have established themselves as only marginally better than placebos, in some cases, or have performed as few as only two clinical trials. He also questions the validity of evidence where research is funded by the founders of the approach or the methodology being researched, thereby having an obvious bias towards their own models. Duncan also draws attention to the alliances and obvious bias of research teams who receive lucrative consultation fees from the founders of the approach or are backed financially by the pharmaceutical industry to promote their drugs. In discussing evidence-based, psychological research, Duncan said:

"I have never seen an advantage of any approach over another that wasn't a lopsided contest that had the winner predetermined".

Duncan (2011, p13)

Most psychological research is conducted by psychologists who are funded by government-supported educational bodies or the pharmaceutical industry, who are deeply embedded in the traditional Western medical model of health. Within this medical model that is adopted by most of the Western world, there is a system in place that provides evidence of the efficacy for the largely favoured mental health therapeutic model of cognitive behavioural therapy (CBT) for dealing with mental health issues.

There is no doubt that, while medication is of great help to many people to achieve some measure of normality, relatively free of disturbances, such as extreme mood swings and neuroses, CBT is often considered by many people in the medical field to be the only treatment, in conjunction with medication, for mental health issues.

Psychologists often make the claim that cognitive behavioural therapy is the most researched and successful therapy, in the treatment of depression, in particular. However, I wonder how valid such a claim is if psychologists research only their preferred modality and do not include research of other modalities in the same manner? Such claims would not stand up to the rigour of true scientific testing.

CBT was developed as long ago as the 1960s, where it was taken into the medical model of treatment as a highly favoured, supposedly scientific, evidence-based methodology, as opposed to Freudian and Jungian long-term psychotherapies that delve into the unconscious mind. Even now, it continues to be the favoured methodology. The modality of CBT has no doubt contributed to the treatment of mental health. However, in recent years, much development has taken place and many ways of working have been created that are also effective. But because many of these processes fall outside the banner of CBT, they mostly don't receive funding for research. Without exploring or researching the efficacy of other more modern methodologies, it's hard to see how new knowledge and practice can be included in a healthy evolution of best practice in mental health.

It is true that many other interesting areas of knowledge are not being researched, perhaps because they are not perceived as useful or potentially profitable by those in power, in our primarily neo-capitalist, finance-driven economies. Why would pharmaceutical companies fund research of modalities that might be effective without, or with a reduced use of pharmaceutical drugs? CBT often claims to manage symptoms with the aid of medication.

More recently, there has been an upsurge in the growth of many natural and alternative therapies that claim to achieve excellent results in not only 'managing symptoms' with medication, in the medical model, but rather in helping to resolve many issues completely or provide significant improvements without medication. These methods are often not dependent on pharmaceutical drugs and, therefore, do not provide the huge financial gains for the pharmaceutic industry and remain overlooked and are not researched.

Simultaneously, there has been another movement in the growth of personal development knowledge by such people as Byron Katie (2002), Eckhart Tolle (1999), Deepak Chopra (2008) and many more, who present alternative ways of thinking that involve the power of the mind and methods of dealing with the complexities of living. These ideas are changing many lives, in terms of empowering people to take on their own personal development and healing. Byron Katie demonstrates through her work that the mind is largely responsible for our suffering and we have the capacity to change ourselves. Eckhart Tolle extolls a similar message in a different way, imploring us to remain in the present and thereby come out of suffering.

Deepak Chopra has been a leader in connecting the effects of the mind to the body and soul. He has shown how thought patterns are directly relayed as messages to body cells, providing the link between mental and physical health. In addition, during the late 1990s to the present time, there has been a continuing explosion of innovation in effective psychotherapies and natural therapies that have not been researched and, therefore, remain outside of traditional medical models with the tick of approval. I don't doubt that many alternative approaches would prove to be ineffective under unbiased, rigorous scientific testing, but there may also be some that are found to be the opposite; reliable and effective. Such therapies could make a significant positive difference in providing speedier and effective solutions and resolutions for a wide range of problems, with reduced or no medication, if they were properly investigated with diligence and an open mind.

All of this means that when I come across areas of knowledge or practices that I or others find give reliable and positive results, but are not yet scientifically or psychologically verified by research, I don't necessarily discount them and wait for scientific approval before using them in my work. I realise that such evidence may not become available in my lifetime. In addition, I believe that caution needs to be exercised before embracing all things that are alternative.

While the medical model frequently relies on medication, it's also true that natural therapies frequently rely on the vitamin supplement industry. It has been my experience that finding healing modalities that treat the whole person and support the body to recover and maintain homeostasis and self-healing, where possible, is preferable to taking medication or supplements for long periods. Particularly if they inhibit the natural recovery or homeostasis that the body has toward self-healing and rebalancing if supported in this. The belief that the body can't recover and needs a constant drip of prescribed chemical, vitamins and hormonal supplements is not necessarily true. There is a danger that therapies that require the constant ingestion of supplements of herbs or pills may give the message that your natural bodily functions are unable to find their own equilibrium.

Overuse of supplements might encourage your natural body systems to become passive or lazy, due to over prescribing rather than allowing it to naturally, given time, the right mindset, good lifestyle and a balanced diet do it naturally. Of course, this is not the case for those with serious medical conditions, that need essential medication for survival. I am referring to those people who do not have specific medical conditions and who choose to take supplements with the assumption that their body cannot get what it needs from a balanced and healthy diet and lifestyle.

There is no doubt that it is important to find someone who can truly treat you holistically by listening to your thoughts and beliefs and what is happening in your life.

By doing this, they can then advise you on your lifestyle and diet in a way that is specific to your age, mindset and body type and not just the treatment of symptoms. I believe that current medical knowledge is valuable and, where possible, should be used in conjunction with or merged with effective, holistic medicine approaches, such as Ayurveda and traditional Chinese medicine or any other effective traditional system that embraces the best of ancient and modern knowledge for optimum health.

Klinghardt (2005) developed a system called the Five Levels of Healing, which offers details of the different levels of healing for human beings. This system shows how knowledge of the levels may be used as a diagnostic tool towards choosing appropriate healing processes and methodologies for each level of 'disease'. This has been further simplified by Madelung and Innecken in Entering Inner Images (2004, p128).

Taken from the work of Klinghardt 2005:

The Five Bodies of Human Beings

Examples of Treatment

5th Level: Prayer, self-Healing

4th Level: Family Constellations, Jungian Psychotherapy

3rd Level: Homeopathy, Psychotherapy

2nd Level: Acupuncture, Body Work

1st Level: Medicine, Physical interventions, e.g. surgery.

In this model, Klinghardt suggests that problems should be addressed at the level at which they arise. He further states that working at a higher level than where problems arise can have a therapeutic effect on the healing process, and the levels below it. Particularly if the lower levels are also being addressed appropriately, e.g. the physical. Interestingly, working at lower levels than where problems arise has little effect on the healing process, because they need to be attended to at higher levels.

So, in short, it seems that there is an effect when working from higher to lower levels, but not so much effect when working from lower to higher levels. This means that working in level 5, prayer or meditation, can have a positively effect on the lower levels, if the cause of the disturbance is in the higher or lower levels. While working at level 3, if the cause it at higher levels level 4 or 5 doesn't have a positive effect.

He further espouses the use of kinesiology (muscle testing) as a diagnostic tool to find the appropriate levels to be addressed for healing. This study is a good indication of how energetic or spiritual processes can have a healing effect on the mental, emotional and physical layers, according to where the source of the disturbance is, hence, showing the value of prayer and meditation to overall health and wellbeing. It also indicates the value of healing methods at specific energy levels in the recovery process.

On another level in looking at unknown spheres, many of us experience unusual phenomena that often go unreported due to their seemingly bizarre nature. So bizarre that they cannot be explained by science as yet. In my case, during the last week of my mother's life in early 2003, she phoned me from England to tell me how much she loved me and to let me know that, even though she was deeply sad that I had chosen to live in Australia, she had come to accept it and loved me and wished me well.

She then contacted or went to see each of my other six sisters and brothers, even a couple that she'd had differences with, and let them know how much she loved them too. She was in good health, but during that same week, as she travelled to see my brother, she was involved in a traffic accident and died. About six weeks later while I was preparing to sleep, I asked her in my imagination to let me know that she was around me and that she was well. That night, I woke at 3 am to a glowing light in my bedroom. I looked around to see where the light was coming from, but couldn't find its source and woke my husband, who also checked and couldn't find where it was coming from either. Eventually, we dropped back to sleep and woke in the morning to find that the clock was an hour slow. The electricity supply had not gone off due to a power cut, because, if it had, the clock would have been 'blinking' rather than being steady. I believe that my mother was communicating to me that she was fine and she wished me well. It is my belief that she was in another dimension and able to merge realms, at least for a while, to communicate her love.

The biologist, Ruppert Sheldrake, is doing research into unknown fields of psychic phenomena and energy fields in nature and human systems, as shown in the Science of Delusion (2012). He researches morphic resonance, telepathy, the psychic power of pets and much more, and challenges traditional branches of science on rigid beliefs, that refuse to look outside accepted scientific norms into new areas. He has been ridiculed and excluded by science for researching mystical and psychic phenomenon by scientists who are unwilling to accept there are areas that they don't yet understand. In more recent times, his research has begun to be accepted as valid. Thankfully, we are entering a new realm, where there are groups of curious scientists who are keen to explore new areas. This has opened up new fields such as quantum physics, string theory and energy field theory, morphic resonance and more. Such research highlights the limitations of linear, rational thinking, compared to open inquiry, that has no agenda to coerce it. This has led to innovation in knowledge that has led to such discoveries as quantum physics, particle and wave duality, basic building blocks of matter, and vibrating strings in 11-dimensional space.

Humanity has vast areas of knowledge at its disposal. Surya has both a left and right brain that gives her the capacity to be rational and logical, and also emotional, imaginative and creative, even though she may favour one side of her brain over the other. Regardless, both lobes are linked and it has been found that the emotional, creative brain develops first in infancy, providing the basis on which the more logical components can flourish. Hence, activities such as art or music, have been found to enhance rational thought development.

Perhaps it's time to appreciate left and right brain properties and embrace wholeness and stop valuing rational thought above everything else. In addition, there are vast areas of energetic healing and psychic practices that might have validity if they were researched or tested, even if it's not yet possible for us to understand how they work. By looking at ways of assisting Surya on her journey, she may explore many approaches in her life and the larger spiritual journey.

In terms of counselling and psychotherapy, this started with Sigmund Freud's 'talking cure.' This evolved into present-day psychology and counselling by becoming an option for many people to heal the mind or pursue personal development. Counselling provides a confidential, non-judgemental forum where we can explore our ideas, feelings and choices. Often, we may come to a new place for ourselves through the process.

I am a counsellor and psychotherapist and have been an educator of counsellors and specialised in methods of counselling, and can appreciate the value of different counselling approaches. Counselling can be a reasonably short to long-term option for many people, depending on the method used and the depth of the issue being explored.

I became a counsellor because of my desire 'to do no harm' with my astrology clients, and also to help them with their karmic patterns. However, even though my counselling skills are invaluable, I soon became dissatisfied with its efficiency, for people with deeper issues, so I began another search for tools and methods that can go deeper and are faster at helping people with change. This led me to hypnotherapy and neuro-linguistic programming (NLP), which I have found invaluable, because it gave me the knowledge and skills that are necessary to help people to make the changes they require relatively quickly in working with the root of problems and feels that are mostly located in the subconscious mind. .

While it is true that talk therapy has a place in allowing you to be heard and talk through problems, from my perspective and experience, it can also result in people remaining stuck in their 'story'. By focussing solely on the 'story', as many counselling processes do, it's often not possible to locate the deeper underlying dynamics, or a better perception or solution.

Talk therapy can often entrench you in your story or encourage you to dissect it and analyse it endlessly, thereby maintaining or replacing one state of anxiety and disease with another. In truth, you are much more than your story. Counselling works with the conscious mind. Alternatively, hypnotherapy and NLP can be very useful to help you change deeply held beliefs and resolve emotional trauma around events or people that are locked into your subconscious mind.

It's true that, for many issues, counselling, psychotherapy and hypnotherapy can all be helpful in rebalancing your mind and emotions, or resolve an issue.

On the other hand, finding a suitable therapist requires diligence on your part. It's advisable to do some research to find a good fit. The task of finding someone who is properly qualified, registered and insured, and is sufficiently skilled in a methodology that is effective for your needs, requires discrimination and research. Don't be afraid to ask questions to find out how they work and which methodologies they employ (if you have some knowledge of this), and learn to trust your gut over what's right for you or not.

In terms of hypnotherapy, the stage hypnotists have done a great disservice to the public's view of hypnosis and also to the hypnotherapy profession. Hypnosis is simply a trance state, which is a natural state that we each go in and out of each day, many times. So, it is relatively easy to use a hypnotic trance to relax the mind, so that the subconscious mind can be accessed to assist you in making positive change.

Hypnotherapy is the use of hypnosis by someone utilising a therapeutic process through a hypnotic trance state. I started to use 'ego state therapy' in hypnosis as an effective way of working with people. Hypnosis by itself is just a relaxation technique, but it is the skill of the therapist to do effective therapy while their client is in trance that is important here. The process of hypnotherapy is normally significantly shorter than the counselling process, in terms of the number of sessions required, due to its ability to go deeper into the subconscious mind, which is where most deeper blocks and problems lie.

Even though I was happy with my tools as a hypnotherapist and counsellor, I came across an even more powerful modality called family constellations, which I will introduce in the next chapter. I came across family constellations due to synchronicity and possibly my own creative intention.

Here is how it happened.

> One day, while browsing in a bookshop in Sydney in 2002, I came upon a small brown book about family constellations, called Acknowledging What Is by Bert Hellinger. Just the first paragraph of this book seemed to speak to me and I felt compelled to buy it. I was so inspired by the depth and sensitivity of this experiential, spiritual, energetic and psychotherapeutic process that, on finishing it, I made a silent wish to see the process of family constellations in action.
>
> However, as I was in Sydney and Bert Hellinger was in Germany, I dismissed it at that time as unlikely to happen. A few years later, while on holiday in India with my husband, we found ourselves in Pune', a four hour train ride from Mumbai. Pune', like Mumbai, was a busy, noisy polluted city, full of choking diesel fumes from taxis and auto rickshaws.
>
> We soon tired of the noise and pollution and were looking for a place to rest when, by chance, we fell upon an ashram that offered a retreat, and took the opportunity to rest. The next day, while walking through the ashram, we saw a large sign, that said 'Family Constellations in progress'.
>
> The sign was an invitation to come and experience the process. Not being able to believe my luck, we went along and was deeply moved by it and eagerly joined the three-day workshop that followed. We

then attended a 12-day training program and another 12-day training in Spain later the same year.

I was thereby happily initiated into the philosophy and practice of family constellations.

In the following chapters, I will present the theory and practice of family constellations for you.

Synchronicity or simply good luck and having the clarity to seize an opportunity that opens up, are probably how each of us create our path through life.

Through several fields of knowledge, I have been able to gain perspectives of my soul journey. Perhaps we are entering a time when staying in one field of knowledge is insufficient, when we have the capacity to consider many aspects simultaneously in order to give us a truer picture of ourselves and the situations we encounter. Maybe there is no need to stay polarised in one area of knowledge anymore. Perhaps the truths from each area of knowledge can assimilate to help us make a fuller meaning of our lives, if we only allow ourselves to be open to both traditional and alternative ways of thinking and being, without feeling defensive. Perhaps the elephant may come into view.

As an astrologer, I am often in awe of the way the predicted themes, events and patterns have unfolded, according to the symbols in my own and other people's lives. This is a constant reminder of how small I am in this life and in my own soul journey within universal cosmic patterns.

As astrology is the map of karma, the map of our actions and our soul journey, I believe that it is incomplete, if it doesn't include a way to resolve or help us on our journeys.

By learning about Vedic astrology, and then becoming aware of a strong past-life connection through this knowledge, I became aware of a need to do it differently this time. In a previous life, as a Vedic astrologer, I was aware of being able to instruct people about opportunities coming their way, or difficult times and marriage compatibility. I had also recommended Pujas (prayers and rituals), mantras (repeating significant words) and gems, among other remedial measures, to help people cope with difficult karma. I knew that these recommendations, if followed with deep reflection, authenticity and positive intention, might indeed help people. But I also knew that many people used such remedies with little or no motivation other than by going through the motions and were not ready to take responsibility for their part in the karma they were experiencing. They were often devoid of any real intention to change their actions or thoughts.

They often did the remedial measures out of superstition and fear, in an attempt to placate an external displeased image of their god. I knew that for these remedies to make a difference, a change of internal attitude or intention was required. Such remedies can be followed on the recommendation of a Vedic astrologer and are known as remedial measures to soothe difficult karmic situations. Through this awareness, I had the beginning of an idea that, in order for remedies to be effective, they needed to be done with conviction. Or with aa genuine motivation for self-exploration and a willingness to be challenged. There needs to be an openness for deep, personal change. How could just wearing a gem or doing a mantra help, if there is no change in intention, belief or action? How could this make any difference to anyone's karma? In modern times, such remedies might make a difference if they help you focus on examining yourself and letting go of belief systems that holds you back, or allow your emotions to bubble up to the surface to be felt, resolved or dissipated. If this happens, it could lead to significant change over time. In fact, I do know that remedial measures such as this can make a difference, but intention and sincerity for change is the key requirement.

If Surya can put together areas of knowledge that appeal to different parts of her brain and life experience, she may be able to embrace more aspects of her experience to help her on her journey as stardust.

Perhaps it's time for many areas of knowledge to come together, each area letting go of ego or defensiveness or the need to be right. In this way coming together to make a greater whole, and expand our consciousness as human beings. Perhaps we can start to see the 'elephant'.

From a Vedic perspective, there are many different levels of knowledge, starting with those involving rudimentary practical survival, followed by those involving skills and technology, followed by the intellectual and then higher learning, involving philosophy, spirituality and wisdom. Finally, as we reach higher stages of development on our soul journey and gained sufficient wisdom, we can develop enough trust and faith in the existence of our inner being, to let go of our attachment to knowledge. Let it rest in the background by allowing our consciousness to merge with 'all that is'. Knowing that as human being, knowledgeable as we may think we are, we may realise that we know little in the presence of universal knowledge and being at peace with that. And yet knowledge is part of our growth journey.

In the meantime, if knowledge allows us to complete this journey, then it serves its purpose.

SHEDDING YOUR SKIN

A snake sheds its skin and, by doing so, it has to find a structure that it can hang onto as it struggles free, leaving it in a very vulnerable state as it does so.

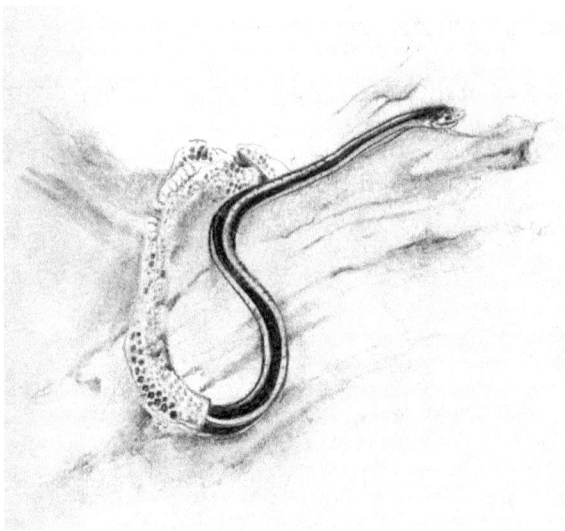

RELATIONSHIPS AND FAMILY CONSTELLATIONS

CHAPTER 12:

KARMA AND THE SEARCH FOR LOVE

Surya is always looking for love. Looking for someone who will dance the dance of love with her, cherish and adore her and fill her up with pure nectar. Someone who will truly see her and 'all that is' sparkling through the stardust in her eyes. Surya is always looking for the beloved in relationships. The 'one' that will transfer her to the bliss that she craves and knows is there somewhere, just beyond her grasp, beyond the misty shade of Maya (illusion). She is always looking for perfection in the other and seeking for the other to see her stardust beyond the sensuality and allure of her eyes, face and form, that she knows will fade over time. Surya is lured by the seduction of some remembered rapture in her search for the 'one', a soul partner, who is someone that she can share her thoughts, wishes, joys, sorrows and anguish with. Someone that she can have children with, bring new souls into the nectar of their union to produce a seed that flowers and bears fruit in a never-ending proclamation of love. It is a dream, a heartfelt craving. A wish so perfect that no mere man or woman could live up to, in their earthly human form. Each of a couple in a mutual search for 'all that is'. A search for a partner, a fellow Surya like herself, who is conditioned by culture with a particular and unique way of looking at the world via the patterns that the planets form on their entry into life. A partner who is on a journey of discovery and an adventure that follows their desire to fill that nagging emptiness.

Is it possible for Surya, once the illusion between the couple starts to dissolve and she becomes aware of her partner's ordinariness, idiosyncrasies and incongruences, to recognise someone much like herself who is in search of the beloved?

Is it possible for the relationship to be a mirror and show each of them their mutual values and beliefs?

Can they continue to allow their dance of love to mellow and mature into respect of each other and their differences?

Can each of them give up the need to be 'right' and walk hand-in-hand into the unknown in this union and the unfolding of each other and themselves?

Can they share their lives through the ups and downs of practical, daily mediocrity and the greater family and culture of their world and the situations that come their way?

Seeking, finding and maintaining a love relationship is a great challenge for Surya, one that she is largely pre-programmed to seek through her hormonal and sexual patterning. Attempting to fill her emptiness through pursuing the divine in her partners in order to discover it in herself and quell her sense of aloneness, in a never ending quest for love. Each of the partners, locked into their own karmic journey, attempting to walk the path of life together.

I wonder if it's possible, as Surya and her partner age and the vigour and beauty of their youth fade, for them to look beyond the flesh and allow the glow of their stardust to shine. In this way, dissolve the need for a perceived veneer of identity that their younger selves struggled to create. This is a necessary creation in their efforts to define themselves. Something they felt compelled to do before they had faith in the existence of their inner lights. I wonder if the couple are able to honour each other enough to embrace the other in walking their own path, achieving goals and aspirations. Be like entwining plants both bonded and also separate, while remaining connected and supported and providing the room to grow and support each other. Dancing the dance of life together, while honouring individuality and togetherness with the freedom to be, grow and connect. Two combinations of planetary energies attracted by their similarities and differences in their quest for love.

She is a woman, potent with fertility, looking for a mate who can match her as an equal and opposite. Someone to balance her femininity with his pure masculinity. Attracted by the law of attraction, much like the poles of a magnet, or yin and yang. Surya's relationships are driven by an almost obsessive search for love and connection, which is a deeply karmic part of her spiritual journey.

Initially, Surya's partner may appear to match her image of a perfect mate. Someone who can fit her like a glove, who exudes a mixture of familiarity, combined with the excitement of a tantalising eyes that are alluring and irresistible. The way her partner watches her and is obviously fascinated by her, encourages her to believe that he understands her, knows what she wants and how to fulfil her needs.

In reality, Surya and her partner observe each other through a mutual illusion. Initially, the excitement of their discovery of each other and the euphoria of falling in love in itself, will keep the romance going for a while. Each of the pair are in a fantasy world of their perception of each other until, eventually, the veil of fantasy between them starts to dissolve.

Surya starts to realise that her partner does not intuitively know many of her most intimate wishes and desires. The couple become aware of the lack of understanding between them and disappointment begins to develop. This is the first stage of the relationship over. Surya may end the relationship at this point and return to her search for her idealised 'real' soul mate, or she might decide to enter a genuine, adult, human relationship with her partner from then on.

If Surya stays in the relationship, she will be challenged to examine her view of the world in many respects. She may begin to notice the many differences between them, as the veil of illusion continues to dissolve. Here begins one of the biggest challenges.

Is Surya willing to examine some of her most strongly held beliefs and be open to looking at other possibilities, she may develop the maturity to understand that, just because she believes something, it doesn't necessarily make it true?

Love, romance and relationships are what we, as Surya, think will make us happy. Most of us without relationships, feel empty and unloved, because this is what the majority crave. We exist in multiple dimensions simultaneously, requiring human connection and also time alone.

Interestingly, while we might crave closeness and connection, we often also fear it, as it can be a source of great pain and disappointment. At times, we may be so disappointed by our relationships that we decide that they are too dangerous and best avoided.

Some of us might decide that the experience of hurt or rejection is far too painful to risk again, while others suffer repeated disappointments and somehow maintain their resilience and optimism as they continue their search for the 'one'.

Many of us keep faith in the idea that good relationships are possible, worth working on, or waiting for. Some of us stay with the same partner for life, for better or worse.

This could mean that either we don't have the courage to leave, due to social, emotional or practical reasons, or we are genuinely content with our choice, or the karma between us is still being worked out.

There is no doubt that next to basic survival, relationships are the biggest area of concern and interest for most human beings.

In my work as an astrologer, I find that these are the two most common questions people ask of me:

Is there to be only one, or several life partners in my life?

Will I be happy?

These are truly perplexing questions.

From an astrological perspective, the house that is opposite the rising sign in your Vedic astrology chart shows your love partner or partners. Your partner is opposite to you in many respects. Most often, your partner is opposite in sex and, if you are an extrovert, you are most likely to attract an introvert or vice versa. Your partners are likely to be different in preferences, expectations, appearance and many other facets. In fact, for the most part, you are attracted to opposites. Of course, this is complex and challenging.

Staying single is an option that has become very popular, especially since the sexual revolution of the 1960s and 1970s, particularly in modern Western cultures. I know that there are also many people who would love to be in a relationship but, for some reason, even in spite of their best efforts, are not able to find or maintain one. Many people have observed the relationships of their parents or friends and judged them to be dysfunctional, controlling, abusive or simply unhappy. Some choose to stay single, rather than put up with a dysfunctional or less-than-perfect relationship. It could be that we come from a broken marriage, bitter separation or single- parent family and don't have the knowledge, experience or vision of relationships functioning well. We may not have witnessed valuable and nurturing relationships and made a decision to avoid them and follow a single path. Possibly, a spiritual path. In this, we can choose anything within a wide range of possibilities, from promiscuity to celibacy or isolation. For some people, promiscuity is a way of enabling them to feel that they are engaging with others with the spin-off of having their sexual needs met.

This may help them to feel attractive and desirable, without having to make deeper, emotional connections, or challenge their thinking or beliefs. It is true that, although you are ultimately born alone and die alone and your journey is primarily a personal one, you are also born into a family in each life and have the desire to form loving relationships. You are a unique individual and a relational one as well. Even so, you may choose to enter into relationships, or not.

People choose not to be in a relationship for many reasons. They may believe that:

"I am spiritual and prefer not to engage in personal, emotional, sexual or intense, intimate human relationships."

"I prefer to love from a distance, through charity, working for a cause, working with compassion or meditation or prayer."

"I find dealing with people and relationships too frustrating."

"People are so difficult and contrary that I prefer to look after myself and purify myself on my spiritual journey. I would rather not have to deal with the complexity of human relationships, in favour of the ultimate relationship with God or the light."

"I genuinely love people and enjoy their company, but feel a deep inner calling to devote my life to my spiritual path."

These are some of the experiences that we may choose when we follow a solitary life.

X It is true that some people need the experience of being single in this life to discover if this is the path that fills their emptiness and brings them what they crave: love. In the lives where people choose to stay alone, they might well gain a sense of independence and autonomy and reach a modicum of calm and serenity, and maybe even a level of perfection in their aloneness.

But how real is it? Where is their mirror? Where are the other intimate people in their life, such as a lover, spouse, children or life situations and the ensuing responsibilities that could reflect how well they are really travelling on their soul journey?

From an astrological perspective again, you are born as a particular rising sign. This means that you and I have a one-sided or a particular view of the world. You are looking at the world through the mask of your astrological and psychological make-up, experience, expectations and also karma, both from your ancestors and past lives. The strength of your personality is shown by the strength of your first house and the position of your moon, showing the extent of your emotional resilience.

Another aspect of your strength is shown by the position and quality of the sun and its relationship with its environment and the qualities of the zodiac it occupies. The sun represents your soul and ego and contributes to your self-esteem. Each life is largely pre-ordained and yet, it is your life to be lived, experienced and developed in anyway you choose.

Relationships and situations become a reflection of the harmony or otherwise of our inner world. How much more difficult is it for us to be spiritual and loving, while interacting fully with family, partners and being involved in the community, and also maintaining our integrity as an individual? Intimate long-term relationships are an important part of our soul journey, helping us to mature and mellow. Our dual desire for aloneness and also the conflicting desire of needing connection through relationships, are part of our human nature.

Sexuality, in itself, has been a challenging subject for most of the cultures of the world. The power of sexual desire and its nature as a wild, untamed primal urge that may be aligned with bodily and animalistic functions, has left much of humankind perplexed in terms of how to deal with it. Sexuality creates life and has consequences. It is how you are brought into the world. It is sacred and it is an essential part of creation, universal energy and manifestation. It is fundamental to life as we know it and yet, as human beings, there is often a struggle with the dilemma of being both creature and animal, but with consciousness.

This dilemma has resulted in most of the religions and cultures of the world creating strict rules around sexuality in order to restrain and control it. This is most likely due to a fear of its supposedly wild, insatiable and animalistic drive and where it might lead.

This thinking has been driven by fear, resulting in an attempt to control sexuality. Many cultures encourage families to stay together for the purpose of childrearing, with sex relegated mainly for the purpose of procreation. Hence, the formation of the institution of marriage to contain sexuality. However, this is often double-edged in promoting marriage, children and monogamy and vilifying and denigrating sex outside of that by the use of shame, guilt and exclusion.

This philosophy has been adopted worldwide, particularly by men in largely traditional patriarchal societies, who seek mainly to control women's sexuality. Interestingly, a curious double standard has developed in many traditional cultures that make sex dirty and shameful, especially outside monogamous relationships, while at the same time, a huge pornographic trade has grown, consisting primarily of men exploiting women and children.

Since the 1960s-70s, many of the structures of society and religion in the West have broken down, resulting in more promiscuity and looser family bonds, while simultaneously, in many nations, another wave has developed that is driven by fear and a need for more control by patriarchal, fundamentalist elements. This is an attempt to shroud or control the beauty and sensuality of the feminine essence for fear of what it might awaken in men. It blames the source of the beauty particularly in women, rather than dealing with the source of the seemingly uncontrollable desire, particularly in men. I believe we have all been men and women in these situations in the rebirth cycle.

By seeking love, relationships and intimacy, human beings seek sex. At some points in our soul journey, this has probably been purely instinctual and spontaneous. We may have been primarily concerned with satiating sexual urges. At times, this can lead to unwanted pregnancies or sexually transmitted diseases.

In addition, having many partners results in the formation of many sexual and emotional connections and the confusion of the deeper consequences of not always knowing who the father of a child may be. Here, we arrive at another dilemma, because children have a right to know who fathered them, whose genes they carry and which ancestral lines they are a part of.

In this, we are faced with the dilemma of our freedom and its consequences and the challenge of being able to follow desires, while also being responsible for its consequences and the wellbeing of our children. In current and in past lives, we may have been part of a religious group where following our libidinous urges was unacceptable.

Such things as duty and virtue were of higher value and sex was relegated to procreation within monogamy and marital relations only. Sexual enjoyment was often a taboo for respectable women, in particular. Even though the same rules may theoretically apply to men too, the fact that the rules are written and controlled by men in patriarchal societies has enabled them to interpret them differently for each sex and use them primarily to control women.

In these same societies, indiscretions by men are often excused, while women are often blamed for seducing men by the allure of their body shape, hair, eyes or scent.

As if men are victims of their lust in the face of overpowering feminine allure. In many cultures of the world, women are given the responsibility of their own sexuality and also that of the libido, drive and choices of men. Women may be told to hide themselves, so as not to be seen or heard, in an attempt to subdue feminine energy. Energy that may be seen as licentious, rampant and so base, as to be responsible for triggering the sexual libido, thoughts and actions of men. Such is the fear of the power of feminine energy.

In some lives, Surya may be homosexual and find that same-sex relationships are a valid expression of love and growth, as sexuality, whether it is heterosexual, homosexual or bisexual, is a valid expression of love from the soul's perspective. This is a potent avenue when looking to fill that nagging emptiness in a search for love and happiness. We are all on a common search, following different paths on a similar journey.

At other times, in a single or celibate life, this may be a soul desire that needs to be experienced and is equally as valid as all others in the quest for discovering what makes us happy.

Not being in a relationship may help to strengthen parts of themselves that could happen while in a relationship. It can provide a cocoon of untroubled and uncomplicated peace in a quest to fill the inner emptiness. Perhaps we lost ourselves in relationships in previous lives and need to find our sense of self in this one.

You may ask yourself if your desire for solitude (if this applies to you) is a reaction to previous wounding, or a withdrawal from possible intimacy, to avoid further risk pain. Or is the need for celibacy just another experience on your spiritual journey while you look for completion? If being alone is your chosen path for this life, it is deserving of respect, as are all lives.

However, attracting, creating and maintaining a healthy relationship remains a challenge for most of us. In many of our former lives, we might have found it impossible to maintain our individuality within a relationship.

Our need for love and connection and the fear of being alone might have been so strong that we stayed in relationships longer than was beneficial and never claimed or developed our individuality. We might have found ourselves in many difficult relationship dynamics in our search for love, such as:

Attracting controlling or abusive relationships

Staying in controlling or abusing relationships

Not having the courage to make changes or leave

Taking on a partner's expectations at the sacrifice of our own

Imposing our will on our partner

Being over responsible

Being irresponsible

Perhaps we were locked in a cycle of victim and perpetrator. The link between victim and perpetrator is tenuous, interlinked and very easily interchanged, even within one lifetime. We can be a victim in one situation and so fearful of losing control again, that we become the manipulating and controlling one in the next. There is a need for all of us to learn how to be assertive, without being overbearing and abusive.

In truth, in relationships, we are challenged to learn to speak up appropriately, debate, discuss, reconsider and give up or let go of the need 'to be right' in all instances. If our view is not the best, highest or most rational, we are challenged to 'let it go'. To expand our view to include the other's view, where possible. To come to a compromise or a position that both can benefit from. Being able to give and take appropriately is part of the challenge of relationships.

Relationships, by their very nature and complexity, have always brought up insecurities and unresolved emotions. They 'push our buttons', resulting in defensive responses of anger or sadness. Toxic, negative or stuck emotions that might never be aroused in a celibate or solitary life, may be brought to the surface by intimate or family relationships.

However, the buttons are ours. They are ours to resolve. They give us the opportunity, if we have enough awareness, to attempt to resolve our turbulent emotions. In a later part of this book, I will look at emotions more fully. Overall, the purpose of relationships is to help us know ourselves more fully.

In reality, you may choose to blame others or situations for 'making you angry'. However, as you become wiser, you might begin to notice that all of the people and events that arouse your anger have a common link between them...You. You are the common denominator. These turbulent emotions or beliefs are coming from your conscious, unconscious, family dynamics, cultural conditioning and karmic patterns.

Here are some exercises that you can try.

Write down your own gender.

Now relax and allow yourself to freely record your thoughts and emotions around your gender. Allow words, thoughts and feelings to be said/written with no editing.

Now do the same with the opposite gender.

Now, take a look at what you have written. Is it favourable, unfavourable or mixed around each gender?

If it is not so favourable for your own sex, you may need to develop some self-esteem and do some inner work, family systemic work or emotional work around the same gender parent.

If it is unfavourable for the opposite gender, this may be the basis of any relationship difficulties you are facing in your life. You may need to do some inner work, family constellation work or emotional work around your opposite-gender parent and previous partners.

If your responses are generally favourable for both genders, then this shows a fairly healthy outlook for yourself and others. An ideal position would be to embrace both the male and female principles within you, as this shows self-acceptance and also respect for the opposite gender that shows an affinity for good relationships. This is a very general and simple impression that should not be taken too seriously, but can be reflected upon. Of course, previous experiences, including those in your family of origin, will also have a large impact on how you perceive yourself, your partners and what you attract into your life.

Love Guidelines.

Act out of love.

Honour the divine in your partner.

Take responsibility for your part in any disagreements between you.

Listen to your partner without making assumptions and, if things are not clear, ask for clarity.

Be respectful in communication.

Don't take everything personally.

Share your thoughts and needs without blame or accusations.

Accept your partner as they are

CHAPTER 13:

KARMA AND FAMILY

Family is part of your karma as stardust. You are always born into a family, which is the culmination of generations of people before you. You carry their genes, their hopes and desires and their love and best wishes for you in the present. These are generations of people with a culture or tradition that have passed on genetic codes. Patterns from your ancestry pour out their genetic imprints for expression in a quest to be seen and played out in a myriad of formats in Surya. This is Surya with an infinite number of faces insisting on expression. Family is karmic, an essential part of each human being's life path through which personal karma may come to fruition. Family is the collective karma of souls coming together in a symbiotic arrangement for interaction and confluence. Family is the seed of love and the source of procreation working in service of creativity, channelling life force into each new human being. The cycle of reincarnation and the karmic imprint in synchronicity provides us with that particular family, mother, father, siblings and ancestors, for our personal and family karma to play out. The family we are born into is fixed karma. Can't be changed. The situation of your birth cannot be changed because it is part of your destiny and can only be experienced, responded to and, ultimately, accepted. It is the means by which all of us enter life, with the creator acting through our parents, in order for us to enter life. We may be born into a family that is functional, dysfunctional, strong or weak. We may find ourselves in nuclear, extended or in separated or single-parent families. Perhaps we have no family after birth, due to being orphaned or, alternatively, are part of a blended family (two separated families living together). There are so many possible combinations, but they are all karmic, all vehicles to bring us into life.

These are all vital means of passing on the sacred life force from one generation to another. These are practical ways of setting up our karma to be experienced and played out in our human form.

This first act of giving and taking, from parents to children, is sacred in the service of life and can't be argued with, even though many of us do just that. Many of us reject where we come from and the people we are born to, or the life that we are given. Accepting the gift of life with gratitude, regardless of how or to whom you are born, is perhaps the biggest challenge for some of us.

You might be thinking, why is this difficult to accept? There is no doubt that children are born with a great loyalty and devoted love for their family initially. However, this is a child's love. It starts as adoration, often putting parents on pedestals in their search for love. There appears to be a tendency to set up their mother and father as god or goddess-like beings, with expectations of qualities that no mortal could possibly live up to. Later, as children mature and the illusions about parents begin to dissolve through the practicalities of living, children begin to see the 'humanness', fallibility and the ordinariness of their parents. This is when they can often feel that they have been fooled or cheated and may become angry, judgemental and blame their parents for not living up to their internally created illusion of the ideal mother and father. This is perhaps a mass illusion depicting the archetypical mother and father that we all seek. It is a challenge for each of us to see our parents as they are. To accept them as they are and also our destiny with them as it is. It can be a challenge to say an unequivocal 'yes' to the gift of life through them. This is all that is required to take in the gift of life in full and free us to go forward in a good way. This sounds simple but, for some people, it can take a lifetime or many lives to come to this place of complete acceptance. It requires wisdom, humility, gratitude and an acceptance of our own fallibilities and ordinariness to be able to also accept those of our parents.

In reality, we are no better or worse than our parents and this realisation is very much at the root of our soul journey. Family is a pivotal part of our karma, full of potency for many possibilities, starting with the acceptance of the synchronicity of the flow of life and the creative forces of the universe in bringing us here.

We are born into the rough-and-tumble of family, ancestral and cultural influences. This includes loyalties and entanglements and also values and belief systems that create a rich tapestry from which to explore and grow. Through these, we can come to realise our nature and tease out our personal values and beliefs from those around us, as we learn to stand in our own strength with humility and gratitude. In truth, each soul has equal value and comes from the same place. Our soul is much like everyone else's. Eventually, we can come to realise that any natural gifts we have, were gained, at least in part, through our genetic line.

This is a simple but undeniable truth, and once we really get it, helps our inflated ego to return to its rightful size. We are not better than them. We are who we are, at least in part, because of them. Once we are able to realise this level of wisdom and maturity on our journey, we will be closer to being non-judgemental and kinder to ourselves. However, this does not necessarily mean that we have to turn a 'blind eye' to our family's idiosyncrasies, values or actions, but we can view them with a little more compassion and take the freedom to make our own choices. We might be able to acknowledge that, if we were walking in their shoes, we may have made similar choices. It is likely that, in our current and previous lives, we have made wise and poor choices too. We remain part of the karmic cycle, as a human being.

Some men are born to a father who is cruel and harsh, resulting in developing low self-esteem, anger and resentment, and even becoming the same kind of father to our own children. Alternatively, such a child could make a conscious effort to become as different to his father as he can, while still somehow trying to hide his psychological and emotional wounds. While he is trying to protect his children from the negative aspects of his own childhood, he may be surprised to find that his children reject him too. It seems that the wounds between the generations still show through in the family soul, often regardless of the best of intentions. The flow of love can be interrupted between generations by a pattern or trauma from the grandfather to the father and to the present generation of fathers, as this may well be a generational pattern going back a long way. The family soul fractured and wounded perhaps by rejection between generations.

The soul tends to remember such imprints and play them back into the present generation in a quest for resolution and harmony in the family soul. The family soul often perpetuates such disturbances until those involved finally reach a point of realisation, resolution, acceptance and compassion for their own, and hence others vulnerabilities. Then the thread of the underlying love connecting them all can be felt beneath the complex web of entanglements and loyalties, to form a healing thread between the generations that allows more freedom in the present.

In reality, few parents want to consciously harm or injure their children, but many act blindly, due to their own wounds. The complex web of situations and unconscious behaviours often block those initially pure intentions of parenthood for each generation and creates yet another generation of people who feel unseen or unheard. This often continues until it can be resolved by each person taking responsibility for themselves, so that love can flow once again, unhindered.

The original connection with our parents is primal, karmic and charged with expectation, vulnerability and need. Parents give what they think is required and mostly with love, but children are often looking for something else and often don't recognise the love that is available.

How well your parents can give you what you need and how well you can receive what is given, is a crucial question. This becomes the blueprint from which you interact with your world. However, even if your parents are devoted and caring, it is very unlikely that you will have received everything that you wanted from them. The relationship is often loaded with unmet desires, needs and disappointments, even in families that did the best they could with what they had. Parents are ordinary people doing the best they can, for the most part, and hoping it is appropriate and enough for their children. The blueprint we operate through may go something like this. Parents are a product of their own families and children have a special love for their parents and are unconsciously aware of any burdens or sadness that they may be carrying. If a child feels the sadness of a parent, their heart will go out to the parent in a desire to help or support them with love.

That child is unconsciously supporting their parent. So, rather than being supported, as is the rightful place of a child, they become the supporter, making themselves 'bigger' in order to attempt to fulfil this role and save their parent.

Having taken on this role in her family, as a woman, she is likely to choose a partner who also requires support on an energetic level, as this role is now familiar and 'normal'. Such a partnership can work well until a time when her partner starts to feel smothered or begins to experience her attention as controlling, and eventually feels resentful. Alternatively, as an adult, she may start to feel exhausted at the amount of energy that she expends to support her partner emotionally. This dynamic in the relationship may also lead her to become unavailable for her children because, ultimately, she remains unconsciously focused on her entanglement with her parent and or her partner. Her children may feel her burden energetically and also feel drawn to support her and so the pattern continues.

As a child, we are always born with an unconditional love for our parents, but that often becomes tarnished along the way by situations, disappointments and the taking on of unhealthy beliefs and burdens from family or society. Our beliefs come from our perception of our experiences. That original young childish love that is so often full of impossible expectations, particularly of parents, is often unrequited or unacknowledged, from the child's perspective, and this may be experienced as rejection.

Parents often do not realise what their child is carrying for them or expects from them. Unfortunately, many families do not know how to express emotions in a healthy way.

This does not indicate a lack of love, but rather a lack of being able to communicate in the language of emotion and, in particular, in the language of love. As children, we have a natural wish to be the centre of attention and to be given everything and to experience ourselves as the centre of a loving focus. Our parents usually do love us, but may also be busy providing and organising the day-to-day practical things in life to making sure there is enough to eat and bills are paid, etc. Alternatively, our parents may be emotionally entangled with their own wounds or belief systems from their past, and may not be fully available. They love us, but perhaps not in the way we would like.

Our family may not yet have had the experience of unconditional love in their own lives, or the knowledge or maturity to experience and practise it openly. In this way, our own pure love is gradually replaced by conditional love and a lack of trust through disappointing transactions with others. We are likely to learn from our caregivers how to manipulate our environment in an attempt to get what we think we need. Remember, we are still searching for 'it', wanting to fill our emptiness, as are our parents.

Generally, if love is experienced in the way we desire, we are likely to be confident and reasonably well adjusted. However, all too often, our parents are so entangled and confused that they are not able to give us what we need, because they didn't receive it themselves. In these situations, we have the greatest opportunities for personal development when we choose to sort ourselves out, come out of entanglement, stop judging those around us, and to have compassion for our own and others' human frailties. We have choices at each point of our experience, whether we realise it or not. Once we can see our parents, just as they are, we may be able to see our likeness to them and let any anger, resentment or sadness dissipate in favour of compassion and gratitude.

We are all human beings looking for love, but perhaps we just don't know how to find it. Once you really understand this as a child or parent and are able to accept your parents, you may find that your children too may also be able to come closer and love may be free to flow through your family, just as you've always wished it would.

Bert Hellinger (2006) in *No Waves No Ocean* explains how the flow of love works in family systems through his family constellation philosophy. Unlikely as it may seem, the way to come out of family entanglements and change your own patterns, is to accept your family members just as they are, with gratitude for the gift of life you've received through them.

Funnily enough, this is all that is required to stand in your own strength. Interestingly, cutting off or rejecting our family members is the way to perpetuate dysfunction at a soul level for ourselves and our children. Cutting off may feel empowering and liberating at first, but often this results in depression and self-sabotage later. According to Hellinger, the individual soul is integrated with the family soul and experiences a strong loyalty, or unconscious feeling of guilt, if it rejects parents or family.

It has been found through systemic family constellations that coming to peace with our family of origin directly affects our self-esteem, relationships and the family that we form.

Parents often struggle between either being too relaxed or too vigilant. By being over-vigilant, they can feel the need to 'save' children from the consequences of their choices and thereby delay their growth and possibly destroy their budding self-esteem and the parent-child relationship in the process. How can a child respect a parent who does not trust them to find their own way? If we are over-protective, we are not respecting them as budding adults. Young adults need to make mistakes and grow their wings in their own way, just as we had to. It is impossible to save someone from life itself. It has to be welcomed and lived in all its shades and ups and downs.

Alternatively, in parenting, we may be too relaxed and not diligent enough in providing enough support and structure for our children, leaving them feeling unimportant and possibly unloved. Again, this may have an impact on the confidence of the budding adult and result in poor consequences for the parent-child relationship.

However, regardless of parenting style, all children, as they reach adulthood, have a duty to themselves, at some point, to move out of the realm of their parents and do their own thing in their own way. In an over-controlling parental relationship, this may take the form of rebellion, at least for a while.

In many tribal or ancient cultures, there are rites of passage that young adults go through to give them a new role and status in the community that paves the way for a smoother transition into adulthood that gives autonomy within structure, place and respect for all.

Interestingly, most parents need only to be 'good enough'. Consciously attempting to be perfect may be trying too hard and thereby not allow their natural fallibility as being human show through. In striving for perfection, this may give children the unspoken message that they have to be perfect too, in order to be acceptable. Attempting to be perfect can lead to self-esteem problems and anxiety, as this is an illusion that is doomed to failure. Of course, wanting to do the best for our children is normal and is also often an attempt to avoid what was done to us. We may have positive intentions, but need to remember our children become resilient through the hurley-burley mess that is life.

If our parenting is too controlled and lacking in genuine spontaneity of feeling and action, how are they to cope with the unpredictable nature of life in the wider world? Seeing their parent as normal or imperfect gives a child permission to relax and be 'normal' too. So, as a parent, relax, do the best you can with what you've got and show your children that you love them. Love is the most important thing. The rest will often take care of itself.

As a child, thank your parents for being the vehicle through which you entered life. It is then the role of each child to develop and to look at themselves and their situation and pursue anything that they wish to experience, and to create their own reality.

A story by Andy Weir called "The Egg":

> *You were on your way home when you died.*
>
> *It was a car accident. Nothing particularly remarkable, but fatal nonetheless. You left behind a wife and two children. It was a painless death. The EMTs tried their best to save you, but to no avail. Your body was so utterly shattered you were better off, trust me.*
>
> *And that's when you met me.*
>
> *"What... what happened?" You asked. "Where am I?"*
>
> *"You died," I said, matter-of-factly. No point in mincing words.*
>
> *"There was a... a truck and it was skidding..."*
>
> *"Yup," I said.*
>
> *"I... I died?"*
>
> *"Yup. But don't feel bad about it. Everyone dies," I said.*
>
> *You looked around. There was nothingness. Just you and me. "What is this place?" You asked. "Is this the afterlife?"*
>
> *"More or less," I said.*
>
> *"Are you god?" You asked.*
>
> *"Yup," I replied. "I'm God."*
>
> *"My kids... my wife," you said.*

"What about them?"

"Will they be all right?"

"That's what I like to see," I said. "You just died and your main concern is for your family. That's good stuff right there."

You looked at me with fascination. To you, I didn't look like God. I just looked like some man. Or possibly a woman. Some vague authority figure, maybe. More of a grammar school teacher than the almighty.

"Don't worry," I said. "They'll be fine. Your kids will remember you as perfect in every way. They didn't have time to grow contempt for you. Your wife will cry on the outside, but will be secretly relieved. To be fair, your marriage was falling apart. If it's any consolation, she'll feel very guilty for feeling relieved."

"Oh," you said. "So, what happens now? Do I go to heaven or hell or something?"

"Neither," I said. "You'll be reincarnated."

"Ah," you said. "So, the Hindus were right,"

"All religions are right in their own way," I said. "Walk with me."

You followed along as we strode through the void. "Where are we going?"

"Nowhere in particular," I said. "It's just nice to walk while we talk."

"So, what's the point, then?" You asked. "When I get reborn, I'll just be a blank slate, right? A baby. So, all my experiences and everything I did in this life won't matter."

"Not so!" I said. "You have within you all the knowledge and experiences of all your past lives. You just don't remember them right now."

I stopped walking and took you by the shoulders. "Your soul is more magnificent, beautiful, and gigantic than you can possibly imagine. A human mind can only contain a tiny fraction of what you are. It's like sticking your finger in a glass of water to see if it's hot or cold. You put a tiny part of yourself into the vessel, and when you bring it back out, you've gained all the experiences it had.

"You've been in a human form for the last 48 years, so you haven't stretched out yet and felt the rest of your immense consciousness. If we hung out here for long enough, you'd start remembering everything. But there's no point to doing that between each life."

"How many times have I been reincarnated, then?"

"Oh lots. Lots and lots. Lots of different lives." I said. "This time around, you'll be a Chinese peasant girl in 540 AD."

"Wait, what?" You stammered. "You're sending me back in time?"

"Well, I guess technically. Time, as you know it, only exists in your universe. Things are different where I come from."

"Where you come from?" You said.

"Oh sure," I explained "I come from somewhere. Somewhere else. And there are others like me. I know you'll want to know what it's like there, but honestly you wouldn't understand."

"Oh," you said, a little let down. "But wait. If I get reincarnated to other places in time, I could have interacted with myself at some point."

"Sure. Happens all the time. And with both lives only aware of their own lifespan you don't even know it's happening."

"So, what's the point of it all?"

"Seriously?" I asked. "Seriously? You're asking me for the meaning of life? Isn't that a little stereotypical?"

"Well it's a reasonable question," you persisted.

I looked you in the eye. "The meaning of life, the reason I made this whole universe, is for you to mature."

"You mean mankind? You want us to mature?"

"No, just you. I made this whole universe for you. With each new life you grow and mature and become a larger and greater intellect."

"Just me? What about everyone else?"

"There is no one else," I said. "In this universe, there's just you and me."

You stared blankly at me. "But all the people on earth..."

"All you. Different incarnations of you."

"Wait. I'm everyone!?"

"Now you're getting it," I said, with a congratulatory slap on the back.

"I'm every human being who ever lived?"

"Or who will ever live, yes."

"I'm Abraham Lincoln?"

"And you're John Wilkes Booth, too," I added.

"I'm Hitler?" You said, appalled.

"And you're the millions he killed."

"I'm Jesus?"

"And you're everyone who followed him."

You fell silent.

"Every time you victimized someone," I said, "you were victimizing yourself. Every act of kindness you've done, you've done to yourself. Every happy and sad moment ever experienced by any human was, or will be, experienced by you."

You thought for a long time.

"Why?" You asked me. "Why do all this?"

"Because someday, you will become like me. Because that's what you are. You're one of my kind. You're my child."

"Whoa," you said, incredulous. "You mean I'm a god?"

"No. Not yet. You're a foetus. You're still growing. Once you've lived every human life throughout all time, you will have grown enough to be born."

"So, the whole universe," you said, "it's just..."

"An egg." I answered. "Now it's time for you to move on to your next life."

And I sent you on your way.

CHAPTER 14:

MERGING FIELDS

Surya is always moving between fields. We are always merging with fields from the physical, spiritual, conscious, intellectual, unconscious and, possibly, many more in each life. These are realms that may include elements of ancestry, dreaming, social and more.

I have discussed many of the challenges on the soul journey and now I come to a way of healing or resolving family system loyalties or entanglements that may have bound us to poor relationships, low self-esteem and dysfunctional patterns through an approach called 'family constellations'.

I am in gratitude to Bert Hellinger, the innovator of family constellations, to Svagito Liebermeister, the author of *The Roots of Love* (2006) and my first teacher of family constellations, and to many other teachers, including Albrecht Mahr, Jacob Schneider and Ursula Franke. I also acknowledge the wisdom or Francesca Mason Boring and the many writers of family constellation theory and practice.

Family constellations is a spiritual, energetic and experiential process with elements of Shamanism that touch every level of our humanity and connect us to our ancestral energies. It is a process that allows the greater system of the ancestral family field to unravel, unfold and find a healing resolution in such a way that it flows in ripples through the mind, body and soul and that of the greater family soul in a healing way, because we are so deeply connected within our family system. Surya, in the present, is the sum total of all that has gone before him, an individual and also a collective of his people in his present reality.

We've come a long way from our roots, as there was a time when Surya could be found sitting around a camp fire with his extended family, listening to the stories of his ancestors being lovingly passed down through the generations by word-of-mouth.

Surya knew the names and the stories of his parents, grandparents or great-grandparents on both his mother's and his father's side. In addition, there was something comforting and heart-warming about sitting in a circle with his people, taking part in the sharing, giving and receiving of stories. I believe that elements of such ancient gatherings are brought into the family constellation process.

Family constellations, as a group process, was brought to the world by the German psychotherapist, Bert Hellinger, in the 1990s.

Hellinger had been a Catholic priest and teacher in Africa in Zululand, where he particularly noticed their system of order in extended families. This consisted of acknowledging each member of the family in relation to the whole, according to their time of entry (who came first, second and so on) and also the nature of the relationships (e.g., father-son or first child, second child, first wife, second wife, etc.) and how these factors appeared to create harmony and respect in family groups. Hellinger took these insights home with him when he left the priesthood to become a psychotherapist in Germany.

A family constellations workshop takes place when a group of people come together to form a sacred space. They sit in a circle with a facilitator and take turns to look at their issues by using people from the group to represent those people of their situation, including one representative for themselves. The representatives are placed spatially in relation to each other, according to the client's inner image. Once placed, the constellation commences and the representatives begin to experience sensations in their body, with the facilitator and the representatives guided by the energetic field that develops. The facilitator enables the energy of the field to be expressed and released, or for the representatives to follow an impulse to move, as the energy field unfolds and reveals what it has to show. The client observes the process from the circle. New perspectives arise and emotions are dissipated through the representatives in the field that ripple through the mind, body and soul of the client and also the greater body of the family soul to find a resolution and a healthier order. The system finds a new equilibrium by allowing the client to reconnect to the flow of love coming through the generations.

This is a powerful, experiential and psycho-spiritual process that is a brief intervention that allows a client to find new perspectives and move forward. The effects of a constellation are often felt for months or longer after the process, as new perspectives fall into place for the client.

Bert Hellinger developed the idea that love flows with life force through families from grandparents to parents and then to children, as long as there is a healthy order in the family, involving respect for the client's own and others' positions. He discovered that where there was a break in the flow of love, this was often due to exclusion, tragedy or trauma, or something that caused shame, guilt or secrets, resulting in the life force continuing, but the flow of love interrupted, leaving those in the system feeling cut off from love.

The family constellations' philosophy and practice presents a revolutionary way to observe and work with human systems to help individuals find their place and receive personal healing within their family system. It is brief, holistic and experiential. The process enables deep psychotherapeutic and emotional shifts towards wholeness.

By exploring family dynamics, Hellinger discovered that a child loves his family far more than we could imagine. So much so that, on entering into a family system that has experienced trauma or disturbances that couldn't be processed, the child will often take on the difficult energy in its wish to somehow 'help', which often results in them 'playing out' a former family member's destiny unconsciously. In this way, relationship patterns, physical illnesses and psychological disorders can be transposed down the family system in an observable manner. Tragedies or dysfunctions may be passed on until they can be resolved by the greater family system in a healing process, such as family constellations. How this process works is not clear. From my experience, family constellations take place in a sacred space where many realms can come together for confluence, sharing, connecting and healing. Realms within realms, like the waves rippling out from a central point in a pond, all connected, with the vibrations of a splash rippling out seamlessly through one realm to the next, until they are absorbed or neutralised and come to rest in the greater body of the pond.

In the process, there are many realms that are touched, such as the conscious, unconscious, emotional, senses (audio, kinaesthetic, touch), family and the greater ancestral family, including their history and, on another level, humankind and universal energy. Each realm comes into balance in the give-and-take between the generations and the individuals concerned in the greater field of 'all that is'.

From another perspective, by looking at how patterns are passed on in family systems, the qualities of family connections are passed on through relationships from one person to another and across generations, and are potent with subtle nuances and vibrations as reminders of each connection.

The children coming into the family have such a strong love for the system that they have a natural tendency to pick up unresolved disturbances in a

wish to 'help'. The effects of this strong love involves the 'magical thinking' of a child seeking to 'help', which is known as 'blind love' in constellation circles. They sense the 'out of order', distress, anxiety or disconnection of a parent, or the tragedy or secret that is held in the family system, and instinctively and unconsciously 'step up' to figuratively support mum, dad or the ancestors. By doing so, the child steps 'out of order' and, similarly, their children too often do the same for them.

And so, it continues until it is resolved by putting out the inner image of their situation or issue in healing processes such as family constellation. Made visible so that the pattern or disorder may be observed and gradually fall back into healthy order through the process. A process where emotions are released or come to rest. At this point, the individual seeking help may be able to 'take in' a different perspective and new possibilities from which to operate.

Here are a few examples of Surya, as stardust, involved in relationship entanglements. These examples show how patterns are maintained through generations.

Here is an example of how generational patterns may be passed on.

Jane, had a poor relationship with her mother and a lot of anger. She'd been born 'out of wedlock' and her mother's parents were so angry and ashamed of their daughter, they rejected her and her child. Jane's mother was subsequently also abandoned by the child's father. Heartbroken and distressed, she struggled to bring up Jane on her own. Jane's childhood was filled with distress, sadness and isolation. She loved her mother and sought to support her emotionally with 'blind love', while also feeling the emptiness of where her father and extended family should've been. Her love turned to anger and resentment over time.

Never-the-less, Jane grew up and eventually had a child of her own, hoping she could create the family she'd always wanted, in filling up her emptiness and disappointment of having a mother, who'd not been emotionally present for her and not feeling nurtured, as was her expectation and right as a child. Jane holds her own distress and emotional pain from her own life that her daughter instinctively feels and start the process of carrying her mother emotionally. And so the pattern continues between Jane and her daughter.

Franz Rupert (2008, p201), in *Bonding Trauma and Family Constellations*, explains how patterns are transferred across relationships and through generations. This is a common example of how children seek to support their parents.

However, when there is a healthy order present, parents give and are able to support and be present for their children and are supported by their own parents or family connections, so that the giving and taking of love is flowing down the generations, one way, thereby leaving children free and unburdened.

From a family constellations' perspective, most parents are doing the best they can, with what they have, or what they know. There is always love at the core of family systems that is often disturbed or hidden by events or situations that caused disappointment, sadness, anger, shame, guilt or trauma. The process of family constellations can allow those blocking emotions or systemic disturbances to be felt, expressed or seen and to dissipate as new perspectives arise and a connection to love is made.

This leaves the individual and the system free to come into their rightful place in the flow of love. This process is a holistic, experiential, psychotherapeutic and spiritual way of dealing with relationships, inner conflicts, mental and physical illness, sexual abuse, personal growth and spiritual development. In truth, coming to a place of peace with who you are and with your ancestors, is an essential first step to spiritual growth.

Acknowledging What Is, Hellinger (1999), and *Loving What Is,* Byron Katie (2002), are books that have significant healing themes throughout, showing that these are foundations that cannot be avoided in dissolving Maya (illusion) and starting the process of deep integration on your journey.

The attitude of the family constellation facilitator is an important factor in the process. In coming from a place of phenomenology in 'not knowing' is vital to hold a space for constellations to unfold. It is necessary to put aside pre-judgements or assumptions and allow 'what is' to emerge in the energy field of the family system. For this reason, a long story of your situation is not required prior to a constellation, just a few facts are necessary in order to set it up, as the story is simply an 'interpretation' of what happened and not necessarily the truth as we each interpret factual information into a story. Other family members are likely to interpret the story differently. Perhaps the truth is what is shown when all parts of the 'elephant' can come together. The facilitator plays a delicate role by trusting the unfolding of what needs to be revealed and also guiding the process to help to restore order and enable an expression of emotions. It is preferable to know very little of the client's issue, other than vital background information, as too much information is likely to have the effect of blocking the natural energy flow of the field.

Of course, knowledge of family constellation relationship dynamics, entanglements and order and also good training are vital, as well as the skill to create a safe space for good facilitation. These need to be in place and held in the background as the facilitator 'empties' themselves to allow the field to emerge, unrestricted through the representatives. In family constellations, we take the view that the person and their family system already have the resources needed to heal or resolve and that the job of a facilitator is to guide the healing process, because all healing is self-healing. The facilitator is in service to the greater family system.

Family constellations make use of energy fields, so now I will talk about energy. Energy is everywhere. Each body cell and in every part of the universe of 'all that is' and is constantly being transformed from one form to another. Energy is in the air you breathe, the food you eat and in everything around you. As stardust, you are an energetic being. I invite you to notice the energy of your body. For those of you that live mainly in your head, you may find this challenging, but I invite you to take a deep breath and, on the out-breath, allow your focus to go down into your body. If you are living primarily in your head, you are missing a lot of experiences that you could gain through being in contact with your body.

You are given a body to experience in its fullness, so it's good to be present in your body.

Many of you might become aware of noticing energy in rooms or buildings or the changing pockets of energy in the natural environment. You may notice the energy when you walk into a room where emotions have been high, even though nothing has been said about a disagreement that has just taken place. In addition, there is always energy between people in relationships, through which it is possible to feel what is unsaid or what the other is feeling.

Studies and research on energy are still in an elementary phase. There are areas of science opening up that are quite different to the physical sciences of mechanics and thermodynamics, that are exploring cutting-edge ethereal realms, of which energy is central, such as quantum physics, string theory and morphogenic fields. William Sheldrake, in *Morphic Resonance* (2012), provides many examples of energetic phenomena in biological and human systems and demonstrates how we are all connected through these systems energetically. Sheldrake is exploring such areas as telepathy and psychic phenomena in nature, humans and animals in order to gain some understanding of how they function.

By working with energy of family systems and relationships, Hellinger found that something could come to light or a new perspective could arise for the person concerned, through the experience. This was the birth of family constellations, which is a dynamic process that has developed considerably since then. It is now being used for relationships, mental and physical health, community and social issues, education, organisations and business, ecology, personal development and politics (in constellations aimed at the healing of nations).

Family constellations developed through the innovator, Bert Hellinger into 'Movements of the Soul' and then to the 'Spirit Mind' and other innovators are continuing to develop it in many areas of human experience to give new perspectives and provide healing on many levels. Hellinger's discovery of the energetic field of human systems is often referred to as the 'knowing field' by those in the world of constellations. This is a field through which information and new perceptions can arise with the intention of providing the space for a resolution or healing of the personal and family soul.

There appear to be realms within realms of energy within 'all that is' that metaphysical knowledge and practices may have always utilised or tapped into by entering other realms of energy to receive experiences or information. Perhaps this is what happens when we look at an astrology chart or read a hand or any other psychic phenomena.

For my part, the integration of hypnotherapy and family constellations into my practice has transformed the way I work. It has enabled me to call myself a brief therapist, in that I see most of my clients for only three sessions in order to facilitate the changes or resolutions they seek in many issues in personal or workshop sessions.

CHAPTER 15:

THE ZEN APPROACH: FAMILY CONSTELLATIONS

Surya may look for the light in many places. She may look for teachers all over the world, often at great expense of time and money. Often Surya can feel that she is spiritual in a group or with a lover or with her teacher or guru, but fall apart when confronted by parents or family members. Surya's genuine spiritual awakening can only start sincerely once she can come to a place of acceptance and eventually, deep gratitude for her parents and family group. This does not mean that she has to agree with, or approve of all of their choices, behaviour or actions. All she has to do is accept that they are her roots and her entry into the world. This is regardless of whether they understood her or not, abused her or not, or had too high or too low expectations of her. Making peace with yourself and your family is the first step in facing relational and personal challenges and starting healthy maturation. Your family members come from 'all that is' and go back to 'all that is', just like you. We are all on the same journey. For some reason, you have a shared relational experience, destiny and karma with them. Once you have accepted your place with them and are open to receiving love from your family system, you're more able to accept and love yourself and those around you, such as partners or children. This is because, at a soul level, there is a deep sense of guilt in rejecting the family soul that can result in maintaining destructive or sabotage patterns.

Interestingly, from a Vedic astrology perspective, the most important houses of the chart that give support for the person are the houses of mother and father, with the house of mother being the root of the chart.

From my experience, family constellations is one of the most profound personal development activities that anyone can do. You have probably realised that external gratification does not fulfil your deeper needs. Yes, it can temporarily distract you, but those feelings of emptiness often return.

As you are reading this book, it is likely that you are at the stage in your spiritual journey, where you know that in continuing your search for that missing treasure, you are now required to look within. You can choose many paths and it is important to find the paths that speak and work for you. However, it is my experience that many of us have not given our roots the respect that they deserve.

Fundamentally, family constellations is about connecting to love. All families have their own karma and dysfunctions. This is part of being human. There is no doubt that the family you were born into is fundamental to this life's journey and an essential part of your collective karma. Family constellations is a process that is perfect for resolving and clearing ancestral karmic patterns. However, not all situations and relationships can be changed. In those areas of life where the karma is fixed and can't be changed, all you can do find a new perspective. So, you may come to a place of peace within and move on to acceptance and letting go. One of the first steps in effective personal development is coming to peace with yourself and your roots. Self-acceptance is a prerequisite to spiritual connection and development.

This is an effective process to help you improve your relationship with yourself and others. However, in reality it may not be possible to have the quality of relationships you would like to have with all the important people in your life. All you may be able to do is to resolve and accept, or make amends for your part in those connections and stop carrying burdens for others. It is up to the others in relationships with you to do likewise, or not. That's their choice as relationships are a shared experience and not entirely within your control. However, having your side of the relationship as resolved as possible may be enough for you to gain some peace and come to a place of self-acceptance, as you move through grief, prior to letting go.

Love flows from one generation to the next from parents to children according to the order of love, according to Hellinger (1999, p93), with parents giving and children receiving life, love and support. Problems occur when parents are not able to take their place as parents emotionally, due to entanglements, trauma and events, and their children 'step up' to support them, which creates disorder in the system.

Entanglements involve being 'out of order', due to blind love, resulting in people carrying the emotional burdens of others in the system.

Interestingly, relationships are also 'out of order' when children fail to accept parents 'as they are' and proceed to judge, as if parents need to fit their idea of how they 'should be', rather than accepting them 'as they are'. Judging is also 'out of order', resulting in an entanglement that will have consequences because judgement of a parent also cuts off the flow of love and is likely to have an effect on how we operate in love relationships, parenting and success in life.

According to Leibermeister (2006, p123) in *The Roots of Love*, in couples, the order is different. In a healthy couple's relationship, the individuals are equal and opposite. Love flows between them, if there is a balance in their giving and taking. The giving and taking of love can be maintained and grow if each of the couple give a little more than they receive. Conversely, when one of the couple does something to upset the other, the balance of give-and-take is out of balance and can be retrieved if the partner who is upset over the actions of the other 'is not too nice to be nasty', according to Hellinger's philosophy. If the injured partner gives back some of the pain, but in a smaller measure than was given to them, then the balance can be restored to the relationship and the give-and-take can resume and the flow of love can start to build again. This is quite a different philosophy from other relationship theories.

There are many possible dynamics in relationship and family systems. For example, a woman is able to feel good about herself as a woman if she is able to connect with the feminine aspects of her family, primarily through her mother's line. A man is able to feel good about himself as a man if he is able to connect with the masculine aspects of his family, primarily through his father's line. In addition, a woman who is able to accept her father is more likely to seek a suitable partner, whereas a woman who has not been able to find a resolution for her relationship with her father, is likely to seek resolution of this relationship by unconsciously seeking him out in her choice of partners. Likewise, a man who is more able to accept his mother is more likely to seek a suitable partner, whereas a man who has not been able to find a resolution for his relationship with his mother, is more likely to seek a resolution of this relationship by unconsciously seeking her out in his choice of partner. Therefore, it is easy to see why a resolution with parents is important to enable better relationships.

Here I will give a few examples of Surya's entanglements as stardust. I had a man come to see me about his relationship. His wife had told him that unless he resolved his anger issues, the relationship was over. His father and grandfather had both been very angry and abusive to their wives and he had vowed in his youth to be nothing like them. He had four failed marriages so far.

In his rejection of his father, from a family constellations' perspective, his soul had unconsciously stayed loyal to his father by taking on his anger. Resolving the issues with his father through constellations and acknowledging that he was much like his father, was the foundation for the change that was necessary for him to transform his anger.

He became calmer and more assertive in being able to express his feelings and needs and was very pleased with the changes over the forthcoming weeks in his personal, social and work life through some very stressful situations. Many people remarked on the positive changes in him. Interestingly, his partner couldn't cope with his new way of being and her own anger became evident and the relationship broke down anyway. So, resolving a personal issue may at times result in a breakdown of a dysfunctional relationship, if the partner is unwilling to resolve his or her own issues too.

Dynamic One

A woman had a pattern of choosing men who had addictions and were unreliable. Her parents had separated when she was young due to her father's alcoholism and unreliability. She hated her father for what he had done to her mother and herself and the family. Through constellation work, she was able to deal with her relationship with her father and through the process was able to find some compassion for his situation with his own alcoholic father and remember some of the better moments she'd had with him. She was also able to acknowledge her own relationship with alcohol too, as she was a binge drinker. She was able to start the process of healing her wounds and unburdening herself to come back into a healthier order.

Although she'd rejected her father, she was keeping an unconscious bond (loyalty) with him by choosing partners that were much like him, in an attempt to resolve the relationship with him. She was also keeping an unconscious loyalty to him through her drinking. By starting the healing process, she was able to gain more freedom, resolve her alcohol issue and also attract a different type of partner.

Dynamic Two.

A man was distressed over his trail of failed relationships. His father had left the family when he was a baby and further contact with him was so destructive and disappointing, that he eventually cut him out of his life. In his constellation, he put himself standing next to his representative mother, in the place of his absent father, and his representative father standing far away. It was clear that his blind love was in good shape in emotionally supporting his mother, demonstrating that he was not free to choose a more suitable life partner, which had resulted in him inadvertently choosing unsuitable women who could not commit to a loving relationship.

By assisting him through the family constellation process with his relationship with his father, he was able to take his place, internally, in the family, as a child, thereby restoring order. This helped him to find more freedom and peace. He is now more hopeful of finding an appropriate partner.

Dynamic Three

A parent came to see me about his difficult relationship with his child. During the discussion, it was apparent that he highly disapproved of his own father, as a result of his choices and behaviour. He had expected his father to be more 'normal'.

It was clear in the constellations that followed, that his child was feeling the rejection or exclusion of his grandfather by his father and had an unconscious loyalty to his grandfather. This was resulting in the rejection of the father by the child. The constellation work helped the parent to start the process of accepting his father, so that his relationship with his son could be rebuilt with authenticity, respect and compassion.

Once we notice the relationship patterns that are running in our lives we may be ready to look at ourselves in our family system to discover what we can do to assist in unravelling ourselves respectfully so that we can heal our wounds, take responsible for ourselves and into a healthier order.

Coming to more peace with ourselves often has an impact on others, practically and energetically, and how we relate. In my experience, it's sometimes the case that an estranged relative will contact the recipient of a constellation soon after the process, with no knowledge of them doing this work. Somehow, the field between them has altered in an intangible manner, allowing new possibilities to emerge. In some relationships the inner change in us can result in changes in others. In other relationships nothing changes and so we have the choice to accept this and the others involved as they are. Change our perspectives. This changes our experience. We all have a choice.

We must be mindful of our intentions when doing family constellations, as the intention must never be to change someone else, but always about changing or healing oneself. Family constellations are aimed at helping the person seeking help. Any healing that takes place is self-healing. Your loved ones may not be ready for this process and their choices and spiritual path must also be respected.

In truth, where one of a couple seeks help, there is always a danger that by healing themselves and becoming more resilient, this change could lead to a breakdown of the relationship because the other person may not be able to connect in the way they did previously. The couple might have been connected through their dysfunction.

One of the couple may have gone into the relationship driven by their family dynamic of wanting to save or look after the other, with their partner happy to be looked after as a result of their own dynamics. Any change in either partner may shift the dynamic between them.

One or both partners may not be ready to look at themselves. However, by seeking help, at least one of the couple already has concerns with the relationship. So, it's already in crisis. Alternatively, as couples are mostly attracted to each other, driven by their family dynamics or illusion, if each of the couple is willing and able to resolve their own issues, they may be able to build a new relationship on more solid foundations of grounded respect, acceptance and love. They might be able to support each other on their individual paths and also as a couple.

CHAPTER 16:

CONSTELLATIONS ON THE MOVE

The purpose of a family constellation is to reveal the love ties in your family system and allow you to become reconnected to love, while you begin to acknowledge the situation or people around you, as they are. This process acts on many levels simultaneously, such as awareness, the senses (visual, audio, kinaesthetic), the unconscious mind and emotions, and also includes ancestral influences and energies. For this reason, it is a very deep and an often rapid, brief intervention that is powerful in enabling change for those who are truly ready to look at themselves and their issues seriously and are ready for growth. Family constellations can take place in workshops or in individual sessions. This is a process that has spread throughout many parts of the world and might be available in your local area. I have provided some links at the back of this book where you might be able to find family constellations' facilitators in your area.

Below, I have set out the process for several constellations of real situations from my practice. In the examples, the names and identities of people have been changed to maintain privacy. In the following constellations, I will refer to the representative with the word 'Rep' before each name. Each constellation must be examined individually; therefore, it is not appropriate to expect the solutions in these constellations to apply in any general way to your own specific relationship dynamics, because each situation is unique. It's best for your own individual situation to be explored with a proficient family constellation' facilitator.

A mother-daughter relationship

Susan came to a workshop concerned about her relationship with her daughter, Emma. She said that she would like to be close to her daughter, but her 20-year-old daughter was keeping a distance between them and had left home as soon as she could. Upon asking more questions, the woman disclosed her own feelings of rejection for her own mother Jane. Susan said that her mother Jane had lost her mother when she was a baby and was raised by an adoptive mother.

In the workshop, Susan was invited to choose one person to represent herself, one to represent her daughter (Emma), one to represent her mother (Jane) and another to represent the grandmother, whose name was unknown. Susan placed her own Rep in the centre of the circle, looking at her Rep daughter, while her Rep daughter was turned away from her. She placed her Rep mother (Jane) facing her Rep daughter Emma. The Rep for her unknown grandmother was placed at the edge of the space, looking outwards.

Diagram 1

D daughter Emma
M mother Susan
GM Susan's mother Jane
GGM Jane's unknown mother.

After a few minutes, the facilitator asked the Rep Susan mother how she was feeling. The Rep Susan reported that she felt a great love and yearning for her daughter (Emma). The Rep daughter (Emma) reported feeling a pain in her chest area and a knot in her stomach and her hands were clenched. The Rep Susan was asked to turn to look at her mother and reported she found it hard to look at her and the Rep daughter also couldn't look at her own mother and looked at the ground.

The facilitator brought the Rep (Jane) closer to the Rep of her unknown mother so that they were looking at each other.

Diagram 2

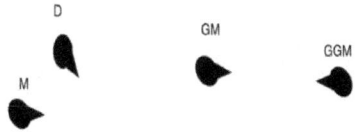

The Rep grandmother Jane was clenching her hands and reported feeling angry and sad. She said to her unknown mother,

"I missed you, I am angry that you left me".

The Rep unknown grandmother's eyes welled up with tears and she told her Rep daughter Jane,

"I had no choice; it was my fate to die early.

However, I am still your mother and I love you".

The Rep unknown great-grandmother noticeably relaxed and smiled warmly and with love through her tears, and slowly her Rep daughter (Jane) moved forward to her and they embraced. After a few minutes the Rep grandmother (Jane) turned to look at her Rep daughter (Susan) and Rep grand-daughter (Emma). Rep Jane was able to look at her Rep daughter (Susan) fully now and say,

I'm sorry I was preoccupied with my loss"

Diagram 3

The Rep grand-daughter (Emma) had, during the process, turned to look at the women and witnessed the expressions of anger, sadness and love between them. She had visibly softened and was crying and felt drawn to move closer to her Rep mother (Susan).

The constellation ended after they made contact and honoured the destiny of Emma's unknown great-grandmother.

Diagram 4

All the women of the four generations were brought into close contact with each other in a close circle. It is clear that the mother and daughter were still feeling the impact of the loss of this great- grandmother in the family system.

Diagram 5

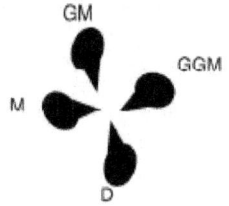

Summary

This is a typical family constellation where the family ancestral energy is put to rest in the constellation without anyone other than the mother herself coming to a workshop.

The disconnection between Susan and her daughter, Emma, appeared to have been influenced by the tragedy of the death of the great-grandmother, leaving the grandmother unable to be fully present for her daughter Susan. Once brought back into the family, the energy between the women was able to relax and the daughter, Emma, was able to connect with her mother Susan. Emma did reconnect with her mother a few weeks later.

Needing male energy.

Jared 32 years old, came to a workshop wanting to explore his issue of not being able to maintain love relationships. He said that even though he loved his last partner and was very fond of others, he found that he sabotaged his love relationships with poor behaviour until they left. He said that he was aware of pushing his partners away and didn't know how to stop it. He said he wanted a partner and family. During initial discussion, he said his parents had split up when he was five years old and he lived mainly with his mother and younger sister. His father moved away and he had little contact with him. He was told that his paternal grandfather had lost his father when he was ten years old.

Jared was asked to choose representatives for his mother, father, grandfather and himself and to set them up in the room. He set the Rep for himself standing beside his mother in the place where his father should have been. His Rep father was turned away looking at the back of his father and grandfather.

Diagram 6

S Jared
M mother
F father
GF grandfather
GGF great grandfather

The Rep for Jared felt very heavy as he stood next to the Rep for his mother, while the Rep for his mother felt quite comfortable leaning on her son Jared. The Rep for Jared's father was looking longingly at his own Rep father's back. The Rep for his great-grandfather was asked to turn to look at his son, the Rep grandfather. Tears welled up in both and they came closer and touched each other on the shoulder. Then both men turned to look at Rep Jared's father, who was moved to touch them both.

The men were reconnecting and acknowledged their shared fate and loss.

Diagram 7

Rep Jared's father turned to look at his son with his Rep father behind him.

Diagram 8

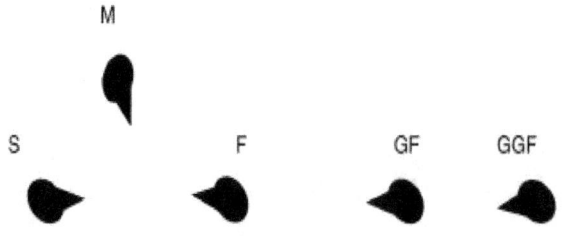

His father was able to look Jared's Rep in the eyes, while Jared's Rep found it hard to look at the Rep of his father. The Rep for Jared felt very angry towards his Rep father. His stomach and chest were churning and he expressed resentment and anger towards his father, and then he felt sadness. His Rep father said,

"I am sorry I couldn't stay".

Rep Jared was angry and confused.

He said, "You left me to cope and to look after my mother and sister. That wasn't fair. It was too much".

The two men looked at each other for a couple of minutes and then nodded in agreement of their sadness for what had happened. The father said:

"I am sorry I didn't have the courage to stay and left it to you. I will take responsibility for my lack of responsibility now."

Once Rep Jared's father had acknowledged his lack of courage and sorrow for what he had done, Rep Jared was able to move over, to let him take his place in the family.

His father took his place a small distance away from his Rep ex-wife, finding it hard to look at her fully, until he offered the sentence:

"Thank you for staying when I didn't."

The father came into contact with his feeling of shame for not taking his responsibility for the family and was able to honour what she had done in his absence.

He bowed and said:

"I honour you for bringing up our children as well as you did on your own", and then turned to the Rep Jared and said:

"I respect your mother. Please leave this with us."

Diagram 9

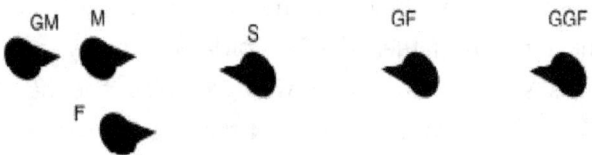

The Rep for Jared's father looked stronger in his place next to his ex-wife, with a distance between them. However, Rep Jared's mother looked very weak, as though she might fall over, so a Rep for her mother, (the grandmother to Jared) was placed behind her to give her some support.

After a few moments, she said she felt stronger and was able to say to her son:

"It's alright now for you to go and stand with the men, by your father."

Jared was now able to leave his parents' relationship with them and take his place with the men.

Diagram 10

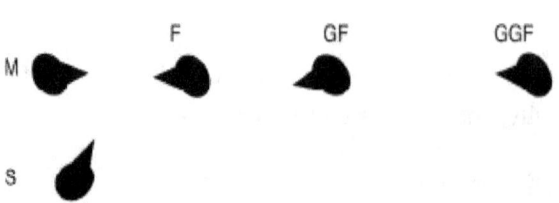

Rep Jared expressed gratitude and respect to his Rep mother and then the real Jared took his place while his representative sat in the group. Jared stood next to his Rep father for a few moments and the Rep for his father looked proudly at him. Then the representatives for Jared's father, grandfather and great-grandfather were put behind them, so that he was at the front of the line of men and could see and feel his male ancestral energy flowing down the line to him.

Some healing sentences were given to Jared and Jared was initiated into the men of his family and was blessed to live well as a man, husband, father and partner, and told to take the male energy and to use it in his own way now.

Diagram 11

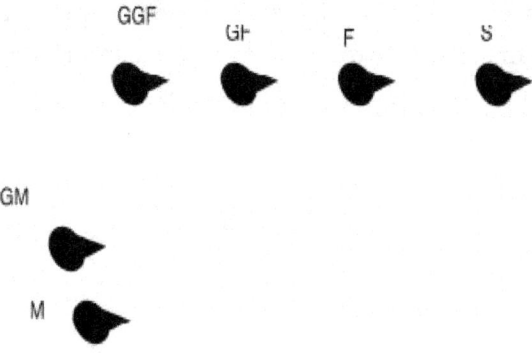

Jared was able to move forward by himself and look back at his family and then look forward again with a smile.

Jared reported feeling very different after this constellation and soon became involved in a new relationship and is very hopeful that he may be able to commit to a more permanent one soon.

Summary

Not having a father meant that Jared was not able to connect with his male ancestry and move into the realm of men. He also couldn't move away from his mother energetically and become a man in his own right in a love relationship.

Daughter's anxiety - difficult divorce

Janet came to a workshop to look at the anxiety and depression of her daughter Kate, who was 15 years old. Kate was too young to come to the workshop. In the discussion, Janet revealed that she had divorced her husband, Kate's father, when Kate was ten years old. Janet was now in a second, much happier relationship with a man who was supportive and who had accepted her children as his own. However, he was now finding Kate's behaviour upsetting and it was beginning to have an effect on their marriage. Upon asking the reason for the divorce, Janet told of years of poor communication and her husband's affair that was the final reason for leaving with the children. The children and Kate were allowed to see their father, David, one weekend out of two and there was no contact between Janet and her ex-husband otherwise, as communication between them was still very poor and often escalated into violent arguments. When asked about her own childhood, Janet revealed that her parents had separated after her father, Denis, had an affair when she was 15 and she'd had little to do with him after that. Her mother's name was Jenny.

Diagram 12

M mother Janet
D daughter Kate
F Kates father David
GM Janet's mother Ann
GF Janet's father Denis

Janet was asked to choose a representative for herself and one for her daughter, Kate, and her first husband, David. The representatives were set up with Rep David, Kate's father looking away at the edge of the circle and Rep Janet looking in the other direction close to her Rep daughter (Kate), who was by her side.

The facilitator asked Janet to put in representatives for her own mother, Ann, and father, Denis.

Janet placed her Rep father not too far away from her Rep first husband, looking in the same direction, out of the circle, and her Rep mother next to the Rep of herself and her Rep daughter (Kate).

Diagram 13

The Rep grandmother leaned on her Rep daughter (Janet) and Rep daughter (Kate) turned to look at them both, mother and grandmother, looking overwhelmed.

When asked how she felt, she said:

"I am so sad. I feel overwhelmed with the weight of it all."

Diagram 14

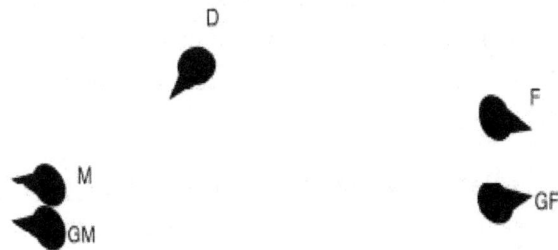

A Rep for the great-grandmother was put in behind the Rep grandmother and Rep grandmother leaned back on her own Rep mother with some relief and appeared to gain some strength from this. The Rep grandmother (Ann) was soon able to stand upright again.

Rep grandmother (Ann) and Rep mother (Janet) were invited to turn around to look at their Rep ex-husbands, Janet's father and her ex-husband Denis.

Diagram 15

The Rep mother looked into the Rep of her father's face, while her own Rep mother looked away. The colour in Rep Janet's face changed as she went red with agitation. When asked, she let the facilitator know that she hated her father; she hated him with a vengeance. Rep Janet was asked to turn so that she faced her mother and offered the following sentence to say:

"I hate him for you. For what he did to you."

The Rep grandmother looked over to her Rep ex-husband (Denis) and appeared to change form as her anger and hate for her ex-husband filled her visibly. The facilitator helped the Rep grandmother to express her anger, disappointment and sadness at what had happened.

Eventually, she was able to leave the responsibility of his affair fully with him. The Rep grandmother was then able to take some responsibility for the part she had played in what happened to their relationship and the Rep for her ex-husband visibly softened. The Rep for the mother moved away from her Rep mother and Rep father and was offered a sentence to say by the facilitator:

"I will leave what happened between you with you two now. This is too much for me. I am just a child here."

Diagram 16

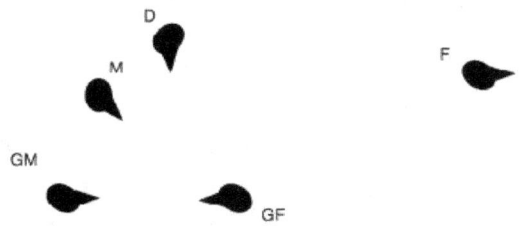

Tears welled up in all three of them.

The Rep father said to his Rep daughter, after a few moments:

"This had nothing to do with you. I never stopped loving you and I have missed you."

Rep Janet easily went forward to hug her Rep mother and Rep father. After a few moments, Rep Janet turned to look at her Rep daughter (Kate), who looked very alone, and also her Rep husband (David) on the other side of the room, still looking away.

Rep David turned to look at his Rep ex-wife (Janet) and Rep daughter (Kate).

Diagram 17

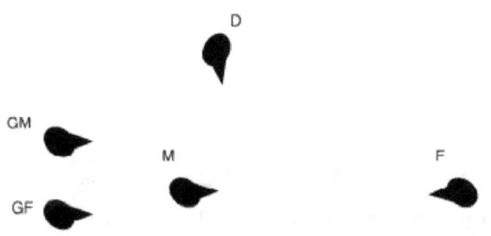

Rep Janet looked back at her own Rep mother and Rep father and then back at the Rep of her ex-husband (David) and said:

"I was looking for my father in you."

Here, Rep Janet was able to acknowledge her hidden love for her absent father and how she had been looking for him in her partner.

Tears welled up in Rep Janet. The facilitator helped her to express her rage and anger at what he had done and how much he had hurt her. Eventually, she was able to leave the responsibility of what he had done with him fully and accept the part that she had played in the relationship that had contributed to the situation. Rep Janet was eventually able to turn to her Rep daughter (Kate) and tell her:

"Leave my anger for your father and what happened in our relationship with us. It's our business. You're just a child here and you're innocent."

She was able to let her daughter know that she had once loved her father and that Kate had been born out of that love and that it was fine for her to love her father. The Rep for Kate was visibly moved and relieved and moved forward to embrace her Rep parents.

Diagram 18

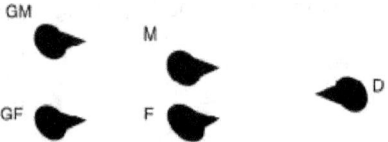

The constellation ended with her Rep grandparents standing together behind her Rep parents and with the Rep for daughter (Kate) looking at them and feeling much relieved and lighter.

Several weeks after the constellation, Janet let me know that her daughter, Kate, was more relaxed and that she felt much more at ease with her own father and ex-husband. Janet was beginning to feel more at peace with what had happened and the communication between herself and her ex-husband improved and her present family was more harmonious.

Summary

This was a situation that showed the pain of separation and divorce that had been repeated in two generations, resulting in the daughter, Kate, feeling the burden of conflicts consisting of loyalty, rejection, exclusion and a love that had not been expressed by her parents and grandparents that she felt as anxiety.

Lack of success.

Jal came to a workshop wanting a 'business' constellation. He was 41 years old and had made several attempts at running his own businesses. He was born in Australia and his father had migrated to Australia to find a better life. Jal had been bankrupted twice so far and his new business was struggling. He was smart, well-educated, ambitious and also prepared to work hard. When asked about his family of origin, he told of his father's struggle to make ends meet to support the family, while his grandfather was successful in his home country. Jal's grandfather had been the leader of the clan in his village and a powerful man. Jal became quiet and said that his grandfather had done some bad things, but that the family didn't speak of it. He said that the family believed that they were cursed. He said that a feud had developed between his own and another family over a business transaction in their home village during his grandfather's time.

The families who had formerly been great friends and had intermarried, were estranged and at war. There were several conflict situations between the families that angered the grandfather, which culminated in him having the son of his once-great friend killed. The family of the murdered son left the village. Jal's father also left later with his wife to go to Australia. Since then, each of the family members had struggled in their own ways, particularly in work and business.

Jal was asked to pick representatives for himself, his father, grandfather and the father of the other family, and his murdered son. Jal put his Rep grandfather in the centre of the room with the other Rep father and his Rep murdered son a long way away and looking away. Rep Jal and his Rep father were standing behind the Rep grandfather.

Diagram 19

S son Jal
F Jal's father
GF Jals grandfather
F* Father of estranged family
S* murdered son

The Rep for the grandfather said that he felt nothing, when he was asked. He was looking ahead and not meeting anyone's eyes. The Rep for Jal's father and Rep Jal said that they felt heavy, as if they were chained. The Rep for the grandfather and the Reps for his former friend and murdered son were turned to look at each other and the tension rose in the room. The Rep for the grandfather's ex-friend said that his hands were clenched and his jaw tight. He said he felt sick and torn with anger and disgust.

Diagram 20

He expressed his outrage and anger to the Rep for Jal's grandfather. The Rep grandfather looked coldly at him and slowly turned away again.

The Rep for Jal's father said to his Rep father (the grandfather):

"We carry the guilt and shame for you."

The Rep grandfather was unmoved.

Diagram 21

The Reps for Jal and his father moved closer to the Reps father and his murdered son. The Rep for Jal's father looked intensely at the Rep for the murdered son. They had been best friends. The Rep for Jal's father fell to his knees and then became prostrate before the Rep of his former murdered friend and his Rep friend's father. He lay there for a long time sobbing. By then, all Reps were sobbing, except for the grandfather. Eventually the Rep for Jal's father stood up. Jal took his place in the constellation by replacing his Rep and took his place next to the Rep for his father.

Diagram 22

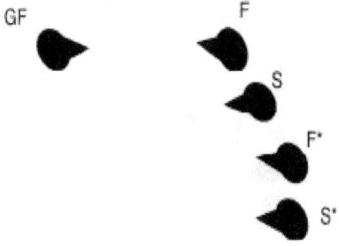

Jal and the Rep for his father bowed together deeply for several minutes to the Rep of the father and his Rep murdered son and expressed their deep sorrow and regret and deep love for them. Then the Rep for Jal's father stepped forward to face his Rep father, the grandfather and said:

"What you did was wrong. They were our closest friends. The guilt and shame is being carried by all of us. We are all condemned to suffer because of this."

Diagram 23

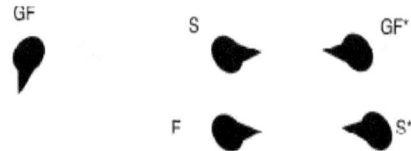

He stood looking at the Rep grandfather for a few minutes.

Then he said, "Please" and bowed to him.

For the first time, the Rep grandfather softened and his eyes welled up with tears. He looked over at his Rep former friend and the Rep murdered son and said:

"I had no right",

"I am sorry. Deeply sorry. I take full responsibility for what I did and the consequences it has had on you and your family, and my own family. I carry the burden of guilt and shame in full. It is mine to pay."

Diagram 24

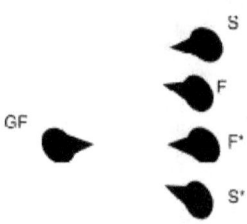

The Rep grandfathers nodded to each other through tears.

The Rep grandfather then took his place next to his Rep former friend and Rep murdered son with Rep Jal's father standing close with Rep Jal. At this point, Rep Jal breathed a large sigh and said:

"It's OK now, it's all in order."

Diagram 25

He turned to look at the Rep grandfather and said:

"I will leave this with you and move on with this as part of my family history."

He heaved a big sigh of relief and said that he felt lighter and freer.

Summary

The shame and guilt was being felt by the present generation because the grandfather had not taken responsibility for his actions. Once this had taken place in a constellation, it was possible for Jal to feel freer.

How this process works is still open to question. People like William Sheldrake (2012) and others are doing valuable work in morphic resonance and epigenetics and opening up more fields of knowledge that could help us to understand the process and the connections within the many levels of ourselves and our family system. These may be genetic, physical, emotional, psychological and energetic connections with each other and the environment. Perhaps, just as dreaming is a necessary process for health, by allowing assimilation, expression and resolution, so too may be the 'movements of the soul', as Hellinger called this process. The process for family constellations somehow provides a medium for things to come to light or to be worked out in a more helpful way towards health and healing.

Those who take part experience deep shifts, new awareness and perceptions of themselves and others. These are often invaluable in facilitating inner change. This process can be used for relationships and wellbeing and may provide an avenue for healing emotions and relationships among many other areas, such as business, mental, physical health and more. The examples given here had only one constellation session, which was enough to enable each of them to move on from their particular issue. Other people might require more than one constellation and also some private sessions to assist with integration.

However, it must be remembered that some situations or relationships may be part of fixed karma. Once you have done all you can do to remedy, resolve or change a relationship or situation from your side, then all that is left is to accept it and let it go. This is also part of your spiritual journey. Many of us carry a heavy destiny in some parts of our lives.

CHAPTER 17:

CLEAR YOUR HEART AND MIND FOR YOUR SPIRITUAL PATH

My journey has come a long way. I wanted to help people like you as Surya make deep changes when you are ready for this, so you can live freer, happier lives. Not everyone needs therapy although most of us would benefit from effective professional help during difficult periods of our lives if we are to sort things out and move on in a healthy way.

My entry into counselling and psychotherapy was a disappointment in this regard, as I found the available methodologies mostly ineffective or slow in providing progress for my clients. My introduction to family constellations was a great gift in providing different and profound way of working that provided deep shifts and changes quickly.

Family Constellations works with what we carry for and with our family system. Many people today are not aware of the power of systemic patterns have on our wellbeing and relationships. Most modern people believe that as individuals we are all powerful. All we have to do is do develop goals that are in alignment with our purpose and desires to assert our autonomy and put them into action to succeed. While this may be so for some, for many this is not so simple. We have invisible connections within our family system that we are largely not aware of. These may be in conflict with the hidden loyalties we hold for our system, that frequently hidden encounter blocks or sabotage. While strongly focusing on looking forward, we're mostly not aware of the power of hidden loyalties. Such loyalties may be linked to a sense of guilt, shame, unworthiness, sadness or trauma holding us back from our goals. This remains so until these entanglements can be resolved and released. This provides an avenue for taking back our dignity and personal power and finding a healthy way to connect with the system as well as stepping out as individuals.

Family constellations is an appropriate way of resolving generational patterns which I believe are also karmic and a great aid to anyone wishing to accelerate their progress on their personal or spiritual path.

I was happy to become a family constellations facilitator and hold regular workshops, private sessions and training to allow people to find more freedom and invite anyone to look for qualified family constellation practitioners close to home.

While family constellations are ideal for generational issues, not all human problems are systemic. I found when dealing with people with non-systemic issues of conflicts, disturbances or trauma, that traditional counselling and psychotherapy was slow and ineffective for most. This put me on another search to find better ways to facilitate change. This resulted in the founding of two new modalities. Emotional Mind Integration and Rapid Core Healing.

I believe we have reached a time in our human development where we have the knowledge and skills from former psychotherapies, hypnotherapy, present day neuroscience and epigenetics to really make a difference. The problem until now has been that knowledge has remained stuck in many fields. Fields that do not enquire or innovate or communicate or share their knowledge.

It's time to put relevant fields together in a practical and coherent manner, that can really make a difference in relieving many levels of suffering in modern men and women.

I have put together systems that are compatible with each other and that work at a practical level to facilitate fast and permanent change for those who are ready.

I founded EMI and RCH in response to helping people who have fallen through the cracks of the medical model of mental health. The medical model attempts to manage symptoms with CBT (cognitive behavioural therapy) and medication. CBT primarily. Attempts to work with thoughts, feelings or behaviours primarily, with logic or behavioural strategies, when the base of the issues is often emotional and locked in the subconscious mind.

Latest studies have shown that the core of problems is often repressed emotional content within the family system or the personal unconscious mind. This means that thinking or attempting to talk it through, or applying strategies to a problem with its roots locked in fear or trauma cannot provide an effectively lasting solution. Rational or cognitive thoughts are not equipped to deal with repressed content or trauma. Further, while some understanding may raise awareness, it often does not result in recovery or a cure.

EMI (Emotional Mind Integration) is a complete neuro-trance-psychotherapy modality that I founded in 2016, with its own unique philosophy, theory, process and techniques. EMI locates and resolves the roots of human emotional and psychological disturbances so that people can be free to fulfil their potential. As the name suggests EMI is a fusion of psychotherapy within a trance state via neural pathways for accurate and fast resolutions.

EMI philosophy takes into account the human requirements for love connection, safety, justice, dignity and autonomy as a foundation for wellbeing knowing that their absence often leads to "dis-ease". The modality facilitates the resolution of depression, anxiety, panic attacks, recovery of sexual abuse, trauma and the underlying dynamics of addiction in a few sessions for most clients.

I recognised that people are held back by personal, emotional and mind-based disturbances that have their roots in their past, personal choices and experiences. These come out in disturbed thoughts, beliefs and emotions and mental illness. These states often become triggers in daily life and cause a great deal of pain and confusion to the person concerned and to those they live with.

I realised that in looking at what was available, a more cutting edge, up to date modality was required that included the vital elements of former modalities and the latest findings in neuroscience.

Through my clients I found that attempting to solve more stubborn, destructive or uncomfortable thoughts, feelings or behaviours with logic or behavioural strategies was ineffective. This is because the roots of deeper issues are often located in the unconscious mind. Attempting to think a problem through, or apply strategies to it misses the mark. This is because logic is not equipped to locate or deal with emotional or painful material in an effective and appropriate manner. They don't speak the same language as emotions and the subconscious mind are not logical.

The good news is the unconscious mind is not only the source of problems, but also a treasure trove of wisdom, creativity, innovation and possibilities. When these are opened up, they are frequently the source of unique solutions and insights and from this place new perspectives and confidence may be funnelled into fulfilling potential and new possibilities.

The EMI process focuses on the presenting issue, locates the source and guides a resolution and integration within a normal session for each disturbed neural pathway. This is a fusion of phenomenology, counselling, psychotherapy, hypnotherapy, ego state therapy and aspects of Family Constellation theory (and practice) and neuroscience in an elegant and streamlined series of processes through innate healing pathways. It operates to guide the client's self-healing.

EMI spans the psychotherapy and hypnotherapy fields in bringing together relevant philosophy, knowledge and techniques in a way that provides a new way of dealing with trauma, mental health and human suffering in a cost effective way for a large proportion of the population.

> a) James suffered with chronic anxiety. He had seen many counsellors, psychologists and a psychiatrist before me, over a few years and was frustrated with his lack of progress. I saw him for four sessions of EMI where we uncovered many instances of being put down by parents, teachers, women and his boss. The EMI process cleared a neural pathway each session and by the end of the fourth session he was quite transformed and happy to move on in his life.
>
> b) Alison had a few sessions for depression that had started six years earlier. She had seen psychologist for several series of sessions and had taken medication to no avail. EMI located a period in her life prior to the onset of the depression six years earlier that had been very difficult and that she not been able to let go of. The sessions assisted in resolving and clearing these pathways and Alison recovered over the course of a month.

Rapid Core Healing (RCH) is a dual psychotherapy, founded by me, that locates the roots of human emotional and psychological disturbances and facilitates self-healing through neural healing pathways and core relational bonds. It is a complete psychotherapy modality with its own philosophy, theory and practice for the resolution of a wide range of personal and generational issues and trauma. RCH requires only a few sessions for recovery of a wide range of relational, personal and trauma related issues for a large proportion of the population (excluding serious DSM5 conditions such as schizophrenia etc)

Rapid Core Healing is a holistic approach.

My experience with clients showed me that human beings carry at least two strands of potential disturbances that can hold people back. These have their roots in either the family system, or personal life choices and experiences, or both. I recognised that each of these roots require a specific approach for accurate and effective treatment. This is why rapid core healing is composed of two modalities, family constellations (founded by Bert Hellinger) and EMI (Emotional Mind Integration).

The RCH modality operates within each sub modality seamlessly and alternates where appropriate. In this way it guides and accommodates the requirements and processing of the client's self-healing through a range of family constellation and EMI techniques and completes each session with integration.

RCH methodology utilises the knowledge that has come out of neuroscience that shows that the brain is neuro-plastic with the ability to heal. This means that change and healing is possible for most of us and all we have to do is find the methodologies that hold a belief that healing is possible for most with effective approaches.

Rapid Core Healing is cost effective in providing treatment suitable for the broad population of the population.

> *a) Jane came to me distressed over the flash-backs that she had of a rape incident several years earlier. She had been to a rape crisis centre and had been on medication over the previous few years. We had three EMI sessions where I facilitated her in clearing the neural pathways that were alive with the trauma of what had happened. She was able*

to recover her power and dignity and take in any wisdom that she had gained. During the sessions she let me know that there was sexual abuse in her family going back at least a couple of generations that could be traced back to her grandmother who was abused in an orphanage. As this was a systemic issue we did a family constellation where she able to leave the fate of her grandmother with her and take her blessing to live a full and free life. This combination of assisting her in resolving the systemic as well as the personal aspects of sexual abuse and the trauma involved was highly effective in only a few sessions in allowing Jane to move into her life with more confidence.

b) George came to see me with intense relationship issues and also anxiety. He had seen many counsellors before me. Because of his intense relationship issues we started with a family constellation that unveiled a very difficult connection with both parents. His father had never been present in his life and his mother was negligent and he had been abused by his stepfather. He was full of rage and a deep sadness. His present relationship had recently split up and he was distressed that he was not being allowed access to his daughter. He didn't want to be an absent father like his own father. In a couple of sessions, I facilitated a family of origin and a present situation family constellation to assist him in resolving his emotional state and find a better place in in his family system and also personally. On the next two sessions I assisted him in resolving his inner disturbances and conflicts with EMI and by the fifth session he was much relieved and planning how he was going to proceed in his life with much more confidence.

I provide sessions and training in Rapid Core Healing, Emotional Mind Integration and Family Constellations. This is presented in my book Rapid Core Healing Pathways to Growth and Emotional Healing (2016)

THE HOW OF MOKSHA

A man wanted to help the larvae of the butterfly to come out of its struggle and complete its transformation in the chrysalis. In his eagerness, he opened up the chrysalis to allow the butterfly out early, but the butterfly was under-developed, couldn't fly and died. The struggle is important to enable the butterfly to complete the straightening and strengthening of its wings. Transformation involves a struggle that cannot be shortened by someone wanting to help.

RETURNING TO LOVE

CHAPTER 18:

FINDING FREEDOM

We come into life in a physical form to experience ourselves in many ways. Our task is to discover our strengths and limitations. To develop the power of our mind and a movement towards opening up and moving towards expansion and move away from limitations and distortion, thereby unveiling our true, creative nature. This is the process of transformation that takes place, much like the transformation of larvae to a butterfly. A movement from inner change that lead towards resilience and freedom. This is a metaphor that I adopted a long time ago and use frequently. I believe it is a useful analogy, whether or not you believe in the cycle of reincarnation, heaven and hell or any other belief system. Here is another story to consider.

> There was a woman called Surya who died peacefully in old age. As her soul left her body, she was aware of travelling towards a huge white light a long way off. As she got closer, she noticed that in front of the light, there was a door with a man standing outside. He told her he was the doorkeeper and he said:
>
> "You've had a reasonable life. Where would you like to go, heaven or hell?"
>
> Surya was surprised at being given this choice, because she had expected that it would be allocated according to her life choices. The doorkeeper said:
>
> "No, it's your choice.
>
> If you like, I can let you see both place first and then you can decide where to go."
>
> Surya agreed and the doorway of heaven was opened up and she stepped in. Immediately, she noticed the high vibrant energy, the blue sky and white wispy clouds and the mountains and forests in the background, with rivers and lakes.

Looking closer, she noticed the rich vegetation with flowers and perfume and the call of birds around her. Then she noticed a long table to her right laden with succulent food and drinks of all kinds.

This was surrounded by many people sitting around the table chatting and laughing. She stayed a while and then asked to see hell.

As the door to hell opened up, she stepped inside. Immediately, she noticed the high vibrant energy, the blue sky and white wispy clouds and the mountains and forests in the background, with rivers and lakes.

Looking closer, she noticed the rich vegetation with flowers and their perfume and the call of birds around her. Then she noticed a long table to her right, laden with succulent food and drinks of all kinds, and people around it. She looked ahead for a few moments and then looked back at the doorkeeper, feeling confused and said:

"I don't understand, the two places are the same."

The doorkeeper replied:

"No, look again. They are not the same. Look at the people."

Surya looked back at the people and noticed that they were looking down with long faces and down turned mouths and mumbling and complaining to themselves. The doorkeeper said,

"It's not the place that's different, it's how the people perceive things. You lived in heaven and hell on Earth too."

Surya smiled and nodded and made her choice.

Surya is seemingly plunged into life with no sense of meaning for what it's about or what she's meant to do. She is plunged into illusion into the material plane from the spirit world. From the start, she is challenged to find meaning and from that, form beliefs, intentions and actions and, hence, create her reality. She continually makes and remakes meaning until she finds those that fit well with her growing wisdom and experience on her soul journey. Luckily, her brain is plastic and able to adapt and reshape constantly.

Surya always creates her reality through her mind, feelings, expectations and actions. She is free to create a new reality and go into freedom at any time, so what holds her back? Her karma or karmic patterns, systemic entanglements and personal beliefs, and emotions and vision may her back.

Once she's ready to resolve these factors, it is just a matter of time, trial and error, until she finds what assists her in creates freedom. With a free and balanced mind and emotions, Surya can become at one with her purpose and passion.

There are no limitations for Surya, as stardust, and it doesn't matter how long this process takes for her to realise and to complete. It is all experience. Experience is the juice of life.

At this level of development, our karma will continue to flow as it always has, but now we can accept it for what it is, what, at some level, we have created for ourselves. We only have to focus on how to deal or respond to it. No need for fear, anger, despair or anxiety about what comes next. One moment at a time is sufficient to focus on, knowing that there are no mistakes and each moment is an experience of equal value to the next, and potent with new possibilities.

Becoming present to each moment and being able to interact, experience and make choices is sufficient.

In this way, we can travel home at any moment to 'all that is', regardless of what is coming our way, because it is an inner, not an outer journey. We are free to see the light in everything and everyone, or not.

We are on a journey as stardust. Perhaps we have been through many lives and experiences and are ready for change, having exhausted many avenues. Perhaps we are aware of our karmic patterns and have made many changes and are ready for more freedom. At this point in the spiritual journey, we may be ready to notice or examine our thoughts and feelings, rather than repressing them. We might be ready for some honest reflection.

The culture, family and parents we are born into highly influences how we view our world and this can often create confusion and turbulence, as we struggle to define ourselves as men and women.

Interestingly, full acceptance of this first experience of our family is often enough to release us from entanglements with them, in a healthy way. We are free to connect to the struggle, history and love of all those who have gone before us, without having to carry them as a burden. Then we can move forward with more freedom and connection to the soul of humanity and all living and non-living things in 'all that is.

This makes it possible for us to develop a sense of humble entitlement and worthiness that enables us to create a vision of ourselves in our world with the creator. Once our inner vision of ourselves is at peace, we can perceive ourselves differently in the world. There is no need to recreate the dramas of old patterns in the workplace or relationships. We can step into a new vision and feeling of ourselves. New possibilities can emerge.

Even though we might have done lots of personal development, we may still be aware of anxiety, depression, irritation or anger and sadness flooding in at times. What Eckhart Tolle (2009) calls the 'pain body' throughout his writing, may still arise when triggered. According to Tolle, the pain body is complex, comprising of personal repressed pain or trauma and also inherited emotional baggage that we all carry. This is pain that has its roots in our childhood, biography, ancestral line and karmic patterns. It may also have roots in the deep psychological structures of values and beliefs going back through many lives. Tolle makes the point, as many other spiritual teachers have, that suffering is a choice and is not necessary to enter a liberated state.

We can choose to ascend into a higher consciousness at any point of our journey. We can come out of the 'story' we have of ourselves and observe any negative feelings or thoughts and let them go. Let go of any attachment to them and allow our consciousness to expand. This is also the essence of Byron Katie's teaching with her 'work' (2002, p9, where she supplies an effective way to challenge and deconstruct difficult emotions or beliefs for those of us who are committed to self-help. In essence, it is very simple, but challenging and effective for those who are really ready to leave suffering behind.

Having read this far, it is likely that you are already consciously on your way home and wondering how you can embrace this further.

Beliefs

Your beliefs are a great monitor of how you are travelling. If they help you to look kindly on yourself and others and are open to being challenged and examined, then they are likely to be healthy and free.

However, if you find that you are constantly being upset or triggered by people or situations that do not live up to your expectations, then it is likely that your beliefs have limitations or may be rigid. Limited or rigid beliefs will create havoc in setting you up for disappointments that can lead to anger, blame and sadness. They also lead to a limited view and lack of vision or possibilities.

The only place where change can take place is within us. It is not possible or ethical to attempt to change others or for them to attempt to change us. However, we do have the power to choose whom we spend our time with and with whom we form love relationships or friendships with. We have the choice to stay or leave.

By staying, we might also have to look at ourselves in the reflection of the other, which can also be challenging. However, there are times when leaving might be appropriate.

Many spiritual masters have gone into a state of higher consciousness after experiencing extreme stress, usually self-made mental stress. Through our karma and choices, we can put ourselves into such extreme anxiety and stress at times, that we reach a point of meltdown (physical or mental), where we can choose to let go or continue as we are. Let it all go. Old mental structures and emotional pathways can dissolve as we enter the freedom and peace of the present. We can enter the freedom of 'now' in each breath and each moment. This is one path to freedom.

For others, it may be a gradual awakening through the refining and purifying of each belief and emotion over time, thereby gradually changing their reality.

You can change your reality. Your reality comes from you; therefore, you're the only one who can change it.

Beliefs can be viewed in two ways. Those that bring pleasure and an open attitude to life encourages growth, enquiry, resilience and perseverance. Such beliefs lead to healthy choices, relationships and wellbeing. The other are those beliefs that bring pain and a closed attitude to life and lead to a restricted and limited attitude that includes fear and suspicion and spoils relationships and wellbeing. In addition, such beliefs create mental and emotional pain. For the sake of ease, I will refer to the former as healthy and the latter as unhealthy beliefs, due to the experiences they create.

Generally, if our beliefs are healthy, then the thoughts that flow from them are likely to be flexible, balanced and easy to live with. Healthy beliefs enable us to be clear about what is important and help us to let go of feelings, ideas or situations that are not in our best interests. If a belief is not so healthy, we will find our thoughts are rigid, disturbing and cause unpleasant feelings. So, it is true that healthy beliefs generally lead to healthy thoughts and feelings and unhealthy beliefs generally lead to unhealthy thoughts and feelings. Healthy beliefs are generally flexible while unhealthy beliefs are generally rigid.

We are always manifesting our reality, but for the most part, unconsciously. Thoughts are creations that come from our conscious and also unconscious mind and the ratio of conscious to subconscious is approximately 7:93. This means that most of our deeper thoughts and emotions are repressed or locked in our subconscious mind. Therefore, analysing ourselves is often difficult, as the more problematic thoughts or behaviours come from our subconscious, so are outside awareness, our blind spots.

Consciousness is a constant stream of information from the senses and the mind, mainly comprised of thoughts, feelings and visions. We create thoughts automatically and continuously, so much so, that it may feel like it's happening 'to' us, rather than being created 'by' us.

However, if we are to gain more freedom, then refining our beliefs is crucial to raise our conscious.

Emotions

By looking at emotions from the view of current psychological research, we see that there has been a long debate in this area of knowledge about which came first, emotions or beliefs. In summarizing Schore's (2003a) idea, the right (emotional) side of the brain is more deeply connected to the body. The right hemisphere, emotional, is developed prior to the left hemisphere, intellectual. According to Schore, it appears that the emotional foundation must be in place before the intellectual functioning left brain can form. The setting down of emotional roots first, enables the higher processes of the mind to develop in their task of logical thought and the ability to make meaning of experiences.

In addition, Maroda (2010 p136), said:

"The critical role of emotions in the transformation of human experience has only recently been recognised."

So, it seems that there is a growing body of agreement that emotions are pivotal to our experience of life. Through your emotions, you can monitor how you are. Whether you're happy, sad, scared or angry gives vital information on which you can base your responses. Healthy emotions are free flowing and are a natural means of letting you know how you are experiencing yourself and your world. Healthy emotions have a requirement to be felt, processed and expressed, in that it is normal to feel happy, angry, sad or anxious at times.

Emotions are part of your essence as human stardust. They flow freely, as can be seen in a new born baby, who can be happy one moment and sad or distressed in the next. It appears that you are thrown into a life where there is no meaning and it is your early emotional responses to formative experiences that enables you to make meaning of it all. Generally, if those early experiences are nurturing and comforting, you will make comforting meanings around acceptance and connection and, if those experiences are cold or isolating, you may make meaning around rejection or disconnection.

From this, your beliefs, thoughts and actions follow. If those early emotional foundations were reliable and resilient, then it is likely that the meanings you formed will be fairly life-affirming and healthy too. However, if those early experiences were chaotic, unpredictable, or even traumatic, it is likely that any meanings you make may be fear-based and not-so-life-affirming or healthy.

Normal, healthy emotions flow. So, what causes emotional blocks? Emotions can easily become frozen after trauma, where deep sadness, hurt, fear or anxiety form blocks to free flowing feelings. These can also form blocks or a distortion to the process of assimilating experiences in a healthy way. This is due to their intensity as painful emotions are often repressed and form the basis on which unhealthy beliefs are built.

These form hidden reactionary triggers or patterns to thoughts, behaviour and feelings. From this state, it can be difficult, if not impossible, to re-evaluate beliefs or process feelings in a natural evolving process of assimilation, that results in letting go that enables growth. I consider these to be frozen, locked in time, due to shock or trauma. Such emotions lead to fixed or rigid beliefs and form a filter by which we view our world that can form a restriction to growth.

Frozen emotions are not processed in a normal manner, due to their intensity, and they remain trapped in the body to become 'buttons' that may be triggered in a seemingly volatile manner.

These buttons have the effect of causing chaos in our personal and relationship life because of their unpredictability, leaving us feeling out of control of our own responses.

The Dalai Lama (2003, p80), in his book called *Destructive Emotions*, used the term 'destructive emotions' because they are formed from traumatic events. They shock the nervous system so the responses are repressed by the subconscious mind, due to the intensity of the discomfort or pain. These can remain locked in our emotional or neurological body and appear as a body sensation.

X Alternatively, they can be locked in the subconscious mind-memory possibly for your life. Such shocks can remain unprocessed and locked up in the mind-body connection and easily be set off by a word, tone of voice, smell, look, facial expression or situation, among many other things. Setting off unpleasant thoughts or feelings can result in fearful, defensive or attacking behaviour. These involuntary emotional reactions can cause havoc, in many people's lives. They are silent time bombs that can be triggered by daily life situations that often render us victims to feelings of powerlessness, unless they are processed appropriately.

When I was living in England, I had a phobia concerning crane flies. They had small wings and long legs and buffeted around at dusk in corners and were attracted to the light of lamps.

This irrational fear had been with me for a long time and was a source of embarrassment, because these insects were harmless and plentiful where I lived. As an adult, one day while I was receiving hypnotherapy, I dropped back to a time of my life as a child that was fearful for me, when my family were going through a stressful period. There, in the bathroom, I could see my younger self feeling the fear or stress and looking at crane flies in the corner. Just making the connection was enough to enable my phobia to vanish soon after. I had attached the fear or frozen emotion to what I was observing, which happened to be the crane fly. The fear had been retriggered each time I saw them. Simply realising the link I had made in my unconscious mind was enough to release me from the irrational fear or phobia.

This is only one example of how frozen emotions can operate in the psyche, that may have quite different root causes and resolutions in other cases.

In another case, a client of mine had a phobia of snakes, even though she was born in England where there are few snakes and even fewer dangerous ones. This fear had been with her all of her life. In regression hypnosis, when going to the origin of this fear, she saw herself as an Indian woman cooking on an open fire with a snake coming towards her.

She said in hypnosis, "It killed me".

On coming out of the trance, she commented that it was strange because she didn't believe in past lives, but the phobia subsided after that.

From frozen emotions, beliefs can be formed that are faulty or irrational, creating the view that 'the world is a scary place' or 'you can't trust anyone', or 'I am not good enough' or 'spiders are dangerous' or any other belief.

Unhealthy emotions and the beliefs that arise from them cannot but poison, limit or colour the experience of your life and relationships and what you create for yourself.

Frozen emotions may also be formed from car accidents or other traumatic incidents, such as intense situations with a parent or teacher, if they are not processed appropriately and disrupt the natural flow of healthy feelings. In addition, these can become the basis of irrational beliefs, from which poor decisions are made. Thoughts and emotions can become inextricably interwoven in the psyche, by either being life-affirming or potentially destructive. Frozen emotions or the beliefs attached to them cannot be relied upon to give accurate information on which to make choices.

For example, just because I felt terror each time I saw crane flies, doesn't mean that I was in danger or that the insects were actually dangerous or threatening. By experiencing stuck or frozen emotions, it is very common for people to blame others for what they're feeling. They might say that someone else is 'making' them sad or angry. However, the emotions are theirs and it is for them to choose to be a victim to their emotions or not.

The first step to coming out of this pattern is to acknowledge your emotions as your own and seek to resolve them. In addition, you may also carry emotions that are systemic, coming from your family system that are both healthy and also not so healthy. Healthy, being life-affirming and unhealthy, being life restricting. For example, you may have been born with a sense of guilt, fear, sadness or anxiety or any other state, such as victimisation, where such feelings make no sense in your personal biography, but are part of your family system.

These become blocks or burdens that you carry. You may be taking on the sadness or anger of parents or the feelings of guilt or shame from someone in the family system, that perhaps was not able to feel or process them adequately. Interestingly, in family constellations, as explained by Leibermeister (2006, p45), the love of a child towards its family is so strong that it will very happily take on other people's emotions in a childish belief that this somehow 'helps' the other. Children are hypersensitive to energy, easily taking on the emotions or burdens of others because of their love and may continue to carry them throughout their own lives.

There is no doubt that thoughts and emotions have an effect on each other. You may assess yourself by reflecting on the following. Notice what is taking place in your mind, in particular, your self-talk, the chatter in your head. Write it down over a few days, so that you can notice any themes or patterns. Notice the messages you tell yourself, what you are reaffirming on a minute-by-minute, or daily basis in your brain cells and into each body cell through the neural network.

These become strong self-determining affirmations going to every cell and neuron of your body or mind so, whether it is negative or positive, it has an effect on you. Deepak Chopra (1993) referred to the mind-body connection that is constantly being verified by further research. If your self-talk is negative, it would be beneficial to change it in order to improve your mental and physical health.

If you notice that you are easily hurt or offended by the attitudes, communication or behaviour of others, you might notice common themes or beliefs that underpin your thoughts or behaviours. Notice if you quickly make assumptions and act on them as if they are real, without checking them out for their validity.

Many people find themselves taking things personally because they are looking for the 'hook' or the 'spike' in words or actions that they can figuratively rub into their old wounds. They make assumptions from a look, word or tone, without checking them out for validity. It is true that we all look for responses beyond words and actions, but wise people check them out to confirm or deny them, thereby avoiding the need to waste emotional or mental energy on creating fear-based, imagined dramas of what they might mean. Blowing small, insignificant things into monumental dramas with no foundation is a way of creating hell on Earth.

In truth, it is not possible to be hurt by others emotionally if our wounds are healed and if we have created newer, healthier, grounded beliefs. Beliefs that are sufficiently flexible to allow us to continue in our growth. Such beliefs can be constantly reassessed as we continue to mature. Those who wish to hurt us can only do so if we have open wounds.

In reality, often hurtful words directed at us are coming at us from their own wounds, in projecting their pain, so it is more about them than you. Knowing this can be helpful to guide you towards your own healing and also towards your choice of friends or relationships. You can choose who you spend your time with. Easy going, happy people are easy to be with.

Some emotions are not so sociably accepted. Anger, as an emotion, has largely been vilified for many of us, but it is a valid, raw energy that lets you know when you are being violated or overlooked in some way.

However, it is your emotion. No one can make you angry. It is yours to help you look at what you are doing, or what is happening to you. Anger gives you the motivation to look after yourself. It lets you know when you need to say 'NO' or shows you where an unhealthy belief or frozen emotion is operating. Healthy anger motivates you into appropriate action and then dissipates once you make a mental shift or take action, whereas unhealthy anger festers and explodes in a volatile way, seemingly out of control for insignificant reasons.

Whatever the quality of your anger, it is yours. No one else is responsible for it.

Anger may also be used to blame and control others, as well as to express pain. It is often felt as a separation from love and is felt most strongly when we feel the pain of that separation.

Anger is a raw emotion that may be felt in a healthy way when a belief system or boundary is violated and motivates us into appropriate action. Alternatively, it may be a frozen emotional trigger from a former unresolved situation that may be projected, like a bomb, onto those around us. Anger will also inform you of your expectations and beliefs, providing a great opportunity to use this potent energy well. Finding ways to embrace healthy emotions and resolve unhealthy ones, rather than suppressing them, will allow your emotional state to revive and flow easily.

Acceptance and change are important dichotomies. Changing what you can and being able to accept what you can't change, are important steps in finding freedom. You already know that you can only change yourself or your choices. It's not your right or in your power to change or influence others and, often it is easier to continue as you are than to initiate change.

Nevertheless, change is a constant in our lives. Change is imminent in us, the world and the universe, but somehow, we often resist it by wanting to stay in our comfort zone. Accepting and embracing change is a choice, one that most of us put off until the stress of the situation has reached unbearable proportions.

Resisting change can cause problems. At a time in my life when I was a school teacher and had been introduced to Vedic astrology and the door had opened on an area of knowledge that enthralled me, I instinctively knew that I was on the threshold of change, even though I loved my existing role of teaching and I loved working with children.

This became the onset of an inner conflict that continued to grow in the following year and consisted of procrastination, over my attachment to my knowledge, skills and security, while I was becoming more seduced by the knowledge that I was absorbing in my astrology studies. My health declined as a digestive problem surfaced and became worse until I had to stop work and eventually listen to what my heart and soul were telling me. I resigned at the end of that year and commenced on my new path and my health gradually returned. Change was imminent, regardless of my resistance.

Self

It is likely that you have been told in many different ways, either through religion, society or family, that you should not be selfish. That it's not acceptable for you to focus on yourself or your own happiness, with an inference that this is a sin. Here we enter another part of your journey, if this applies to you, and another belief to unravel. By believing this, you might feel honourable in putting the wishes and welfare of others before your own. However, this may be followed by feelings of resentment because you deny your deepest wishes, along with a surge of guilt over the resentment. It is true that there is a need to take responsibility for looking after what is yours, such as children, older parents, relatives and possibly friends who depend on you for care. Therein lies the dilemma. How can you be fully present for others if you are depleted or confused and not keeping yourself in good order? How can you be authentic in your generosity if you are not taking care of yourself first? Looking after loved ones who require your help is appropriate, but must also be balanced with the need to look after yourself. Only you can do that, emotionally and spiritually.

No one else, no matter how well meaning, can do that for you, or you for them. If you really understand this, you will know that there is a limit to what is appropriate or healthy for you to give or do for others.

In reality, no one else knows what you need, as you don't even know this for yourself until you take the time to explore what makes you happy through many lives.

Expectations

By seeking freedom, it is necessary to look at expectations. Expectations can be the source of great disappointment, such as expecting others to live up to your wish or you to theirs. This is fraught with problems because it is each of our responsibilities to do that for ourselves. Not being real or grounded in this is fraught with problems. The only person you are primarily responsible for is yourself: your emotions, beliefs, perceptions and your own soul journey.

In addition, you might also be aware of your imprint or effect on your loved ones, society, the environment and your part in mass consciousness. Understanding this can help you to find appropriate boundaries and to avoid taking the world on your shoulders or blaming or relying on others, so you can be appropriately responsible.

We are living in times of great wealth and depravity, freedom and enslavement. In a world where poverty and hunger are rife in the midst of abundance, with capitalism ruling and benefitting the 'haves' over the 'have nots.'

This situation might cause you to feel the pressure, as I do, to find ways that can make a difference. There are many ways that you can share your compassion and material wealth, skills or knowledge in your local community and in third world countries. You can support groups or cooperatives that demonstrate clearly that they make a difference. However, it is impossible to be responsible for everything and everybody. You are stardust, Surya, on your soul journey. You have been born into this life, this place and time and you can become active in those areas where you feel drawn, in having an impact and making a difference. Also, you can let go of those areas where you have no control, while remaining informed socially, politically and financially for the developing and changing environment of your world. You can also use your political vote locally, nationally or internationally to support those ideas that call you.

Manifestation

Surya is a co-creator and creates through her vision, intention and emotional and mental state. If they are strong and healthy, her creations are fulfilling or enjoyable and, if not, she creates destructively and painfully. In addition, she has the ability to feel and choose her responses and make sense of her experiences.

When she is free in her beliefs and emotions, generally she finds it easy to feel good about herself and project that into her world. She can be more conscious of her choices and how she uses her emotional energy. You have a powerful mind. Look at what pain and chaos it can create. This same power can be used to create consciously too. It is possible to create a new reality and manifest a new experience, regardless of what is happening in the world around you. You create from your inner state and from your inner reality. You can make changes in yourself over time through honest reflection and a conscious effort to change your thoughts and behaviour. In addition, you can resolve stuck emotions with a competent psychotherapist or hypnotherapist, or resolve systemic issues through family constellations, in order to gain more emotional freedom. These are all powerful aids to gaining freedom of the heart and mind.

Interestingly, those people around you might not want you to change and might feel threatened or offended by your new choices. You may at first take that on, feeling responsible or guilty for their feelings.

You might even consider letting go of your wish to grow and go back to the way you were. Remember, this is your journey. Your life.

At some point, you might realise that it is impossible to please everyone and, even if you devote your life to this purpose, it is unlikely that you will succeed. Each person is ultimately responsible for their own life and spiritual journey, while, where possible, remaining compassionate and respectful of others' choices.

Only when your mind, values, beliefs and goals are free and in line with your life purpose, will you be able to manifest your vision of yourself fully. Opportunities might frequently present themselves, but if you are not open to their possibilities, due to the limitations of your conditioning, you won't notice them. So, it is important to free yourself from your conditioning as much as possible, as this becomes the filter through which you view everything. You view your world through the blueprint of former experiences, until they're set free; a filter putting forward the familiar, even when it's unpleasant or painful, will be noticed above others.

If you have a filter that sees only rejection, sadness or poverty, then that is what you will see around you. You will be blind to other more comfortable, loving or prosperous possibilities. Your filter becomes your blind spot, the part that is so familiar that you don't even know it's there. How are you to find your blind spot or change your filter? Most often, this happen through your interactions with others and most especially when the mirror is turned on you and your feelings of anger, disappointment or misunderstandings.

At these times, you may feel like a victim to your emotions that result in confusing or painful thoughts. At some point in your spiritual journey, you will begin to question the level of suffering you are experiencing and begin to notice that, wherever you go, the same themes arise around you. Perhaps you will see that you are the common denominator and ultimately, the source of your unease and creating your own dramas. At this point, you might come to notice what your filters are selecting and the nature of your blind spots. In the present, you might be greatly helped by utilising 'The Work' of Byron Katie to help you change unhealthy beliefs or feelings. You can look at any emotion, thought or belief through this process and start to conscious change your deep-seated conditioning and open up to new possibilities.

As you evolve, you will become more aware of your thoughts, whereas previously they may have seemed to have had a life or will of their own. Having clarity about your thoughts and feelings means that you can be clearer about what you're creating.

As your growth continues, eventually, you can become so fine-tuned and conscious of your thoughts that you can easily witness them manifesting into reality relatively quickly, even in small ways, day by day. Likewise, if you are fearful, you will constantly find yourself in scary situations. You can make changes at any point, once you understand the power you have at your disposal, to become anything from the very highest to the lowest of humankind.

Change

When looking at why change is so difficult for us to make, it is a reality that many of us are very much attached to the 'story' we have of ourselves. In fact, many people believe that they 'are' the 'story'. Alternatively, we may have a belief that is underpinning the 'story' that makes it advantageous to keep.

To let go of the 'story' might mean:

"That it wasn't so important, painful or traumatic as I once thought."

"I'm letting them off from what they did to me."

"Having this story gives me power and control, as I get sympathy".

"If I let it go, I will have to take responsibility for my behaviour."

"If I let it go, who am I?"

Or...anything else.

Most people will only let go if they can see a benefit in doing so.

In reality, not letting go always means punishing yourself by damaging your relationships and life experiences.

You're always creating your reality with universal energy, along with your karmic patterns and life purpose. If your values, beliefs and thoughts are not so clear or healthy, then you may be creating a lot of confusing thoughts to take into your reality and, hence, chaotic events unfold. If they're healthy, you are more likely to be in contact with your passion, life purpose and have a clear intention. From this point onwards, you will be able to manifest your reality relatively easily, if you are also willing to do the work involved to build and maintain it in a practical, physical and grounded way.

Dreaming or visualising alone is often not sufficient, unless you have some strong positive karma heading your way. Having a mind and emotions means that you create your image of the world through your experiences, ideas, values and beliefs. The experience of your family, culture and events in your formative years all provide you with a blueprint of how to experience the world through which you create your life.

If this is not how you would like it to be, then it is up to you to make the changes necessary for more freedom. However, your filter is often so effective, that you see only what you expect to see, rather than what is present. This selected set of information becomes what you project into the world, although you may not be aware of what or how you are doing it.

In addition, much of what you project comes from your level of self-worth. You pursue goals that fit with your view of your worth and don't pursue what appears to be outside your view of your worth.

As an adult, regardless of your childhood, it's your responsibility to create yourself in your own image.

How quickly you are able to recover your equilibrium after an upset is a good measure of your personal development.

Freedom Checklist

Do you take everything personally?

Are you critical of yourself or others?

Do you find it difficult to accept others having a different point of view?

Do you make assumptions without checking them out?

Are you a glass-half-full or a glass-half-empty person?

Are you able to recover from an upset in a reasonable amount of time?

Do you accept your life as it is, including your family?

Do you stay mainly in the present, or do you focus mainly on the past or future?

Are you able to let things go, or do you hold grudges?

Are you making the most of your life?

Are you able to love easily?

Are you able to receive love easily?

Can you say 'no' clearly, when necessary?

Can you let go of the need to always be right?

Remember, your life is to be lived and experienced. The clearing and refining of thoughts and emotions takes place by being totally absorbed in living, experiencing, reflecting and changing. This is the spiritual journey.

CHAPTER 19:

ESSENTIAL EGO

Ego is the shell that protects the developing embryo of spiritual essence, so the ego is essential on the path to awakening.

It's like the larvae of a butterfly in its chrysalis that needs the restriction of its container to push against, in order to strengthen its wings. The ego is an invisible, psychological structure that is so familiar that we don't even know it's there until we dare to look within, or are made aware of its out-pouring's. The ego is both an individual and also a collective structure that is in symmetry with an illusion of ourselves. Surya falls into life and, according to Vedic thinking, proceeds through four basic stages of growth in a normal life span, where he is ruled by the moon. The elusive moon represents his mind and emotions and how he manifests his soul energy through the ebb and flow of daily life. The normal lifespan of a human being is comprised of four main periods of life: childhood, adolescence, adulthood and old age. Life span can range from sort to long and anything in between.

As a child, Surya is the universal student, ruled by Mercury, the planet of intellect, reasoning, communication and knowledge. It is early in this stage of development that he forms an ego. At this stage of his life, Mercury enables him to learn, to be adaptive and to be conditioned into family, culture and language with practical and intellectual knowledge. This continues until he enters adolescence.

As an adolescent, he enters the next stage, completing his studies and entering a role in life where he is ruled primarily by the sun. In this stage of life, the sun encourages him to find an identity or role that can sustain him and enable him to be noticed or recognised. He is very aware of how he appears to others and is ruled by his ego. During this period, he creates a stronger identity and more independence and begins to socialise until he becomes aware of his need for love and romance and enters into the next stage of life, adulthood.

In the stage of adulthood, Surya might find a partner and might start a family. If he does, he takes on the responsibilities of managing a household and parenting. This is the stage of life that is ruled by Venus, Mars and Jupiter, which collectively give him the drive and perseverance to sustain him through this tumultuous period of his life, where if he has a family is often forced to put the needs of others before his own.

Eventually, Surya reaches the last period of his life, old age, which is ruled by Saturn. This is a time when his children, if he has any, move on into their own lives, leaving an 'empty nest' and the freedom for Surya to follow his desire in how he wishes to spend his time. He may simply rest, or turn his focus to deepening his spiritual Life, as he continues into old age. If Surya has not had children, he may simply reach a crisis where Saturn will help him to let go of what no longer serves him, as he reviews his life and embraces his deeper essence.

By this last stage of life, we are often able to let go of our gender roles, to some extent, because they have served their purpose. Couples might now live together, more as companions, regardless of whether or not they still have sexual relations. By this stage, we've had the opportunity to gain wisdom and insight from life's experiences. We may realise that our intellectual or rational and practical knowledge does not speak the language of the soul journey or understand its synchronicity with universal energy and can't answer the bigger questions of life. We're offered the possibility of letting go of intellectual knowledge, status, materialism, craving and identity, in favour of more connection with the essence of 'being'. This is Surya, the universal soul that is part of 'all that is'. There are many things said about the ego and most spiritual teachings talk about the need to 'let it go'. The ego is often discussed as if it is a demon or a trickster. What is not spoken of is that the ego is a necessary part of our psyche and our journey.

The ego is the structure that provides us with an identity involving the roles that we take on in life, such as parent, child, sibling, friend, colleague, banker, teacher, cleaner, etc. Identity is important for the developing persona because it provides an anchor to hold us steady while we don't know who or what we are. We cannot let go of ego before we know that there is something much deeper and richer to sustain us. While we fear that there is nothing else, we hold onto our ego.

The egoic self is on a journey of transformation, just like the butterfly that transforms from the caterpillar. The chrysalis acts as a firm and restricting holding space that allows it to be nourished and grow in pushing against boundaries to strengthen its wings. This is the same for the ego, which is the structure against which the inner essence of the soul expands against to deepen its resilience and develop its sense of presence. Ego and illusion are perfect companions. Desire and aspiration are also part of illusion, as are the challenges and goals to be achieved through the pushing and growing of the ego in the chrysalis of life.

Ego is the shell that protects us from the disappointment of finding ourselves in a fantasy, before we have grown sufficiently to meet this reality. The ego requires a strong identification in the physical world of thoughts, beliefs, emotions, drama and identity. Ego can make us think that we are better or less than others, because it feeds on insecurity and fear. Fearful of letting go of its constructs and the need for identity, power, 'being right,' the glory of me as my 'story', that leads to annihilation. The identity obliterated, dissolved or doomed to nothingness. Like the fear invoked in a nightmare of falling into a never ending black hole.

There is always a struggle with who we are. So much so that we form stories of who we are. We become our story, if we over-identify with our ego. We may identify ourselves as victim or hero, or some other role. A role that gives us the attention we crave, whether it is positive or negative. For the ego, any role is better than none. It seeks to rationalise or justify our behaviours or attitudes. While we are fully engaged in these roles or dramas, why would we want to come out of them? In reality, we play them out until we have exhausted all possibilities, and until we realise that this is not IT.

We find this doesn't give satisfaction or connect us to the bliss that we know is there somewhere. Also, from the ego's standpoint, what is the point of existing if we are not seen or recognised, or do not have a role to be remembered by? The ego is responsible for giving us a face or a role before we are aware of our deeper self. It is responsible for over-confidence, name- dropping, to impress, shyness, the fear of failing or being ridiculed and bullying or feeling victimised. Beliefs that involve attachment to fame, notoriety or over-identification of roles or qualities, such as power, wealth, poverty, control, fear, anxiety and many more, are all-ego related. Ego has a place.

The shield of the ego helps us initially to operate in our physicality and to practise the art of creation and manifestation on the material plane. It gives us a sense of purpose and importance and distracts us from the perceived void and disconnection within. Interestingly, only when we have developed a strong and healthy ego, can we begin to appreciate its shortfalls. This is when we realise that the job, relationship or new item of clothing did not make us happy for long, nor did it fill the void. The intellectual and practical knowledge that appeared to be so meaningful is not able to be sustained. The objects we obtain are empty.

Relationships constantly change form. Eventually everything dissolves, due to their temporal nature, leaving us pushing the boundaries of our chrysalis in Maya, in search of new dimensions.

The experiences of life are temporal. Nothing lasts. While we enjoy our successes, we also have to experience the loss of youth, loved ones, relationships, our health, career, wealth, objects and, eventually, life. Each of these experiences of loss provide us with the opportunity to 'let go.' To begin the process of peeling back the egotistical mind to allow our sense of 'being' to emerge that, unlike the ego, is formless, nameless, stateless, limitless and free.

By travelling towards liberation, there must be a letting go of the illusion of self, others and the material world.

Letting go may happen naturally over time, through the satiation of unlimited experiences through many lives., Letting go often takes place through extreme stress, where situations or experiences are so overpowering, that it becomes easier to let go than to continue. Let go of the craziness of ego and illusion, through a meltdown of the mind or body into the simplicity or 'beingness' of oneness.

Alternatively, those who go through a near-death experience are frequently transformed. The experience of death informs them that this is not the end and in showing them that there is so much more beyond this material plane. In reality, it's always possible to let go now, or at any moment, but for most of us, a crisis is required to trigger the shift.

We might let go of ego gradually through a gradual refining and mastery. This is mastery that happens through eons of lives and can result in desires that can lose their addictive, obsessive quality that enable us to continue to enjoy material and sensory experiences without being attached to them.

During the later stages on our spiritual journey we have experienced and mastered many elements of life. Mastered our material world and the basics of survival. We have mastered vast amounts of knowledge in many spheres in our search to fill our nagging emptiness. Through other desires, such as the thrill of romance, sex or finding that perfect relationship. The soul mate that can complete us, fill us up and save us from our sense of 'aloneness'. Or we may pursue thrills and adventures in many other ways. In our search for fulfillment we have pursued dharmic paths in an attempt to come into symmetry with universal and cosmic law in doing the 'right thing'. Being of service or learning, teaching and guiding others. All of these pursuits provide us with valuable experiences on our journey of forming our identity or ego, until we finally realise that such pursuits do not provide us with what is missing.

At this point, we are challenged to free our mind, beliefs, thoughts and emotions so that we can let go of our ego and allow the essence of 'being' to arise in our awareness. This is our true nature.

Practicing the skills necessary to create and manifest physical reality starts with creating and manifesting the image we have of ourselves and of our possibilities. Our identity. Our ego. This is an endless task for which we have unlimited time in the cycle of life. Initially, in each life, we experience ourselves as a woman, man, doctor, farmer, engineer, cook or mystic, etc. These are all necessary identities or roles that can help us to develop our wings, thereby helping us to develop a strong and healthy ego. It is necessary to have a strong ego before it can be let go. The path to letting go of the ego includes mastering and refining feelings and beliefs. Emotions, as I have said at length, are a perfect way of monitoring wellbeing. If you have trauma or unresolved emotions from your past, your task is to resolve them or find help to do so.

This means that you take full responsibility for your own emotional state. Once you do this, no one can MAKE you happy, sad, angry, jealous, ashamed, guilty or anxious. This becomes fully under your control and is easy. It's not an effort. You may indeed feel any or all of these emotions periodically, but now you can feel, acknowledge and process them as they arise and take full responsibility for them. They are yours and they tell you something of value.

Any beliefs that make us 'right' and others 'wrong', or give us the non-accepting attitude of 'why me?' or complaining that 'it's not fair' or looking for fault in others, keeps us very much attached to our egoic mind, creating a conflicting, competitive illusion of separation.

We are challenged to come out of these patterns. Of course, once we've taken full responsibility for ourselves, there may still be some situations or relationships that challenge us, but now we have the capacity to find our equilibrium again more easily. We can choose to take action or simply to let it go. We won't blame anyone or any situation for our emotional state, or complain, take things personally, name-call or gossip again and, if we do, we will notice and stop until this pattern is no longer a part of our way of being. Taking full responsibility for ourselves is an essential step towards letting go of ego.

We won't stay in damaging situations or relationships if it's in our capacity or best interests to change them or simply leave.

There are many ways of doing this through reflection, wisdom, spiritual practice and personal development. However, don't rely completely on therapy or any other therapeutic or spiritual practice to 'make' you let go of ego, because that final leap into the unknown is yours to do alone.

Becoming addicted to therapy or processes may become just another ego game because these can form another distraction.

The role of being or becoming 'spiritual,' or constantly providing something more to 'work on' or 'do' in therapy can become a delaying tactic to avoid the next step that is fully yours to take. Only you can take it. At some moment..., and why not now? you can let go of ego.

Many people do this with no external help at all. Letting go is both simple and complex. To be genuine, letting go needs to be done in a state of gratitude and awareness of what the ego has taught you.

This includes family, partners, career, status, wealth, poverty, betrayal, culture, rigid or unhealthy beliefs and stuck emotions. Letting them go is only possible once you have come to the end of them, done them in their entirety and truly see the value of what they have shown you, so that you can take the wisdom from them and then let them go, with gratitude. Only once you have reached this point with any situation, can your ego dissolve.

Many people say that they have let go of many things, people and beliefs, but often, all they've done is turn away, become resigned or cut off, rather than letting them go. Letting go is liberating freedom. There are no repressed feelings of resentment or hurt in really letting go. Repressing or denying feelings or thoughts is not letting go in the sense of what I am proposing here.

It's often the case that many spiritual seekers are really seeking the parents that they would have preferred to have by turning to their vision of God, guru, or some other idol, in their search for love. They often turn their backs on their families in deep disappointment of their human dysfunction, fallibility or ordinariness, thinking that they deserve better, rather than accepting them as they are and thereby accepting themselves as ordinary too. Themselves equal to all others. Not more, not less, but equal. No soul is more or less than any other. That is dissolution of the ego. WE are just at different points on the same spiritual journey.

Many people put on a smile to cover up pain or repeat affirmations or mantras in an attempt to change their state or focus. While this can have some benefits as reminders of a task in hand it often masks much deeper psychological or emotional structures, that are still very much in place. However, once deeper changes are in place, such affirmations may be of great benefit towards transformation. Once we understand karma and the power of our intention, we can become increasingly aware of what we think and do. From this point, we can frequently notice our thoughts and words and appreciate their power and their possible consequences to others and, ultimately, to ourselves. Then the process of change can be escalated to refine our intentions, thoughts and actions towards freedom and love.

We can choose to use the knowledge of our experiences and infuse them with our inner essence. The essence for which there are no words that can only be felt as we become aware of our 'beingness'. Once we are aware of 'being', we can allow ourselves to sink into its vastness and start to dismantle the structures of the ego and its beliefs and attitudes. There is no need to be 'right' or to remain attached to who we think we are. We are much more than any story created in illusion. As we break out of our egoic and illusionary structures to dance in the light of our essence of 'all that is', we can accept life, as it is.

There are five indications that you are letting go and moving towards a state of liberation. You mostly experience:

> Peace
>
> A clear mind
>
> Contentment
>
> Happiness
>
> Harmony

Even in the midst of chaos. Those around us may be in very different places.

Ego serves its purpose by allowing us to grow in our physicality and giving us confidence in our ability to create and manifest. It has allowed us to live our beliefs and projections and experience them in many ways in the cycle of reincarnation and the karma we create. So, we might eventually refine each intention, word, thought, emotion and action to dissolve our illusion of separation. Once we are connected to our 'oneness', there is no need to inflate ourselves with pomp and ceremony or titles. No need to put others down, so that we can feel big. This is now immaterial.

The point I am making here is that the ego is an important part of our growth. The ego is an important part of our quest to fill our emptiness and to provide us with protection from the agonising pain of our seeming disconnection. Without defining ourselves through ego and creating a place for ourselves in this world, we would die in the 'chrysalis'. With our ego in place, we are able to grow our 'wings' and strengthen them by creating an illusionary structure that enables us to survive our physicality and our sense of isolation, while our inner essence rises to awareness. Then we can start to let our ego go and allow ourselves to fall into the 'not knowing' of the cradle of 'all that is'. Gradually, as each layer of illusion is illuminated and dissolved, intellectual knowledge can also recede into the background of a greater wisdom.

Intellectual knowledge answers the rudimentary aspects of our physical plane only. We still don't have the language or capacity in our physical form to conceive the infinity of 'all that is'. From here, we can let go of that too and spread our wings to dance in the light for a moment in this egoless form, in this life, knowing that we will return to the womb of the universe, the centre of creation.

CHAPTER 20:

PERFECTION

Surya is always looking for perfection in our outer and inner world. We seek perfection in our mother, father, children, partner, friends and environment and are often disappointed by what we find.

So, ring the bells that still can ring

Forget your perfect offering

There is a crack, a crack in everything,

That's how the Light gets in

That's how the Light gets in.

Leonard Cohen (2012, online) Perfection.

What is perfect? There are probably millions of opinions about what a perfect world or lifestyle might be. Each person has their own view at different points on their spiritual journey. All of us are in different stages of illusion and awakening, with unique life purposes and ambitions while we create and live our karmas. I don't know if it is possible for new and old souls to agree on an idea of perfection? Many are immersed in their purely physical plane seeking gratification through their physical desires, while largely unaware of their deeper spiritual journey towards moksha. I wonder if it is possible for the people of the world to agree on a vision of perfection when they are all pursuing different goals of what they think will fill their emptiness and make them happy. It is true that many people have a vision of a utopian world of justice and equity, with no poverty, hunger, greed, power, violence or corruption and ample opportunities for a life of meaning. I don't know if this is possible, probable or desirable.

Alternatively, perhaps the world is perfect as it is by providing us with all of the situations and the free will to create and experience the consequences of our actions in the cycle of rebirth and its ensuing depravity, chaos and stunning beauty.

Perfect families.

We all come from families. Many parents strive to be perfect and to give their children the very best experiences and the best start in life, perhaps not realising or remembering that the ups and downs of family life and not always having everything perfect, is actually a perfect start to life. Such a start has the ability to make children resilient and self-reliant to prepare them for their journey. By attempting to be a perfect parent, we are sending the message that our children must be perfect too. Perhaps this can be interpreted to mean that 'only perfect is lovable'. Such unrealistic goals become the source of insecurity. Whereas, accepting yourself as fallible and ordinary, can free your, your children and partner from impossible expectations. Happy, accepting people are easy to live with.

Many people look for the perfect partner, someone to make them happy and fill their inner emptiness, like the man in the story that looked for the lost treasure outside his house when he knew he had lost it inside. This is a search that cannot be successful until the need to focus inwards is realised. We can embrace ourselves completely in the grounded acceptance of our sacred ordinariness and fallibility with all fellow travellers. From this place, it is possible to take full responsibility for our creations, knowing the full power of our intentions, words and actions in manifestation.

Another quality that many people treasure is the idea of truth. Like perfection, there are many perspectives of truth; for example, wars have always been waged on a version of the truth. The truth of one side versus the truth of the other. Truth, like perfection, is objective and has many faces or many aspects to it, much like the story of the elephant.

In my life, Vedic Astrology showed me very clearly in my chart where I have fixed and mixed-strength karma. With parents, and also children, this would be very painful because it includes losses of people, situations, expenditure of energy and poor choices, depending on the planets and houses involved. This is why a chart with a big twelfth house can lead to imprisonment, or alternatively, self-imprisonment or confinement in a retreat of some kind.

Such an arrangement in a chart can create such stress and suffering that it can produce a meltdown, with the possibility of choosing to wake up, let go and come out of illusion. By understanding and using the philosophy and practice of family constellations, I have been able to find a place of peace and gratitude with my parents and to acknowledge the geographic distance I have placed between my siblings and myself by leaving England. I know that I have caused pain to both of my parents, even though that was not my intention and, inadvertently, to my children, through my actions and unconscious patterning.

This is mine to put right now as best I can. Attempting to be the perfect parent while, in reality, being highly imperfect, has consequences as I continue to live, create and resolve my karmic and family patterns. I am aware that each of my family members is also playing out their own patterns and making their own choices, which is exactly as it needs to be. The symbiosis is perfect.

I feel gratitude to astrology for showing me my challenges and letting me know that the patterns are mine; my karma and my soul journey to be accepted and resolved. The cycles of reincarnation have brought me to this life and given me the opportunity to face the consequences of my actions. In fact, my spiritual journey is at a standstill until I can do this in a good way. Such processes as family constellations have helped me find a way to come to peace with myself and my family in a way that can resolve and create harmony and find a way forward for me.

My heart is full of gratitude for the knowledge, synchronicities and the people in my life that are an intricate part of my soul journey as stardust.

Many people think of Moksha (liberation) as an energy rush or bright lights or some other altered state, and perhaps it is, or perhaps it is simply being at peace, at 'one with all that is'. Enjoying every moment of the ordinary: breathing, sunrise, the glow of the moon and the smile on a child's face. Perhaps, even our final illness is perfect because of the way it can gradually make life too difficult to live and make it easy to let go when the time to leave has inevitably come. How else could we be persuaded to let go of each life?

It all has a place. Perhaps it is perfect just as it is.

Maybe we shouldn't be too surprised if we never find the answers to the big questions surrounding our existence while we occupy this body and mind. Perhaps it is arrogant of us to expect to know everything from this place on our journey. The more we let go of our image of perfection and our need to know everything, the more we might be able to observe the 'elephant' fully.

The universe is in a constant state of evolution so, as stardust, why do we often expect to reach a state of perfection or completion that would leave us with nothing left to create or do? Perhaps the idea of perfection is that of illusion, as we and 'all that is' are perfect in our imperfections and disarray.

Perfection is different to different folk, as the following common story makes clear.

> A very wealthy man was on holiday on a tropical island. One morning, he walked past a native man, who was fishing, and they began to talk. He asked how the native man lived on the island. The man said that he loved to watch the sun rise and set and follow the path of the moon each night, and he enjoyed fishing for his meals regularly. He also loved to work on his land and collect the wide variety of fruits and vegetables from the fertile soil and, most of all, he loved being with his family and friends.
>
> After a while, the wealthy man said, "You know, if you got a boat, you could catch more fish to sell and make money."
>
> The native man asked, "Why would I want to do that?"
>
> The wealthy man replied, "Because then you could get a bigger boat and hire people to work for you and catch even more fish. Then you could make even more money and buy a better house and car."
>
> The native man asked, "Why would I want to do that?"
>
> The wealthy man replied, "Because you could make so much money that you could do whatever you wanted. Move somewhere where you could make even more money and buy more things to make your life even more enjoyable. Then, when you've made plenty of money, you

could buy a holiday home as a retreat for your time off. A place to relax after working hard, where you could spend some quality time with your family. Then, eventually, when you've made enough money, you could retire to a tropical island and enjoy a more relaxed lifestyle and just go fishing."

The native man smiled and asked, "Is that so?"

The men parted affably with the wealthy man feeling a stirring of irritation for the native man's contentment and apparent lack of ambition, natural easy smile, and a stirring of doubt over the native man's lifestyle choices.

In this tale, there are two souls at different points of their spiritual journeys, with the wealthy man looking down on simplicity and contentment that he doesn't yet know is what he is searching for.

CHAPTER 21:

BECOMING ONE

The journey is all about becoming 'one', to realise ourselves in our true nature, in multidimensional levels, with our essence having many different faces and opportunities to present itself. It takes a while to realise the connections and the 'oneness' and to allow the many veils of illusion to dissolve so that we can allow our inner jewel to arise. While individual souls are on the same journey to become one and integrate all of their levels of consciousness, so perhaps the world as we know it, is also in the same process. This appears to have been in motion, particularly over the last hundred years or so. We are in the midst of a huge shift of people and cultures that has bought us into chaos. For many centuries we have been in relatively stable cultural groups and these are being thrown into chaos by war, famine and politics. Many nations of the world are being challenged by accelerated change and this affects all of us.

Becoming one is both a personal and collective challenge. By becoming 'one', there is a need to let go and transcend those factors that separate, because they raise conflict and lack love. We are challenged to be inclusive to life-giving and loving qualities or to exclude and deny welcome and love. This can be a conflicting and even painful process of raising consciousness. To refine personal and collective consciousness to let go of the ancient structures that have kept us separate and find connection with each other and 'all that is'. We are all part of this movement at the personal and social levels and we can say yes to it, or resist. With resistance comes denial, anger, fundamentalism and racism.

On the personal level 'becoming one' is a long process, a process of countless lives on the soul journey that allow us to view our world through many different eyes, as men and women with different cultures, religions and attitudes. Just as all rivers arrive at the ocean, all breath is one with the atmosphere and the colours of a rainbow returns to white or golden light: The light of 'oneness'. We need to experience ourselves in myriads of ways, in order to transcend the barriers between us. To transcend family culture, religion and geography. We each come to points in our soul journey where we are spurred on by desire and curiosity in our search for completeness and to expand our boundaries.

This search is driven by a powerful force for new experiences and is in direct opposition to our need for comfort and familiarity, which is also strong. The growth coming out of such a struggle assists us in the assimilation of our expanding consciousness. There is a natural personal and collective soul movement that can merge with others and transcend difference to move towards a bigger identity.

At this time in history, this movement is on the rise because many of us are being pushed by political or financial forces to leave the familiarity of our homelands, culture or religions and move to foreign lands. This is a challenge for both the host countries and also the immigrants involved.

Change is a reality because physical reality is impermanent. Everything grows old, decays or changes form, and change in the last century has accelerated significantly. Time, lifestyle and technological advancement appear to be moving faster than ever before. This is scary for those who don't like change and find it hard to accept impermanence as inevitable. For such people, there is a tendency to attempt to stem the natural flow of change and hold onto a former vision of reality that is predictable and comforting. These are the foundations of fundamentalism, marginalisation and, ultimately, racism.

About 2,000 years ago, several world religions came into being. Perhaps this was a period where the masses had reached a new state of consciousness that required the guidance of formal religion. Many people were conscripted into world religions. Of course, identifying with groups, such as a culture and religion is a natural drive because humanity craves the need to belong, connect and find an identity to fill the void within. Religion has a place in giving us an identity and sense of community and guidance. The problem is that religions have an ego of their own and frequently believe consider theirs is better than others. This has led to wars being waged on identity, ideology, power, religion and cultural differences for thousands of years.

Having been born between nationalities, I have always had a fascination for culture and religion. In my studies of multicultural religions, I could not help but be touched by the simple truths of love and peace that showed through each faith in their pristine beauty and simplicity, that were so similar at their core. So much so that it is my belief that the founders of those religions would not have agreed to have their teachings used as doctrine, to divide and conquer or judge each other, which has been the case in world history.

We are now in a process of the movement of many peoples in the world, that is driven by commerce, desire, tragedy and politics, resulting in the merging of nations, religions and cultures. This has created an upsurge of nationalist fervour by traditionalists. Conservative groups deny the natural flow of peoples and cultures and view change as fearful and alien just because it doesn't fit their view of the world of things remaining the same and familiar.

The protest and struggle of Surya, the traditionalist, denies the merging of humanity that is taking place now, that is being driven by forces outside of our control.

All groups form a community and have value but, as we grow on the spiritual journey, we are frequently challenged to let go of groups in our awakening authenticity and identity and metaphorically stand alone vulnerable, naked, humble in our connection to 'all that is'. This leaves us with no labels or groups to hide behind. We stand as equals with all other souls on the same journey to 'oneness'. How can this take place if I call myself a Christian, a Buddhist or a Sufi? We are all much more than these labels. The label and the need to identify ourselves with a group and to give ourselves validity, are unnecessary as we progress in our journey. We are children of the universe.

Nevertheless, human beings at earlier parts of their soul journey, have a need to belong and to find an identity in order to appease their innate sense of 'aloneness'. So much so that, even belonging to groups that hold peace and harmony as an ideal, they may still be trapped because they are still part of a group with an identity. People either belong or don't belong, so this can still be divisive in a subtle way. When our consciousness has gone beyond the need to belong to collective religious or spiritual groups, meditation styles, ashrams or practices, we will no longer need to put labels on ourselves, or on others. We do not have to consider ourselves better, or less worthy than others, because being at peace with ourselves entails not being judgemental and not making comparisons. At peace, the focus is away from the label. It's about the inner experience and it is personal. There is no need to be seen as this or that if we are authentic in seeing ourselves as ordinary, the same as others, not special or superior. There is no judgement, just genuine gratitude and humility. True spirituality has no label.

Tapa, in the following metaphor, is at a crossroad. He is torn between leaving his familiar world, with its intrinsic value, and going to a more confused collection of realities, driven by the desire for growth, experience and curiosity. Tapa is a story of Surya considering moving away from his people, due to a peak of curiosity after his brush with modernity. If he accepts the challenge, he can gain experience and expand his consciousness.

He will experience the struggle between comfort and discomfort, belonging and not belonging and have feelings of guilt in standing alone if he chooses to take a different path and accept its consequences.

> *Surya was born as a youth called Tapa in a tribal African village. Tapa had learned to hunt, build huts, how to find and collect honey, and his senses were highly attuned to his environment and to something more, a sixth sense of feeling or knowing that helped identify when something changed in the air around him. Tapa enjoyed the tribal dances and the festivals that follow the seasons. He enjoyed the camaraderie of his peers and knew his place in his immediate family, extended family and tribe. He admired the leaders of his community and modelled himself on one in particular, who was a great warrior. Tapa was officially a man since his 'rites of passage ceremony' that took place when he was 13, three years ago. Entering manhood was significant because he left his family's hut to go off with his peers and the male elders.*
>
> *The ritual involved saying goodbye to his boyhood and the close relationship he'd had with his mother and grandmothers, to move into the realm of the men of the tribe. He had given his mother a gift to thank her for all she had done for him, a gift she was still wearing around her neck. Tapa noticed it when he passed her and they briefly locked eyes with fondness and remembrance.*
>
> *Tapa was now learning the ways of the men with a sense of pride. He had a lot to learn and aspire to, as the men of his tribe were skilled warriors and hunters. He also had a lot to learn about their history,*

culture and conflicts with the neighbouring tribes. He learned about the boundaries of their native territory and the spiritual knowledge that was woven into their daily life. One of the tribe's rituals was to go into a trance dance during special occasions, to connect with their ancestors for guidance. One day, while Tapa was hunting, he looked around him at the savannah that was his home and felt a deep connection to it and the intricate comradeship and support of the teamwork of the menfolk as they approached their kill for the day. He felt at one with his people and his land. While walking back with their kill, they approached the village.

As they got closer, they became aware of a different energy in the air. They arrived to find three strange-looking white men in the village. They were talking with a group of elders in a loud, strange tongue and were gesticulating with their hands, while the women and children looked on. The white men had an African-looking man from another tribe with them and it appeared that he was translating the conversation.

The men sat talking as they all ate a congenial meal together. They continued talking into the night with the help of the translator. The white men slept in a tent next to their vehicle.

Tapa had seen white men before, as well as their strange vehicles, and was fascinated along with the rest of the tribe by their clothes and strange belongings and, for a while, he watched their every move with curiosity.

After a couple of days, the tribe was called to a meeting where the elders let the tribe know that the white men would be accompanying them on their hunting trips to gain knowledge of how they lived on the land. Tapa, along with others, was appointed to go with them and to let them see how they hunted. Over the next few days, Tapa began to enjoy the company of the strangers and their guide and started to learn a few of their words. These visits with the tribe were repeated several times until, by the end of the year, Tapa was able to communicate with them in broken English. The researchers had grown *to like and respect him and to appreciate his intelligence and his quirky sense of humour.*

One day, Tapa was called to see the chief and the other elders. As he entered the hut, he noticed his father was present with the chief and the group of white men. Tapa was told that the researchers had asked if Tapa would be interested in training with them to become an interpreter as they travel round the bush tribes in the region. This took Tapa by surprise, because he had never considered going outside his village which, until now, he had been more than satisfied with. Now he was faced with another possibility. Tapa asked for time to consider the idea and spent the evening talking to his friends before falling into a restless night's sleep. In the morning, he awoke knowing that everything had changed. He no longer lived fully in his world and his innocence was no longer complete. A door had been opened and his curiosity awakened.

Tapa accepted the opportunity and left his village a few days later, feeling a deep physical pain in his chest as he waved goodbye. He noticed tears running down his face. This was a choice that changed his life. He learned quickly and did the job well, interpreting and learning English. He learned so well that another research team hired him for more work. Through his new role, he saw lands far away from his own tribal land, including unfamiliar mountains, valleys, waterfalls, forests and deserts. He had no idea that such diversity existed away from his place in the village. He saw so many different people with different shades of skin and facial features, dialects, customs, spiritual and religious practices. He realised that there was so much more to see and explore. For a while, he was lost in this new world, but eventually he felt pulled to go back to his homeland. He was overjoyed to see the familiar landscape, the faces and the comforting food.

The tribe was happy to welcome him back and held a celebration for his homecoming. He felt his heart full in his homeland for a couple of weeks. Then he began to notice that he had lost his place among the young men and that he no longer found the jokes and camaraderie as funny, or as satisfying as he had before.

He tried to tell the others about the places he had been to, the films and TV shows he'd seen, and the strange foods he'd eaten, but his friends soon tired of his talk and went back to their chatter and games. Eventually, Tapa realised that his experience had changed him. He no longer fully fitted into his home. He had lost his place in his home and with his people. Tapa knew that he could get it back if he persisted, but now he didn't know if he wanted to do that. He didn't know if he wanted to stay in this world of simplicity, comfort and familiarity, when he knew there was another world out there where he could learn and experience so much.

Tapa stayed on for a month, feeling distressed and sad, and then one day his father took him aside and asked him what was wrong. He looked into his father's eyes and knew that he had to be honest with him. He told him of his deep love and respect for his father, mother and the tribe, and also his insatiable curiosity for the other world. He told him how this was splitting him apart, hurting him in his chest and his head and how he couldn't rest or sleep properly at night anymore. His father laid his hand on his son's crown and pulled him close and held him there for a few moments. His tears welled up as he looked into his eyes for a few moments.

The next day, a meeting was held for a trance dance and the tribal elders asked the great spirits to speak through them to help Tapa to make his choice. Tapa and the medicine man started to dance, as the trance developed, Tapa felt totally taken up by the spirit of the dance until he was completely engulfed in the experience. He felt light as he danced with the tribe in trance and then he saw himself in the other world, having adventures, meeting new people and changing much more than he already had. He had a vision of women he would meet and then leave as he pursued his work. He saw himself meeting a woman, having children and forming a family with many other possibilities opening up for him.

In another vision, he saw himself feeling sad and alone at being away from his people. Then Tapa had an image of himself at home, becoming one of the tribe again. He saw himself looking at one of the young beauties of the tribe and becoming a husband in the not too distant future and enjoying the closeness and love of the relationship of family around him.

He saw himself as an older man sitting with his children and grandchildren and passing on the tribe's sacred stories of their special place in the world. He saw himself being able to help his people through the encroaching advances of the modern world on their lifestyle. He then collapsed in trance. He heard the medicine man dancing around him and then felt a deep silence settling in his head, going through into his chest, deep into his heart and his breath flowed easily as his body relaxed.

When he awoke, he saw the sea of faces all around him. He looked from face to face and smiled. Later that night, he fell into a deep sleep and felt at peace. He knew that he had contacted the spirit world to ask for guidance and that it would come in a vision or a symbol very soon. He knew that his soul would make the right choice for him. The trance dance had connected him to his ancestors and the greater spirits. He was reminded that his soul would make the right choice and that all would be well, so that he didn't have to trouble his mind with making a decision. He also knew that there were gains and losses on each path of his crossroad.

Perhaps you are frustrated with not knowing what Tapa chose. There were positives and setbacks with each of his choices. Each path had great value. Some of you, as Surya, would have stayed and some of you would have gone. This is a story about growth, emigration and education and, although each of these may be viewed as positive, they can have detrimental effects as well. For many of us, staying with what we know is what is required in this life. A more settled, predictable existence can often provide enough drama through family and community life, and the changing political or financial landscape can provide enough impetus to make life exciting and challenging enough. There is enough experience to be gained from relationships, family, work, health and the natural aging process, as well as the impact that world movements, politics and environmental or technological influences can have on the lives of ordinary people, even if they stay in their home place. For others, the drive to leave and to explore is paramount. Perhaps Surya, at this point, requires this new experience for some reason. Perhaps Tapa has become entrenched in the conditioning of one culture or religion and needs to grow and allow himself to be challenged.

In growth of any kind, even through education, people become separated from others if that knowledge gives them a different perspective, or if they become wealthier and move into a different socio-economic group. This has implications of separation involving losing their place with the people they came from.

This is the same with emigration. Leaving a homeland has implications that can have an effect for generations to come, even if people move to a different or better life or work.

Losing their roots, connections and culture has a deep effect on their identity that can be seen as both positive and also detrimental.

The story of Tapa is a metaphor for situations we all face in life at many different times. Leaving behind family, beliefs and patterns, gaining knowledge or experiences that give us different perspectives to those around us, changing jobs, moving house, or moving into new cultures, are all examples of situations that we face constantly. We also face these if we belong to a host nation that is receiving people from other lands.

Tapa's story speaks of belonging, being part of a group, tradition and the comfort to be found in that, and also the expansion and restriction of growth. Many of us belong to or have belonged to religions, political groups, spiritual or meditation movements from which we have gained a lot but, at some point if we are to continue to grow, we must leave. Take our experiences with us as we move deeper into our own essence and away from a need to justify ourselves through being a member of a group or religion. We can experience conflict and grief by moving from one group to another. There is a need to move on so as to fit the image of growth that we have of ourselves until, at some point, we reach a place where there are no longer any groups that are left to join. We might come to a point where we are not seeking the label of a group any more, even that of being seen as spiritual. We simply 'are' and have nothing to tell anyone about or compare notes on. This is a lived experience that is so rich that words do not suffice.

Ultimately, becoming aware of ourselves as souls with no need for a label or external identity anymore, and being happy to stand seemingly alone, naked, humble, but infinitely connected to 'all that is', in being at 'one'.

Over the last 200 years or so, and even more so in the last 50 years, there has been a strong movement for nations of the world to expand or open up through invasions, wars, tyranny, natural disasters, technology, trade and the ensuing spread of refugees. Perhaps Surya, as humanity, has a need to go beyond the strong polar cultures of the world, to find more similarity than difference, and to go to the next step in evolution to recreate itself.

This merging of people is being accelerated by intermarriage that results in a 'melting pot' of humanity. However, this situation is not without conflict because, when we marry outside our race, religion, socio-economic group or colour, this results in integration and also polarity. We and our children may no longer fully belong to any group and are challenged with having to redefine ourselves. We are excluded.

We are excluded. However, eventually assimilation is taking place as we can see in many places in the world, such as Europe, North and South America and Australia, where people are coexisting and belong to new groups and can identify themselves within their nation.

This movement is also accompanied by a resistance to change driven by fear. Turbulence accompanies change. A move towards merging to create one race, one nation, one humanity, standing together, yet accepting diversity and difference. Only time will tell how it will develop

CHAPTER 22:

SURYA AS BANDHU, THE BEGGAR

The wheel of karma and the flow of destiny are always in motion, drawing us into life, a new body, situation and experience and then drawing us into death as we continue on the cycle. Who knows why some lives are so full of suffering compared to others? We cannot know the reasons because we are part of the larger cycle of the cosmos on our karmic journey towards liberation.

> *When I was in Kerala, in the south of India in 2011, I came across a beggar who appeared to shine as stardust. There were many beggars in the town and many looked very sad and withdrawn, while others appeared to be making the best of their situation with ingenuity and humour. Bandhu appeared to have a different presence, compared to the rest of the beggar community.*
>
> *Bandhu was a crippled beggar of around 30 years old who lived in a coastal tourist town of Kerala in south-west India. He had thick, shiny, wavy, black hair, large almond eyes, dark skin, a wide face and a big smile. Bandhu had a strongly developed upper and emaciated lower body, with twisted legs that trailed behind. He was slightly lifted from the ground because he walked on his hands from a squatting position. From a distance, he looked a little like a spider. On hot days, he placed his hands on rubber thongs to protect them from the heat and the harshness of the roads as he walked. He sat at various points along the main tourist drag that was lined with restaurants, jewellery and gift shops facing the beach. He was there throughout the day and evening with a small begging bowl.*
>
> *Regardless of his disability, Bandhu had a quiet dignity about him in the way he thanked each person for their donation with a wide smile and steady eyes. The shopkeepers had grown to like him and often sat chatting with him when business was slow, and gave him cups of chai or water. The restauranteurs often gave him leftovers if they spotted*

him at the end of the day. At night, Bandhu slept in an outhouse behind a local café on a few pieces of cloth on the hard clay floor.

Bandhu had only vague memories of his mother. He remembered her as a young woman with a kind face and manner, who was often busy 'working'. His mother ushered him out of their room each day when men visited her.

Men came and went throughout the day and night. When he was about seven or eight years old, while he still had the use of his legs, he remembered that his mother's waist had become larger and he noticed that the men stopped coming. Then one day, his mother doubled up in pain and he was pushed outside as two older women went in with her. There were many shouts and screams heard coming from the room over the next two days, as Bandhu waited and watched the door. A neighbour gave him some rice and water on several occasions. Then it suddenly went quiet. The women came out with tears in their eyes and told him that she was gone. The landlord of the building came by to find out what had happened. When the women had gone, the landlord pushed Bandhu out, telling him to go someplace else. He said that he would see to the disposal of his mother's body by selling what she had, but that Bandhu could not stay anymore, because he needed the rent money. Wondering down the street, Bandhu felt lost, dazed and numb with sadness. He was not aware of anyone besides his mother that he could call on.

A vision of his mother's kind face was competing with the memory of the screams coming from the room. This generated a thick feeling of fear throughout his body in the imagination of the eight years old on his mother's pain tortured him. He didn't understand. Later that night sitting by the roadside a young man of eighteen or so stood by him and asked if he had anywhere to go. Bandhu shook his head. The man said he could come with him so he could have food and somewhere to sleep. He was taken to the edge of the town where there were many children. Some were blind, while others were crippled and hobbling along on sticks. They were all eating quietly from a large, flat plate of mainly rice in the centre of the room. There were several men in another adjoining room talking loudly and they grew silent as Bandhu and the young man entered. The young man went over and whispered to them and an older man came over and beckoned Bandhu in, inviting him to eat. Later, Bandhu joined the children as they slept huddled together on some cloths on one side of the room. The next morning, when Bandhu awoke, the children were up and leaving the shack, hobbling or walking towards the town.

Bandhu was taken into the adjoining room and told to sit down on the floor in front of the three men. After he had answered their questions, he noticed that they looked at each other in turn and then nodded. One of them gave him a cup full of brown-coloured liquid, which he was told to drink. Soon, Bandhu felt himself becoming very drowsy and was finding it hard to sit up. As he lay down, he lifted his head to see what was happening and saw the older man with an iron bar lifted behind him.

He felt the blow on his lower back and then he was aware of nothing else. Bandhu doesn't know how long he was unconscious. When he awoke, he found that he couldn't move his legs and there were sharp pains running up and down his back. Over the many weeks that followed, he hovered between life and death until the pain began to subside and he started to move around using his hands.

Then the older man told Bandhu that he would earn money for his keep through begging. Bandhu was taken each day to a street in the town and left there all day with a begging bowl. Over the next few years, he learned to master his handicap and became mobile by walking on his hands to beg.

Bandhu and the other children understood that their injuries helped to attract more money in their daily begging for the consortium. A few years later, Bandhu escaped after he persuaded a truck driver to give him a lift to the coast using some cash he had managed to hide. Since then, he had been living in this tourist town.

Bandhu knew that his life was hard and that it had been unfortunate, but he was also aware of the kindness in it too. In this area, he had made some connections and, from his place on the street, he'd had a lot of time to think about his life, his mother and the brutality that had made him a freak. Bandhu was no longer bitter about his past. He'd had lots of time to view the people who passed him by as he sat begging. There were those who walked straight past or turned their heads away from him as they went and those, the majority, who refused to meet his eyes when they put money in his bowl and moved on. He was grateful for all donations. Bandhu met people with his steady gaze and noticed their reactions. His intention was not to challenge or confront because, it appeared to me, that he had come to a point in his life where he accepted himself and his life just as it was.

Bandhu looked straight into my eyes each time I saw him and, as I met his smile, our humanity merged for a moment. I was always struck by his courage and dignity in facing the world each day, as a man. I have an image of Bandhu looking at the sun setting into the ocean each evening, as it emits its warm glow and sinks into the horizon and again watching the sunrise from the hills behind the town. He is there as it gradually infiltrates the dark, velvety mystery of the night with its amber tones, and knows that he has existed for one more day. Bandhu knew that he was lucky to have survived as long as he had and he appeared to savour each moment. He had no fear. Perhaps this was what Surya, as Bandhu, required in order to connect with the treasure within.

He certainly appeared to be a wise soul: Stardust entering Moksha. Perhaps this is the life he required in order to be awakened.

CHAPTER 23:

FUEL FOR GROWTH

We are all on the same journey, just at different points on the road. However, it is wise not to judge others because many people have chosen, at a soul level, to experience the tragedy and suffering that may be necessary to accelerate their awakening. It's possible that such lives are more spiritually awakening than those of a conventional, easy 'good life'. We cannot know, so I believe it's best not to judge.

As I have mentioned before, in the experience of my astrology practice, some people are here for lives that have maximum stress, many losses and unfortunate circumstances to be experienced. Yes, it is karma that might be present as a prompt, to encourage the possibility of making new choices or to let go of attachments to old patterns.

I met Leonora (not her real name) in my astrology practice when she came to me feeling frustrated and stuck. She was at a crossroad, astrologically. There appeared to be some difficult karma for her to experience, but also lots of possibilities for change. Here is her story.

> Leonora was a 25-year-old Afro-Caribbean woman, well-built and of average height, with thick frizzy hair that was teased back off her face into a plait at the back of her head. Leonora had full lips, shiny with red lipstick and dark blue eye shadow accentuating long eyelashes. She wore a short skirt and a small, tight tee shirt and denim jacket, from which her generous bosoms protruded. Leonora was a sex worker in Sydney who worked in alleys and occasionally in a room when her clients were willing to pay more. She shared a unit with two other sex workers and stored her cash in a shoebox under her bed, under piles of shoes and clothes because she didn't have a bank account. Leonora was a stow-away from Trinidad and had been living in Sydney for nine months, without a passport or papers of any sort.
>
> She had a strong American accent and talked very loud and fast, and she had a lot to say. In addition, Leonora had a wild sense of humour

and easily fell into fits of screams and laughter. Even though Leonora was aware of staying in the background, so as not attract too much attention, her appearance and exuberant nature often found her becoming the centre of attention especially when she was with her friends.

Leonora liked to look on the bright side of life and was grateful to have landed on her feet, so to speak, in Sydney, but she was beginning to worry about where she would go from here. It had never had the intention to be a sex worker but, with no papers, she had found that she had little choice.

Leonora had fallen into bad company in America and had naively delivered brown paper parcels to various locations in her town. She had been careless and the drug barons for whom she was delivering parcels, were after her because she'd delivered a parcel to the wrong location and it had ended up in the hands of the police. Escaping to the local harbour, Leonora had managed to get on board a ship unnoticed, only to find out later that it was going to Australia. She managed to hide herself with the help of one or two sailors, who were happy to provide her food and a place to sleep in return for sex. On her arrival in Australia, she disembarked in Sydney and found herself in the city centre with nothing but what she stood up in. A man struck up a conversation with her as she rested on a park bench in Hyde Park. He was interested to know who she was and what she was doing., He offered to find somewhere for her to stay and give her some work for a regular commission. That's how she was introduced to her roommates and became a sex worker. The money was good, but Leonora was feeling troubled by the limitations of her situation, because her future looked bleak.

Feeling a little down one day as she sat in a café, she'd picked up a magazine with a picture of Jamaica on the front cover. Leonora saw the image of the idyllic tropical island, conscious that her experience there had been quite different. Suddenly, she saw herself as a ten-year-old girl living with her mother and step father in their tiny shack in Trinidad. Her mother was drinking in the corner with her friend and becoming louder and more argumentative throughout the day, with no meal prepared as the day turned into night. She remembered her stepfather smoking marihuana, while her older brothers fought outside. Leonora was suddenly overcome by a deep sadness and an intense feeling of loneliness, as she saw her younger self in her bedroom falling asleep with hunger pains in her belly and being woken up by her stepfather in her bed. He was stoned and ran his hands all over her. He didn't hear her screams of protests and neither did anyone else in the house and, over the next few months, this became a regular pattern. One night, as she stood by the side of the road she decided to hitch a lift. Leonora decided to run away to America.

She was resourceful and courageous and managed to find a job at a corner store. A little while later, someone she had befriended introduced her to an additional way of earning money, by delivering packages around the town. Leonora reflected on her past as she sat drinking her coffee. She had escaped from a dangerous situation with a drug baron, but had found herself trapped again in Sydney.

One day, as Leonora walked through the Sydney CBD, she noticed a sign on the front of a pub saying, 'Come and Audition' to be a performer. Leonora felt drawn to go inside, where she found a small group of people sitting nervously with two men, who were in charge and taking down contact details and notes of each performance.

A young woman sang on the stage, screeching to hit the notes in her song with a pianist accompanying her. Next, a young man stood up and nervously told a few jokes. Others had their turn and eventually she was the only one left. One of the men asked here, in a rather tired and flat voice, if she wanted a turn. She remembered a song she used to sing along to as a child when she heard it playing on the radio in Trinidad. The pianist in the pub didn't know the song, so Leonora made a snap decision to sing it unaccompanied. She knew that she had nothing to lose. For a few moments, nervousness chewed at her stomach and her throat closed so that she couldn't speak. Then something happened as she heard and felt the song in her head. She heard the beat, tempo and pitch. Leonora closed her eyes and didn't hear the impatient coughing of the men in front waiting to finish their long day of auditions. Feeling the song and the music inside her, she started to sing. Her voice came out in full volume, in a deep, rich timbre. The words poured out easily with the music in her head. It was clear that she had the song inside her, as she listened to the beat in her body. Leonora's voice was rich and deep with a natural rhythm and quality of its own. Keeping her eyes closed, she allowed the background music in her head to support her. Leonora didn't see the look of amazement on the faces of the two men in front, or notice that people from the street were coming in to see who it was that was filling the space with such an evocative melody.

By the time she had finished, the room that had been nearly empty, was full and she opened her eyes to loud applause.

Leonora was hired to sing. She let them know that she had no tax file number and required 'cash in hand', which meant that she was able to reduce her hours of sex work. However, the original man who had got her that work, was constantly pressing her for more and more 'commission' from her new role. Eventually, another performer who had been sidestepped because of Leonora's popularity, reported her to the authorities and she was deported back to America.

Leonora spent some time in prison. Fortunately, this was not so bad for her, as it was a relatively safe place where she could take stock of her life. She began to notice the things that were not within her control and to accept the decisions she had made and their consequences. As she'd had very few opportunities for education in her life, she decided to take advantage of the educational opportunities in the prison.

During this period, she began to form a new image of herself and how she would like her life to be. Leonora had a great imagination and was generally optimistic. Following her natural talent and what soothed and gave her joy, she often entertained her inmates with her singing and became popular with them. By the time she'd served her *sentence, she had formed a new image of herself and had a plan of how she could sustain herself in a better way.*

On her release Leonora auditioned for work in her local area and soon became a much-loved entertainer. She also joined a gospel church and quickly became a valued member of the community. I have a vision of her now, still looking much the same. The plait and the shiny red lipstick, but now she has a close-fitting, long sequined dress and silver stiletto shoes. I can envision Leonora sitting at a bar sipping champagne after her performance in the nightclub with a good-looking, powerfully built, tall black man. A man with a wide easy smile, who finds her enigmatic and is mesmerised by her stardust. Leonora looking and finding him attractive as someone who had overcome many problems who is making new choices too.

Leonora's astrology chart showed someone who is born into a difficult set of circumstances with many challenges and little support. A person with a beautiful moon well-placed for entertainment and recognition and a strong twelfth house that could easily result in incarceration, at least for a while. The second half of her life looked easier with more opportunities for personal power and more conscious choices. In such a life, there are many opportunities to wake up and to raise consciousness as stardust on her journey.

CHAPTER 24:
THE EVOLUTION OF SPIRITUAL PRACTICE

Surya, in ancient times, was always involved in spiritual practice, embracing 'all that is' in his or her daily life, in such things as planting, harvesting, food preparation, the cycles of day and night, and the seasons. There was a spiritual experience to be found in every moment, in every breath that flowed in and out of the body, through the rituals, celebrations and the tragedies of life. This is a spirituality that is deeply woven into the folklore and mythology and the soil of the land. More recently, in the last 2,000 years, with the rise of formal religions, there has been a distance placed between Surya and 'all that is' by some priests and clergy that seek to control and alienate us from our human right to a direct connection as stardust in the universe. They suggest that we are not capable or good enough for a direct connection with creation.

So, you may wonder now in the 21st Century what spirituality and spiritual practice is. In a time where life has become so separated from the environment, nature, mother Earth and the stars, it can seem that spirituality is totally separate from daily life. Something we have to 'do', invent or create, or dip into at regular intervals. So divorced are many of us from our roots, our bodies with our minds conditioned to focus on the linear, rational thinking of 'advanced' technology, that we often divorced from our physicality and who we are. We've lost our sense of animal and intuitive instincts. Due to being so separated from our natural environment. We are often found in high-rise, windowless, artificially lighted, heated or cooled buildings, staring at computer screens and navigating cyberspace, lost in other worlds. This is so in both our work and home environments where we enter the realities of media, TV, movies, intoxicants and consumerism. In short, we often allow ourselves to be drawn away from our physical life, purpose, passion, feelings and bodily sensations through endless distractions. Such constant distractions result in becoming tired and depleted as we begin to feel the pointlessness, lack of meaning or passion and emptiness of our lives. Hence, in the present, we can often be seen 'dropping out' of society in our attempt to escape. Many of us may be found embracing alternative lifestyles, personal development groups or cults, and pursuing gurus or teachers of all kinds.

It is interesting that, in this time of technological advancement, the interest in personal development and spirituality has risen to epidemic proportions in some nations while, at the same time, many formal religions are declining.

Many of us are tired and frustrated by our lack of fulfilment through the excesses of technology and consumerism and consciously choosing to change our focus and seek what 's missing. Trying to fill our emptiness. The part that we have always been searching for, with that vague remembrance of something much more, something precious and fulfilling that is there, somewhere, if only we can find it. We are more consciously searching for something to help us feel whole, complete and connected. By doing so, we are looking at many religions and, in particular, at some Eastern religions. Coming to understand the ideas of reincarnation and karma and wanting to take responsibility for our own choices and personal development and discovering a wide array of spiritual practices, such as meditation, yoga, Tai Chi and Chi Gung. The list is endless.

Gurus and teachers can indeed be helpful if we are lucky or discriminating enough to choose those who are genuine. Authentic and coming from their hearts in their wisdom and generosity who impart knowledge and also encourage us to develop our own ideas. Beware of those who say theirs is the only way. However, we need to remind ourselves that our guru too is on the same path as ourselves in the river of reincarnation in seeking the light. Each soul ultimately has to find its own way while incorporating the learning, skills and knowledge of each experience into its evolving wisdom. So, it is important to learn from those who are wiser than us, but to remember that their path is for them. Their way back to the light is theirs and it is our challenge to find ours.

Many people are confused by the vast array of spiritual paths or techniques when they look at books or listen to different teachers or guides, and may wonder if meditation is an essential component of spiritual practice and personal development.

All this can be confusing and overwhelming because it seems that there is a long list of do's and don'ts with most spiritual schools advocating their own methodology of spiritual practice, not unlike the traditional religions of the world.

However, coming back to looking at you through your Vedic astrology chart and viewing your psychology, personality and the stage of your spiritual journey, it makes sense to realise that any spiritual practice should be specific to you and not necessarily the same as anyone else's. It could be that sitting in a lotus position chanting "Ohm" and being able to meditate deeply is not possible or necessary for each person in this life.

I will now go through some of the possible spiritual practices that you can try.

Vedic Astrologers often give their clients a mantra to repeat, as a spiritual practice, when they are going through difficult periods. These are sacred words that help the person to align themselves to the energy of the planetary period that they are experiencing.

The mantra is sacred if done with conviction, because it can open up the person's heart to the energy of the period and the benefits that it has to offer. The purpose of a mantra is not to attempt to change the destiny of the person, but to help to align the person with planetary energies so that they can reap its wisdom in whichever form it comes. If this happens, the person might adopt a 'yes' attitude to life and stop denying or resisting their karma and make the most what comes. If we are in flow with cosmic energy, it must flow easier. The intention of the mantra is important. If it is done out of superstition or an attempt to gain favour with the gods, these are not the highest of intentions and are coming from a place of fear, superstition or control, rather than a wish to be receptive to what karma is unfolding and what cosmic energy is offering.

Passion as a Spiritual Practice

I take the view that experiencing life is a spiritual practice if you can be present to whatever it is you are being or doing. So that being lost in the art of creation, action, movement, sport or sound in the form of music or writing, gardening, cooking, learning or sharing knowledge, if done with presence or focus, might be meditations in their own right. The experience of silence, laughter and movement and the fullness of body sensations can all be considered spiritual practice, from my perspective.

It is likely that you have experienced spirituality through following your passion and life purpose in ways that might not be recognised as spiritual, in a conventional sense. Maybe you have been wholly focussed in the present moment in an activity that fills your heart and soul. Some of you might experience dancing as being at one with creative energy by allowing yourself to be fully immersed. Being at one with the dance is an expression of creative joy.

Or if your passion is music, you might allow the music to play you, sing you or flow with you in rapture. Alternatively, you might have a passion as a long distance runner, to somehow find a place of elevation through the physical enjoyment of allowing your body to flow like a well-oiled machine, in perfect time, as you pace the floor beneath you. Your heart beating steadily and rhythmically as you enter a calm, meditative and altered state.

Or you might be a tennis player who becomes entranced by the pace of the game and the sound of the ball on the racquet, as you allow your instinct and senses to magically recover each shot with ease, while maintaining focussed accuracy.

Each of these experiences is a form of meditation in their own right and just a small example of moments of unity. These are special moments when you find yourself in the flow of life, as your body, feelings and desires unite and come into synchronicity through a creative focus and reality. There is no ego or pretension in those moments, just pure being, pure ease and 'oneness' with your embodied physicality and creativity.

These are powerful expressions of creative energy and co-creation to channel desire, creative potential and manifest into the physical world, similar to the creative frenzy of an artist or excitement of a surfer in full flow. Each has the skills so well embedded in their psyche, that they no longer have to think of the rudimentary steps of their practice. They just have to allow themselves to enter the state where they transcend the mediocre, the ego and the ordinary, to the extraordinary. They tap into the creative energy of the 'oneness' of universal energy and transcend physicality.

CHAPTER 25:

MEDITATION AND SPIRITUAL PRACTICE

We, as Surya, are physical in a physical realm and require good nutrients, exercise and rest to provide for one level of health, but what of the mind? The mind the powerhouse of the body as it controls all body functions. It's also the interpreter of our experiences and may harbour fears, wishes or possibly a fleeting nature, as it jumps around constantly. Many of us have a fidgety mind that somehow disturbs the body and the nature of our focus and rest, until we find a way to befriend it. Stay with it, so that we can learn to trust a quieter way of being.

For me, meditation is essential to my health and wellbeing. We know that good sleep, regular exercise and good nutrients are essential to our health and energy levels. However, my health, wellbeing and energy levels increase many-fold when I include meditation every day. Meditation is a way of nurturing the mind because it increases my sense of peace and, ultimately, my focus. I am able to work hard and not become depleted when I meditate.

When your spiritual path is to enter the experience of meditation, you will learn to focus inwards. Focus on the present moment, of each breath and each moment of your bodily experience, at least for the period of the meditation. Each second is your life. Meditation helps to train your mind and body to be fully present to 'now', to be fully present in yourself and also aware of your connection to 'all that is'. Notice your breath, bodily sensations, thoughts, images and emotions. Observe them coming to the surface, unravelling, coming up to be acknowledged, witnessed and released. If this meditation takes place daily for a minimum of 20 minutes as a genuine desire to witness your inner world, the effects of this practice may be transferred to a peaceful backdrop for the rest of your day. The practice can allow your conscious and unconscious thoughts, feelings and desires to bubble to the surface to be observed as they drift by and dissipate, so that more harmony can develop within you. There is no need to dwell on any aspect, rather just be a witness to the flow of consciousness. Through such meditation, you can clear your mind and possibly your emotions, so that you can come to understand yourself with compassion and love, as you open your heart to 'all that is'.

You might find that you are be able to release any emotional imbalances and find a place of peace.

Exercise as a Spiritual Practice

You are an embodied spirit. The body is your temple, the vehicle that houses your spirit. Without it, you cannot be in this life. It is inseparable from your mind and soul; therefore, you must look after it. Nourish it, maintain it, stretch and tone it to keep it at its optimum level of functionality. In the modern world, unlike earlier periods of history, we often need to exercise purposefully or more consciously because for many of us daily life doesn't provide the physicality that we need to stay strong and supple. While others have a highly physical existence.

Through the process of exercise, pheromones, hormones and many other chemical triggers are released and harmonised and emotions unlocked, as each body system receives a plentiful supply of movement to oxygenate the blood and body tissues. Therefore, some form of regular exercise is a vital part of maintaining balance to regulate your mind, body and emotions. This is an essential part of your spiritual wholeness as an embodied spirit in a physical world. Your physicality needs to be gloried and celebrated.

Meditation as a Spiritual Practice

Meditation is not 'blanking out' or going to sleep or escaping to somewhere else. It is being present and staying present. This is a discipline in itself; staying present with yourself. It is normal to find your mind active and wanting to escape from the present moment of breath or stillness and feeling, into a stream of thoughts or images, initially. It is important, if you want to master the art of meditation, to repeatedly and compassionately bring your focus back to the present. Everything else is a distraction. You may start with five or ten minutes and go up to 20 or 30 minutes, or longer each day, as you become more comfortable with the process.

There are many possible ways to meditate. You will need to experiment and find the ones that you feel comfortable with and change them when you feel the need to move onto something else.

If you are new to meditation or have a very active mind, it might be wise to start with a guided or a moving meditation like yoga, Tai Chi or Chi Gung, or even a walking meditation.

A deeper, more focussed meditation is appropriate for those who are ready for this, with no other agenda other than to connect with parts of themselves and merge with the ocean of oneness of 'all that is'. This may be experienced in the 'being with yourself' meditation ahead.

Meditations are generally best done in the morning after exercise or stretching, so that the body is oxygenated and energised and you are fully awake. However, it's important to tune into your own bio-rhythms and lifestyle to find the best time for you. It is important to sit with your back straight, either on a chair or on the floor with your legs crossed, only if this is comfortable.

A straight spine allows the body organs to be in their rightful place. Nothing is being squashed and the energy centres, called the chakras, are lined up. Each stacked above the next through your spine, so as to allow your energy or Qi to flow easily. You will need to experiment with different types of meditation to find the ones you resonate with and are likely to find particular meditations suitable for different periods in your life.

MEDITATIONS

A Guided Meditation

These meditations are useful for training your mind to be present and to help you maintain focus through imagination and visualisation.

The Secret Garden

Sit comfortably with your back straight. Shut your eyes and see yourself arriving at your secret garden. Open the gate. Step inside and notice the energy of this place.

See the hedged garden with tall trees all around and the richness of the lawn. Now notice the stepping stones opening up in front of you, guiding you through the grass, winding through the flowers, bushes and trees.

Feel the sunlight on your skin, soft and warm with a gentle breeze. Hear the call of the birds. Notice the shafts of sunlight coming through the canopy of trees above and falling onto the ground all around you, forming streaks of light and shade. Notice how your breath is flowing gently in and out.

Each breath takes in calmness while the out breath releases stress, anxiety and mental over activity, as you begin to relax in this sacred space. Feel the quietness of this place soaking into your body and awareness. You are walking at your own pace, deciding on your own direction and, at each turn, the path opens up before you, guiding you deeper into your sanctuary. Soon you start to hear the sound of trickling water and, around the next bend, you notice a stream ahead coming off higher ground and falling into a deep, natural rock pool. The sound of the splash and trickle of water reaches you with its brilliance sparkling in the sunlight. As you get closer, you find yourself looking into a deep pool. Notice its colour and crystalline quality. Feel its sacred, cleansing power. Allow your thoughts to drift and to come and go, unhindered.

Soon you find yourself undressing in this private place and then drifting in the pure crystalline water and floating for a while. It cleanses and revives you.

Come back when you are ready and notice the surface of the sparkling water and the birds calling all around with the sunlight gently bathing your skin under the wispy clouds overhead.

Give gratitude for this experience, find yourself stepping out and getting dried and dressed. Now turn to start the calm walk back. Take your time. Again, notice the pathway opening up in front of you as you meander around the bushes, shrubs and flowers and through the shafts of sunlight coming through the canopy of tall trees above and around you. This path leads you back the way you came, through the vegetation, the smells of dampness and the perfume of shrubs and flowers. A mass of colour, sounds and smells are around you and within you. You have returned to the beginning of your journey. As you turn and look back at your secret garden with gratitude, you know that you can go back there whenever you like.

2. Furnishing Your Headspace

Take yourself to your favourite place in the whole world. Your special place. See yourself looking through your eyes to view the landscape in front of you. Notice the energy of this place, the light and shade and the colours. Notice the smell and feel of your special place. This is your special place and no one else can see it quite the way you do. From this place, with your eyes looking outwards through an opening of your making, you observe the landscape. As you look, you become aware of the room behind you. It is a room in the shape of your skull. Notice its shape, colour, light or shade.

Fill your room to your liking. Choose any colours, textures, furnishings or furniture. This is your room, so you can make it just what you want it to be. Notice its furnishings, their textures and design. Fill it for your own comfort and pleasure. Make it as full or as empty as you like. Fill it with beauty, essence and colour. It's up to you because it's your space. Your room. Make it what you want it to be. Now, sit in your room and enjoy its ambience, energy, atmosphere and survey it from this spot. Stay there for as long as you like, taking it all in…

Come out of the meditation when you are ready, knowing that you can recreate it at any time. This is your space.

Creative Visualisation

This is a meditation to help you manifest your desires into reality. For this to work, you need a clear vision of what you are manifesting and to be as free as possible of any self-sabotaging tendencies. You might notice these through your behaviour, language or thoughts, as previously discussed.

Be able to see yourself in the vision clearly and be prepared to do the groundwork to gain the skills, knowledge, connections or money, or any other structures necessary to enable the visualisation to come to fruition.

Go into the body of your vision.

See it, feel it, paint the picture of the image in your mind, so that you can see yourself in it clearly.

Feel it in your body and notice the excitement you have for the vision. Stay with this for a few minutes. Repeat several times each day.

Simply wishing alone is often not sufficient. See my book *Be Rich AND Spiritual*.

For this to work, you will need to be in full connection with your passion and life purpose and be prepared to do what is necessary to allow it to grow. Notice that what you focus on is what you create, so focus consciously.

This should not be at the expense or demise of anyone else, if you are to create positive karma for yourself.

Meditation

Being with Yourself

Sit comfortably with a straight back on a chair or on the floor with crossed legs. Focus on the present moment. Become aware of your body, mind and breath. Focus on your breath for a few breaths. Notice the thoughts and images that flow through your mind. Let them flow, but don't focus on any particular one. Allow them to move through you as a breeze would blow through an open window. Notice any sensations in your body. Is there any lightness, pressure, heaviness, joy, or other emotion? If you notice a difficult emotion like anger, resentment or sadness, allow it to arise. Allow yourself to feel it. Let it bubble up to be felt. Don't go into the story of what or who is responsible for it. Just feel it for a count of ten seconds and then let it go. If it is still present, repeat for another ten seconds and let it go. If it is a very strong emotion, allow yourself to feel it for longer. Go back to focussing on your breathing and to witnessing your thoughts and images flowing through your awareness.

Stay like this for ten minutes initially and extend the time to 20 minutes or longer. Finish your meditation by stating your gratitude for at least five things in your life Repeat this daily, preferably at the same time each day and in the same place. With practice, just sitting in the space will settle you and your meditations will go deeper and more quickly. Each time you meditate, you will experience them slightly differently. Occasionally, you might be aware of messages, colours, smells or sounds. This is unique for each person.

The practice of meditation has a build-on effect in that you may not feel

its effects straight away but, over time, you will notice subtle or more pronounced effects on your ability to focus, experience inner peace and happiness and feel differently about your interactions with others and the situations in your life.

CHAPTER 26:

HAPPINESS: COMING HOME

Moksha. Coming home to happiness is what your journey has been all about. Reconnecting with yourself, your 'oneness', joy and bliss. You are always looking for the 'beloved' through each facet of your life, whether you are aware of it or not.

You come from a state of bliss or happiness in the spirit world and fall into the mists of Maya into your physicality. Encased in an earthly, tactile environment of creaturehood and sensuality in the cycle of life where your locked in a constant wheel of entering and leaving from life to life.

I have been privileged to witness new life entering this world through the birth of two of my grandchildren, each with their own aura and unique vibrational energy. I watched my tiny grandson in the first moments of life, breathing. Moving his hands and legs with small, involuntary spasms as he looked up into the harsh, bright light above him as he lay in a glow of his own. His aura was clearly visible around and within him. This was my first grandchild, a boy. Embodied and yet not fully so. He was still transposing as he completed his entry from the spirit world, playing with the light and shadows and the sensations of his new body and the beginning of a new adventure. A few years later in the mystery of another long night of waiting and preparing for another new soul to enter, I noticed a ball of golden light dancing, hovering on the ceiling in the early morning, as my daughter was in labour in the next room. The golden light ball hovered on the ceiling prior to dawn, until it magically disappeared as soon as the baby girl was plunged into the fresh morning light and took her first breath. This was the birth of my second grandchild. A new life intoxicated by the physical sensations at the beginning of a new adventure. The next phase of her journey as stardust.

You know that you will not always be here in this body and this mind. There will be a time when your existence in this life will be no more and yet, the waves from the ocean will continue rolling, the wind will still blow and the rain will continue to fall, with new days unfolding and closing continuously.

You are aware of that feeling inside, that remembrance of something more. Of a continuing theme, a familiarity of a search and a striving for that which is just beyond your senses and your grasp.

You might also be aware of your fear of not 'being', not existing and your growing curiosity about what. Not sure if anything, lies ahead, as you take your last breath and are taken into death, one more time.

As your lives unfold on your spiritual journey and as you pursue your dreams and visions of yourself grow and your knowledge mellows into wisdom, you begin to understand your creative potential. You begin to search within, to feel your void and to examine your fear and your emptiness. You begin to exhaust many avenues in your search for that missing part, your treasure. There is a growing vague memory of the lightness and fullness that you return to at death, as you return to your source, where you are bathed and nestled in the glow of pure love and light and continuous bliss.

As you progress and engage with your purpose in each life, you become more conscious and more finely tuned to the search for the spiritual connection to universal energy. Your growing wisdom develops an inner 'knowing' of how or where you might look this time and how you might somehow create bliss on Earth inside you, in every waking moment.

You are here to experience and enjoy and eventually to find completeness and happiness through each of your life experiences. Interestingly, happiness is your natural state at source, because each of your desires have been about returning to happiness. Indeed, you often do find happiness at the end of each quest, adventure or achievement. You notice too that, often the journey itself, when you are totally absorbed in the task of pursuing your goal, is more satisfying and more joyful than the reward at the culmination of the goal. The culmination of your experiences results in all aspects of yourself being synchronised 'into 'oneness'. The act of 'being' and experiencing is the most fulfilling part.

Happiness is an emotion that is an expression of the heart. Your heart is the centre of your emotions and is a crucial part of human experience. Indeed, all of your emotions are valid; are all to be noticed, felt or expressed. They are an accurate monitor of your state of being and provide a compass of how you are and where you need to go. When your emotions are flowing freely, your mind, body and soul are in synchronicity as they rise and fall and flow with each thought, vision and sensation. Anger, sadness, joy, jealousy and passion, all flowing, being felt and dissipated and providing information of how you are at each moment. This is a crucial part of being human.

There are elements of my own life that I am happy and grateful for and others that I regret and am sad about, because I am Surya, like you, stardust. On my journey and living my karma. Karma is what I do to myself and others through my thoughts and actions and it helps form the filter of the world through which I see and create my reality.

This is universal law, a cycle that is ultimately under my control on my soul's journey. What I do to others, I do to myself. I am immersed in the illusion of Maya until I make those deep psychological and spiritual shifts to let go and wake up. Enter into a new reality, a new way of being in my body and mind in the world.

At this stage of our spiritual journey, we know that this is not easy to achieve and maintain, until it becomes our way of being. It is challenging to observe each of our thoughts and images and question the validity of our beliefs and to come out of the 'story' we have of ourselves. The story that makes it easy for us to hold onto our old ways of being, seemingly punishing others with accusations of 'shoulds' and 'coulds' and holding onto hurts of unfulfilled expectations, thereby keeping us victims of our suffering, if we allow it.

It's true that we often face difficult people and situations. This is the ebb and flow of life. However, we do have the capacity to choose how we deal with them. We can see ourselves as victims or each event as an opportunity for experience, change or growth. There is always a choice to be made in how we perceive or deal with each situation. There is no doubt that it requires commitment and courage to embark on this journey consciously and to make inner shifts. Once started, it might be that our progress feels slow, cumbersome and clumsy, and positive change may feel too small or subtle to be noticed at first but, as we persist on this path, we start to notice that the progress begins to snowball and become more noticeable. We might quickly feel stronger, more empowered, compassionate and loving. It is true that we might alternatively feel angry, sad or deeply distressed at times, depending on the situation. However, we now have the capacity to find our equilibrium again relatively quickly, process our thoughts and emotions and decide if there is a course of action to be followed or not. We can do what has to be done and return to our free emotional state relatively quickly. We are free to feel our emotions instead of shutting them off, thereby dissipating them in a healthy way. This shift in consciousness is available to those who have reached a level of maturity, awareness and development and is always available to us, at any time.

At some stage, you decided to come on this great adventure into the physical world, lose your way, become intoxicated by your physicality, sensations and attachment to your world through your thoughts, beliefs, emotions, people and situations.

We often don't know what our purpose is. We don't know and cannot know who or what could have engineered such a bizarre adventure, such a soul journey. Perhaps the experiences and development in this physical plane are necessary to prepare us to enter into other realities and experiences, other realms or other worlds, in ways that we cannot envisage in our present, limited human form.

On one level, you are infinitely small in universal terms. You are housed in a physical body that has limitations of feeling, senses and physical strength. The atoms that make up your body are the same atoms that form the basic atoms and molecules of all things in the universe. You are an intricate part of the universe because you are a part of it and it is a part of you.

Just as an ant in a jungle is totally enmeshed in its world and has no notion of what lies outside its experience, so you are totally involved in your earthly human experiences. On the other hand, you are part of universal energy and the universe at large. You are both small and great simultaneously. All you have is this moment, this breath, feeling, vision or thought. This and each moment of consciousness.

You are a creator. You are always creating, but often chaotically, fearfully and destructively, due to confused thoughts and emotional states.

You create your experiences by the power of your thoughts, beliefs, emotions and imagination, with your personal 'soul' joining the greater soul at its 'source', as it rests between lives, becomes 'one' and yet somehow maintains its essence to decide what it needs to experience on your next soul chapter. It has no interest in how much pleasure or pain or anxiety this might cause in the physical life. Its only interest is in the experience and the opportunity to grow. It knows that any pain is self-created and that once the soul is able to let go of what it's doing to itself, there is no pain. The good news is that difficult or limiting beliefs and toxic emotions that have blocked your creative energy, can be resolved so that you can manifest more consciously and freely in the physical world. At this stage of your growth you are able to satisfy its physical, emotional intellectual and spiritual needs and connect to happiness and love on a more permanent basis.

You are constantly looking for love and satisfaction in all of your pursuits. There is ultimately only love and a perceived lack of love. Perceived lack of love is demonstrated as emptiness, lack of trust or faith and, ultimately, fear.

Happiness is often fleeting because it comes and goes like a wave. You hope that your relationships, mother, father, lover or spouse, children or friendships will help you to find love and happiness and they do for limited periods of time. Then they may leave, die or focus elsewhere for their own fulfilment or amusement.

These situations may result, ultimately, in disappointment and sadness or even anger, if you feel let down, unheard or unacknowledged. Nothing is permanent because, even the best situations or relationships end eventually. As you advance on your spiritual path as stardust, you begin to realise that it is your task alone to make yourself happy.

No one can do it for you. It is your task to refine your thoughts, beliefs and values and let go of those that are the root of suffering. It is your responsibility to peel away unrealistic expectations of others and of the world. You can resolve unrequited or frozen emotions so they flow freely again, resilient and robust.

Life will always have its ups and downs. Situations come and go and you will be faced with decisions and stresses. You are in charge only of yourself and your reactions to life, but life still happens and rolls on. In an advanced stage of development, you will not waste your thoughts or energy on worrying about what might have been, what might come next or what someone thinks of you.

If you are clumsy or forgetful and cause unnecessary hurt or harm to others, you will be quick to apologise and make sincere amendments, where possible, and move on. You won't spend much, if any, energy on self-flagellation. You will accept that you are human, that you still make mistakes or poor choices at times, but will be able to be fully responsible for yourself and the consequences of your actions. This means that through your growing compassion towards yourself, you can be more genuinely compassionate for others.

You are always looking for the beloved in everything you pursue in life. The beloved, the loving one, the nurturer, the blissful one, the Creator. You know it can be found in your environment: mother Earth, the sun, moon and the stars, and the stardust all around and within you. You see it in your lovers, children, parents or friends and in the twinkle of an eye or smile, and you notice it in each radiating dawn and mellow sunset. In the gentle rain, flowing rivers, valleys and mountains. In a new born baby and in each flower bud, in the vastness of the ocean and the rich clusters of stardust in the night sky.

Stardust is all around you and within you; the beloved, so abundant in your life and yet, so hard to grasp and hold onto. The creator is so prolific that it has too many faces for you to comprehend as you look out on your world. The abundance of life is so wide and deep and complex, spreading out into the universe and creating such a rich soul journey that it's awe-inspiring or possibly unbelievable.

Perhaps the greeting of 'Namaste', the Indian traditional greeting, is a timely reminder of our godly state.

'Namaste' means 'May the God in me see the God in you'.

This forms a frequent and timely reminder for those who use this greeting, to treat each person with compassion and respect because they are co-creators, just like you. Those who use this or similar greetings are frequently and consciously reminded of the importance and the equanimity of each soul. It is a timely reminder that all souls are on a similar journey, but at different points along the way. We are all within and part of universal energy.

The Indians and many others from ancient cultures have attempted to capture the vastness of creation through their symbolisation of multiple gods and goddesses depicted as the many possible faces of 'all that is', each one symbolising one area of life, rich in mythology and potent with magic. Hindus have created a rich culture and religion that weaves all elements of life into a deep colourful tapestry, depicting the cosmos through many symbols of universal energy. Starting with the god, Krishna, who symbolises the source of creation, with his beloved goddess, Radha, who is a manifestation of him in feminine form, symbolising devotion and pure love. There is another manifestation of goddess Sitar, Sarasvati, who is depicted as the infinite goddess of art, music and knowledge, which results in Lakshmi (wealth), sweetness and comfort. The goddess Lakshmi is the deity for those who sincerely pursue art, music and knowledge. The worshippers of Lakshmi create a relationship through the creation and expression of their art, as a form of devotion to and with cosmic energy. Another god, Ram, is the highest symbol for ridding the world of sin and cruelty and represents living in righteousness and harmony. Yet another popular god, Ganesha, the elephant man, symbolises the removal of obstacles and, of course, we must not forget Kali, the fierce goddess of destruction, representing death and reminding us of the cycle of life. The end of one life to make way for another, like the circle of a ring; each circle completing a round and starting another in a continuous cycle. This is the same way that your body cells are continually dying and being replaced by new ones each second, making each moment potent with the possibilities for death and new beginnings. Death making room for life and new thoughts, ideas and perceptions to replace the old, and make a new start possible in each second. There is no need to dwell on the past or focus too much on the future. Just enjoy the moment. This is a unique space. When you engage in true devotion in your relationship with the 'divine', by dancing, singing, playing music, creating art, new ideas, gardening, cooking or making love, as if with your creator, are you not embracing your stardust and the wonder of the universe?

If you allow the wind to breathe you, the music to play you, the song to sing you, the music to dance you, the expression or appreciation of art to inspire you, love to move you and joy to sing you, then you are using your earthly human form well in the devotion and celebration of your existence with universal energy.

These are all seen as expressions of devotion through creative articulation and the experience of 'all that is' in your relationship with creation as 'Stardust on the Spiritual Path'.

ENDNOTES

Namaste: May the God in me see the God in you.

Ohm. Shanti, Shanti, Shanti.

Ohm means 'yes' to universal oneness.

Shanti means 'yes' to peace.

Shanti 1. Yes, to peace and acceptance of self.

Shanti 2. Yes, to peace with the world.

Shanti 3. Yes, to peace with the universe.

Ohm. Shanti, Shanti, Shanti.

Finally:

All that matters is:

* how well you lived

* how well you loved

* how well you learned to let go

My wish to you is: may your stardust continue to shine.

Special Offers

10% off Yildiz's certified online training

If you love the book then consider taking your practice further.

Simply scan the codes below to receive 10% off Yildiz's:

- Certified Family Constellations online training
- Vedic astrology online

Or go to: https://familyconstellations.com.au/buy-fc-training/

Family Constellations Online training with experiential learning- 12 weeks

10% discount coupon **BRFC10**

Or go to: https://vedicastrology.net.au/buy-your-va-course-now

Vedic astrology online 12 week training

10% discount coupon **BRVA10**

Family Constellations training is certified in Australia and allows the student to obtain insurance and immediately start earning income and helping others.

Please read on to learn more about Yildiz's online training courses.

Family Constellations Online training

Family Constellations is a modality that shows the underlying dynamics, entanglements and generational trauma of individuals in their family systems. Also how these manifest in the present in relationships, parenting, patterns, wellbeing and mental health and their ability to fulfil potential.

This may take place in groups and private sessions, in person or online. The process is brief, experiential, psychodynamic, solution-focused, phenomenological and client-centred. A powerful way to re-order our inner perception of who we are into healthier places. The Constellation process works at the core of who we are as human beings, in a way that is limited or inaccessible with other approaches: Particularly in such a brief intervention.

The process works at several levels of awareness and experience simultaneously. Intellectual, visual, somatic, emotional, energetically and generationally. For Relationships, family, parenting, relational bonding, generational patterns, generational (systemic) trauma and incest. This results in several levels of change taking place simultaneously, as multiple levels of neural pathways realign. Suitable for existing and new practitioners.

The training is fully online with experiential learning component.

Learn Vedic Astrology Online

Learn how to read the magic and mystery of Vedic astrology.

How Yildiz developed the course

After Yildiz was introduced to Vedic astrology she spent years in study, research and practice. She went to courses in India, USA and in Australia and took part in lots of personal study and hundreds of Vedic astrology books. She found some information really useful and applicable and lots of information, confused confusing and not helpful or accurate. She has put in hundreds of hours of study and practice to find out what works accurately.

This is what she offers you this this course.

An honest open and practical approach to Vedic astrology in looking at the soul's journey.

Learning Vedic Astrology

You will learn by listening. There is an audio for each lesson.

You will learn by reading. There are course notes and charts for each lesson.

You will learn by doing. There are exercises at the back of 11 lessons for you to test yourself.

You may check your answers with the answers section included.

You may repeat each lesson several times.

You will listen and work through the course notes at your own pace.

Do it as fast or as slow as you want – It's up to you.

The course is designed to build your knowledge as you go through it.

You will be shown how to develop your skills in practical applications as you are shown how to navigate through chart information and build up an analysis.

All that's left after this is, Practice, Practice, Practice and ENJOY

APPENDIX A

Insert Retrieved September 2012 from Vedandtechs

http://www.vedandtechs.com/wiki/ancient-vedic-knowledge-spirituality-and-science

Vedic Literature and "Classification Kaushitaki – Karma.Chandogya – Reincarnation, Soul.

About Vedas

Vedic literature signifies a vast body of sacred and esoteric knowledge concerning eternal spiritual truths revealed to sages (Rishis) during intense meditation. The Vedas are considered to be full of all kinds of knowledge and an infallible guide for man in his quest for the four goals – Dharma, Artha (material welfare), Kama (pleasure and happiness) and Moksha (salvation).

Vedic Literature and Classification

The Vedas are four in number: Rig Veda, Yajurveda, Samaveda and Atharvaveda. Due to the different ways of reading (pata bedha) in different kulas (family traditions), different sakhas are manifested. The RigVeda was divided into 21 branches, the Yajurveda into 100 branches, the Samaveda into 1,000 branches and the Atharvaveda into nine branches (Kurma Purana: 52, p19-20). Furthermore, every branch has four subdivisions called Samhita (or Mantra), Brahmana (contains mantras and prayers), Aranyaka and Upanisad (contain philosophical contents). So, all in all, the Vedas consists of 1,130 Samhitas, 1,130 Brahmanas, 1,130 Aranyakas and 1,130 Upanisads, a total of 4,520 titles. Over time, however, many texts have been lost, stolen or destroyed. Some scriptures were so intimate that they were buried and hidden so as not to be misused by anyone in Kaliuga.

Vedangas ('limbs of Veda'): Siksa (pronunciation), Canda (poetic metre), Nirukta (etymology and lexicology), Vyakarana (grammar), Kalpa (ritual),

Jyotisha (astronomy and astrology). The first two teach how to speak the Veda, the second two teach how to understand the meaning of the Veda and the last two teach how to use the Veda.

REFERENCES

Bhaktivedanta Swami Prabhupada A. C. (1978) Srimad Bhagavatam. Bhagavad Gita. California. Bhaktivendanta Book Trust.

Chopra, D. (1993) Ageless Body, Timeless Mind. New York. Harmony Books.

Cohen, L. (retrieved 2012) Lyrics of Perfection http://www.elyrics.net/read/l/leonard-cohen-lyrics/love-itself-lyrics.html 2.

Coleman, D. Narration of the Dalai Lama (2003) Destructive Emotions and How to Overcome Them. London. Bloomsbury Publishing.

Duncan, B. L. (2011) Evidence-Based Practice (EBP). Talking Points on Becoming a Better Therapist. The American Psychological Society. Australian Counselling Association. 2- 2-.

Flaherty, D. (2001) (retrieved 2012) An Interview with Dennis Flaherty. http://vedicsciences.com/interview.htm

Frawley, D. (1999) The Astrology of the Seers. A Comprehensive Guide to Vedic Astrology. Wisconsin. Lotus Press.

Hellinger, B. (1999) Acknowledging What Is. Phoenix. Zeig, Tucker & Co. Inc.

Hellinger, B. (2006) No Waves Without the Ocean. Heidelberg. Carl Auer-Systeme Verlag.

Katie, B. (2002) Loving What Is. London. Harmony Books.

Klinghardt, D. (2005) (retrieved 2012) 5 Levels of Healing. http://www.klinghardtacademy.com/images/stories/5_levels_of_healing/Klinghardt_Article_5_ Levels_of_Healing.pdf

Liebermeister, S. (2006) The Roots of Love. Cambridge. Perfect Publishing.

Madelung, E. and Innecken, B. (2004) Entering Inner Images. A Creative Use of Constellations in Individual Therapy, Counselling and Self Help. Heidelberg. Carl Auer-Systeme Verlag.

Maroda, K. J. (2010) Working with Emotion in Psychodynamic Techniques. Working with Emotion in a Therapeutic Relationship.

Maslow, A. (1943) (retrieved February 2013) Maslow's Hierarchy of Needs. http://psychology.about.com/od/theoriesofpersonality/a/hierarchyneeds.htm

Novak, P. (1997) The Division of Consciousness. Charlottesville. Hampton Road Publishing Company Inc.

Robertson, J. (1994) Seth Speaks. The Eternal Validity of the Soul. California. Amber Allen Publishing and New World Library.

Ruppert, F. (2008) Trauma, Bonding & Family Constellations. Frome.UK. Green Balloon Publishing.

Schore, A. N. (2003) The Effects of a Secure Attachment Relationship on Right Brain Development Affect Regulation and Mental Health. In affect regulation and disorders of self. New York. W.W. Norton & Company.

Sharma Girish C. (2010) Brihat Parasara Hora Sastra. Vol. 1. A Compendium of Vedic Astrology. New Delhi Sagar Publications.

Sheldrake, R. (retrieved June 2012) Morphic Resonance. http://www.sheldrake.org/homepage.html

Sheldrake, R. (retrieved June 2012) The Heretic at Odds with Scientific Dogma.

http://www.guardian.co.uk/science/2012/feb/05/rupert-sheldrake- interview-science-delusion

Sheldrake, R. (2012) The Science of Delusion. London. Hodder and Stoughton.

Strahan, D. (2008) The Last Oil Shock. A Survival Guide to the Imminent Extinction of Petroleum. Man. Hachette Livre, UK. John Murray Publishers.

Tolle, E. (1999) The Power of Now. California. New World Library.

Tolle, E. (2009) A New Earth: Create a Better Life. United Kingdom. General. Penguin. UK.

REFERENCES

Vedandandtechs. (retrieved 2012) Ancient Vedic Knowledge Spirituality and Science. http://www.vedandtechs.com/wiki/ancient-vedic-knowledge-spirituality-and-science

Ward, V. W. (2008) (retrieved June 2012) The Soul Genome. The Reincarnation Experiment.

Webster, R. (2001) Past Life Memories. Minnesota. Llewellyn Publishers.

Weir, A. (2009) The Egg http://www.galactanet.com/oneoff/theegg.html

Weiss, B. (1988) Many Lives, Many Masters. New York. Simon & Schuster Inc.

Zammit, V. (2009) (retrieved Sept. 2012) Evidence of Past Lives. http://www.victorzammit.com/evidence/childrenwhorememberpastlives.htm

REFERENCES

www.ingramcontent.com/pod-product-compliance
Lightning Source LLC
Chambersburg PA
CBHW051938290426
44110CB00015B/2021